PENGUIN BOOKS
THE LAD DONE BAD

Denis Campbell saw his first match in 1979 by bunking off school in Belfast one Wednesday afternoon to watch Northern Ireland lose 5–1 to England. Football, he quickly realized, had to be more of a laugh than a game. At Manchester University he read politics, history and the back page of the *Daily Mirror*. He works in Edinburgh as a reporter for *Scotland on Sunday* and has written for the *Guardian*, the *Independent*, the *Independent on Sunday*, the *Irish Times*, *Time Out*, *Elle* and *The Face*. He supports West Ham and Glasgow Celtic – teams with great shirts, amazing fans and illustrious histories but, sadly, no chance of winning anything any more.

Andrew Shields was born in Middlesbrough in 1959, and cultivated his fervour for footballing underdogs by watching the Boro during their inglorious Second Division days. Since moving to London, after reading English at Warwick University, he has developed an equally unrequited passion for Leyton Orient. His uncle was capped by Wales, while his father played locally alongside members of the Clough family, who lived in the next street. He is Sports Editor of *Time Out*, having previously edited the Sports Council's magazine, *Sport and Leisure*, and with Denis Campbell is co-author of *Soccer City: The Future of Football in London* (Mandarin, 1993). He was highly commended in the 1993 British Sports Journalism Awards. He lives in east London with his wife, a lifelong Spurs supporter, and two young daughters.

Pete May was born in 1959 in Bishop's Stortford. He grew up in Essex and attended his first football match in 1970. Educated at Shenfield School, his firm but fair performances at centre back for the school side earned him the moniker 'Animal May'. Unexpectedly passed over by West Ham United, he graduated in English from Lancaster University. In 1984 he appeared at Wembley in a Milk Cup Final – although sadly only in the guise of a giant walkabout milk bottle. Since 1987 he has worked as a freelance journalist. Between matches he writes for the *Guardian*, the *Independent*, *Time Out*, the *New Statesman & Society*, *Loaded*, *90 Minutes*, *FC* and *Goal*, and he has a weekly column in *Midweek*. Pete was a founder editor of the award-winning West Ham fanzine *Fortune's Always Hiding*.

The Lad Done Bad

Denis Campbell, Pete May
& Andrew Shields

PENGUIN BOOKS

PENGUIN BOOKS

Published by the Penguin Group
Penguin Books Ltd, 27 Wrights Lane, London, W8 5TZ, England
Penguin Books USA Inc., 375 Hudson Street, New York, New York 10014, USA
Penguin Books Australia Ltd, Ringwood, Victoria, Australia
Penguin Books Canada Ltd, 10 Alcorn Avenue, Toronto, Ontario, Canada M4V 3B2
Penguin Books (NZ) Ltd, 182-190 Wairau Road, Auckland 10, New Zealand

Penguin Books Ltd, Registered Offices: Harmondsworth, Middlesex, England

Published in Penguin Books 1996

1 3 5 7 9 10 8 6 4 2

Copyright © Denis Campbell, Pete May, Andrew Shields, 1996

Filmset in Sabon and Meta

Printed in England by Clays Ltd, St Ives plc.

Contents

Picture Credits

Preface

The modern-day professional footballer is a highly trained athlete – a miraculous combination of cardio-vascular efficiency and finely honed, God-given skill. After a hard day spent in dedicated pursuit of mental and physical fitness, he likes nothing better than to dine quietly on pasta and salad and retire to bed at a sensible hour, where, tucked up alongside his loving wife, he slumbers soundly, dreaming only of sweeper systems, wing-backs and Christmas tree formations.

If every modern-day professional foot-baller was as clean-living as his manager exhorts him to be, this book would not exist. Instead, the frequency of headlines like SOCCER ACE IN SEX ROMP simply prove that our heroes are as unreli-able as the rest of us – only considerably richer.

This is not an exhaustive chronicle of every minor misdemeanour committed by footballers in their tired and emotional moments. Rather, it is an affectionate guide to the game's Hall of Shame, a celebration of lads done bad – with some, inevitably, badder than the rest. Regrettably, legal restrictions mean that many more stories must, for the moment, remain untold.

Credit where it's due to Stuart Cosgrove, author of the magnificent *Hampden Babylon* (itself a homage to Kenneth Anger's *Hollywood Babylon*). We are particularly grateful for their help to *On a Mission*, *A Large Scotch*, *There's Only One F in Fulham*, *Heroes and Villains*, Bill Williamson, Steve Rapport, Alex Fynn, Razi Mireskandari and the respective staffs of Colindale Newspaper Library, Sportspages in the Charing Cross Road, and Walthamstow's Sporting Bookshop. Nicola Baird, Elaine Burgess, Helen and Isabel were as classy a back four as you'll ever hope to find; Ken's Cafe kept things bubbling away in the middle of the (Upton) park; while Penguin's Tony Lacey, David Watson and Caroline Sanderson did the business up front. Finally, we must thank all our sources, particularly those who, for various reasons, go unnamed in the book.

Denis Campbell, Pete May and Andrew Shields
London, September 1996

'I WAS AT AN AGE WHEN I COULD STILL PARTY ALL NIGHT AND GET UP IN THE MORNING AND DO MY JOB': GEORGE PROVES HE'S SIMPLY THE BEST.

1

George: Original and Still the Best

'It's like George Best once said to me, "When you've had the last three Miss Worlds, then you can start talking."'

Maurice Johnston – a hell-raiser *par excellence* with Celtic, Watford, Everton, Rangers and a host of others – on the dubious wisdom of any footballer apart from Best himself boasting about his sexual conquests

It all began not with a coconut on a beach in Rio de Janeiro or a bundle of rags in the back-streets of Buenos Aires, but with a tennis-ball on the green open spaces of the Cregagh council estate in east Belfast. There, in the late fifties, a matchstick-thin kid called George Best honed the almost supernatural skills which would later make him a legend – and, in the process, transform the simple game of football into The Greatest Show On Earth. Best was the first player to be treated like royalty, a Hollywood idol or pop star. He was exciting, flamboyant and eccentric, capable of sending fans into ecstasy with his on-field brilliance and managers into despair with his endless indiscretions away from the stadia which reverberated to the chanting of his name.

Best symbolized the glamorous, liberated new era of the sixties. He was a money-making phenomenon and one-man sexual revolution, a rule-breaker *extraordinaire* and target of unprecedented media fascination; he was a handful on the pitch and pretty much unstoppable off it too. Never before had such a mischievous, maverick maestro set foot in English foot-

ball. The authorities had experienced nothing like it, and didn't really know how to cope. But they did, somehow. In so doing they learned the vital if uncomfortable truth that bad boy footballers are as much a part of the sport's appeal as Geoff Hurst's hat-trick in 1966, Gazza's tears at Italia '90 or Arsenal losing to non-League opposition (*any* opposition, in fact) in the third round of the FA Cup. Best's ultimately self-destructive genius forced football to grow up and adapt, sometimes painfully, to the voracious media interest in its protagonists. His antics established a gloriously troublesome tradition which hundreds of wayward geniuses (and not-so-geniuses) since have sought to uphold, albeit few with quite the same verve and vigour. George Best broke the mould of the professional footballer, and refashioned it for ever in his own unique image. In many ways the spectacular rise and disastrous fall from grace of Georgie-boy, soccer's first superstar, was also the making of the modern game itself.

The world probably should have seen Best coming. At fourteen months, an age at which many youngsters can't even walk, he was already learning to dribble. At three or four, taking a football to bed at night. At nine and ten, running rings round all comers. Then, at fifteen, the shy but richly gifted young prodigy was on his way to Old Trafford, despatched by a scout who sent his employers a telegram which simply read: 'I have found a genius.' Bob Bishop was not exaggerating. In time the Belfast boy became, to quote Pele's expert testimony, the greatest footballer in the world. To many, he remains the best player there has ever been, and that's including the other likely candidates for that accolade: Maradona, Di Stefano, Cruyff, Eusebio, even Pele himself.

The man who turned football on its head was born on 22 May 1946 into what he proudly recalls as 'a solid, working-class family, Protestant by religion, decent and honest in its beliefs'. Best's parents, Dick and Ann, both worked long hours – he as an iron-turner in Belfast's famous Harland and Wolff shipyard, she in a fish-and-chip shop and ice cream factory – to give their son and his sisters, Carol and Barbara, an upbringing as secure as the post-war peace itself. Luckily George got to know Belfast long before the Troubles erupted and was never scarred by sectarianism. On the Cregagh estate, in his time at least, Protestants and Catholics lived peacefully side by side.

Young George had a happy childhood, unremarkable except for the incredible ease with which he could make a ball perform tricks. The dark-haired boy with the mischievous smile did all the usual things besides playing football: visited the cinema, went on trips to the seaside, rode his bike and attended both church and Sunday school regularly. Football, though, was everything. 'Soccer didn't dominate my life completely,' Best explains, 'but it certainly made a good attempt.' He and the other lads from the Cregagh estate kicked a ball around any chance they got: at school, over lunchtime, after school, in the evenings at the local youth club. Come lunch-break, George would race home from Nettlefield primary school, wolf down two pieces of toast and a cup of tea and be back in the playground ten minutes later to take his place in the kick-around. After final bell, the same routine – only at that time everyone from around the area wanted to play, and games quickly developed into thirty- or forty-a-side. In such frenzied surroundings Best learned how to beat one opponent, then leave another in the mud, then another, then . . . That special talent, as First Division defences across the land later found out, was to become his trademark. Though no slouch at school – George was the only boy in his class to pass the eleven-plus – football was his only real passion in life. Even when he dreamed, his reverie ended in him scoring the winning goal in the FA Cup Final – not, however, for Manchester United or Tottenham Hotspur, but for the perennially unfashionable Wolverhampton Wanderers, to whom the soccer-mad schoolboy had rather rashly pledged his allegiance.

In a foretaste of adventures yet to come, Best also displayed in his youth a rare talent for getting into scrapes. He was, by his own admission, a bit of a nutcase. 'I was always trying to do things people said you couldn't do,' he recalled later. 'And I was always getting bruised for my efforts.' That brief admission of misdemeanours committed years before he began going AWOL, drinking too much and giving Matt Busby headaches, could serve as the ultimate epitaph for his crazy, colourful, controversy-filled life and times. Indeed, the words would not look out of place if eventually inscribed on Best's gravestone.

Manchester United were lucky Bob Bishop's fifteen-year-old 'genius' ever joined them at all. Best had just passed the exam to become a printer's apprentice, and his father was urging him to pursue this solid, if uninspiring, career rather than his dream of becoming a professional footballer. Then, when he finally got to Old Trafford, the future legend was so homesick that he walked out after two days of his two-week trial and went home to Belfast. Only Dick Best's telephoned plea to Sir Matt earned his errant son another chance, and unwittingly set up one of the most volatile but gloriously successful chapters in football history. It was not the last time George Best would walk out on the Red Devils.

The young apprentice settled in quickly second time around, thanks in part to the hospitality he found in the digs run by the legendary Mrs Fullaway. Best's confidence grew, and not just in his footballing ability. He enjoyed the first of his countless romantic liaisons with a girl called Maria. That she was already going out with someone else – Steve, Mrs Fullaway's son – was an obstacle, but not for long. The teenage temptress provided early proof of George's irresistibility to women. 'Her aunt owned a cake shop in Manchester and we went to bed for the first time in the flat above the store,' Best reminisced later. 'Then we rushed downstairs again and helped ourselves to cakes.' Couplings

with willing females in the back-seats of cars soon became a regular occurrence. Then he transferred his scoring exploits to where it really mattered, on the field of play. He signed as a professional on his seventeenth birthday, 22 May 1963, two weeks after United had won the FA Cup. On 14 September Best at last made his full debut, against West Bromwich Albion, then returned to the reserve team until a Christmas-time encounter with Burnley. His goal in that game, paving the way for a 5–1 thrashing by United, was the first of the 179 he would score in 466 appearances for the Old Trafford side. It marked the beginning of the George Best phenomenon.

When Best arrived in the autumn of 1961, football was very different from the game played now in all-seater stadia, broadcast on satellite television and crowded with players from Europe, Africa and even America. When the human cyclone hit, the sport had not changed much since its Victorian origins. Match-balls were brown, grounds had no Tannoy systems, few spectators travelled away, tickets cost a few shillings and teams played 2–3–5, not 4–4–2. Although soccer was even then the vast popular religion – a mind-boggling 28.6 million people paid to watch it in 1960–61 – it had no real media image. While football had its big names – Wright and Milburn, Finney and Matthews – fanaticism was more about teams than particular players. Film stars were the only celebrities instantly recognizable to a general, non-sporting audience. Politicians were remote figures. Pop music didn't yet properly exist; Beatlemania was still two years away. The cult of the sexy, controversial, media-friendly individual did not yet hold sway.

Players were honest, working-class lads who wore Brylcreemed side-partings, not perms or goatee beards. If they did get involved in night-club brawls, run-ins with policemen and sex scandals, the papers didn't report it. Managers were gents, such as Bill Nicholson, boss of the Spurs team which had won the Double not long before Best got to Manchester (only to get instantly confused by the taxi-driver asking him which Old Trafford he wanted). Games in those days were reported in a non-judgemental, almost dignified way, where criticism was rare and managers were always referred to as Mr so-and-so – the method still preferred by the *Daily Telegraph* in its Monday morning match reports.

It was a bumbling, amateurish era, innocent compared to today's big-money, high-exposure game. Plain Alf Ramsey was still managing Ipswich Town. The country that invented football had not yet won the World Cup. Soccer had not been established as a vital ingredient of national self-esteem. Then George Best exploded on to the scene and changed all that. If football was a woman, you could say that the Belfast boy came along, shamelessly took her virginity and taught the lady in question a few harsh but vital truths about survival in the modern world.

After that goal against Burnley, Best became unstoppable. He remembers that playing for United was not only 'fun and the most exciting thing I could possibly have been doing', but also easy, 'just as easy as it had been on the streets of the Cregagh estate. I discovered that I could go past the big men, the hard, seasoned professionals with big reputations, with the same ease I had gone round the bigger boys I played against as a child; and I revelled in it.' Hugh McIlvanney, the legendary football writer, memorably summed up George's gifts thus: 'With feet as sensitive as a pick-pocket's hands, his control of the ball under the most violent pressure was hypnotic. The bewildering repertoire of feints and swerves, sudden stops and demoralizing spurts, exploited a freakish elasticity of limb and torso, tremendous physical strength and resilience for so slight a figure and balance that would have made Isaac Newton decide he might as well have eaten the apple.'

Almost single-handedly, Bestie made soccer sexy. The fact that he was blessed with looks to match his talent did him no harm; football's first pin-up was born. He earned £1,000 a week, drove a Lotus and even opened a boutique with Mike Summerbee selling paisley shirts, velvet jackets and other crimes against fashion. 'That was the way it was in the sixties,' Best explained. 'Everyone was "doing their own thing" and I was in there, right at the beginning of it all. It was a time of experimentations and change in fashion and hairstyles and music, and they even wrote a song about me.' Happily, unlike Terry Venables, Gazza and Hoddle and Waddle after him, the Belfast boy chose not to sing it himself. As the idiosyncratic Irishman recalled in his aptly titled autobiography, *The Good, The Bad and The Bubbly*: 'The springboard for all of this was foot-ball and it was a glorious time to play the game. The sport was full of great characters like Stan Bowles, Rodney Marsh, Charlie George, Alan Ball, Eddie Gray, Peter Osgood and, of course, [Denis] Law and [Bobby] Charlton, people you were happy to spend money

AND BEST MUST SCORE: GEORGE CONTEMPLATES LIFE AS FOOTBALL'S FIRST SEX SYMBOL.

to see.' No star shone brighter, though, than George Best's.

With the Law-man and balding Bobby the net-buster, simply the Best turned Manchester United into a team typical of the times: exciting, glamorous, bursting with flair. They won the League in 1965 and then again in 1967. After success at home, they became the first English team to make a major assault on the European Cup. 'I think that week in, week out we played against great teams both here and in Europe and beat them,' boasted Best later. 'In 1967 when we won the League there were some special sides around like Arsenal, Spurs, Liverpool, Leeds. West Ham had three World Cup members in their team; the Everton midfield was Kendall, Harvey and Ball.'

Though the 1968 European Cup triumph at Wembley is often cited as genius George's finest hour, his performance in a quarter-final of the same competition two years earlier is more worthy of that description. United were playing Benfica in their famous Stadium of Light in front of 75,000 hysterical fans. This was the Portuguese champions' nineteenth home game in Europe in seven years, and they had won all the other eighteen. Though the Reds fancied their chances, most neutrals expected Benfica, led by the peerless Eusebio, to triumph. With United leading 3–2 from the first leg, Busby told them to forget their normal game, not to bother too much with attack and instead keep things tight. He didn't want any mistakes. Best takes up the story. 'So what did I do? I went out and scored two goals in the first twelve minutes and we went on to win 5–1. Sir Matt's remark, referring to me, was: "I wish he wouldn't listen to me more often."' The fact that the Old Trafford side lost in the semi-final to Partizan Belgrade made no difference. His display in Lisbon had seen Best dubbed as 'El Beatle', and the nickname stuck. 'El Beatle'; 'The Fifth Beatle'; fan-mail, sacks of it, poured in; screaming schoolgirls turned up at Old Trafford for his public appearances. Until those goals against Benfica, the dark-haired, red-shirted number ten was just another football player. Afterwards, as Best recalled, 'Suddenly I was one of the biggest pop stars in Europe.'

While the 'El Beatle' performance sent the Best phenomenon into overdrive, the night in May 1968 when soon-to-be-Sir Matt Busby lifted the famous trophy with bigger ears than Prince Charles probably did show Best at the peak of his footballing powers. He scored once in United's 4–1 demolition of Benfica. Just a week before, Best had turned twenty-two. Both the British and European Footballer of the Year awards found their way on to his mantelpiece around that time. The attention, hysteria and adulation grew, with George appearing as much in pop magazines as in the sports pages of newspapers. The money poured in, making him Britain's best-paid sportsman, from endorsements such as George Best boots (over 250,000 sold, earning the golden boy a golden pair of boots).

Soon after, though, it all began to go horribly wrong, with alcohol at the root of his downfall. If Isaac Newton had been around, his faith in the theory of gravity would have been fully vindicated. After all, what goes up – in this case, Best's rise into the stratosphere of fame – must come down. And down he came, not so much with a bump as a hiccup, a hangover and headlines that told of horror at his booze-fuelled antics. The sessions in the Brown Bull, his favourite Mancunian watering-hole, which he called 'a hard-drinking pub in a hard-drinking town' – and a place Sir Matt unlovingly referred to as the Black Cow – became longer and heavier. At first, such excess didn't matter: 'I was at an age when I could still party all night and get up in the morning and do my job.' But then the problems began mounting.

In the months and years that followed, Best blazed a trail which established him as the prototype bad boy footballer. No British player since has behaved quite so appallingly as George in his heyday. The superstar became a soak, a sad case who referred to alcohol as 'the demon who keeps beating me'. He began going AWOL from United, hurting and baffling his legion of admirers by announcing: 'I preferred to stay in bed.' He wrecked relationships with women most men would die to get near – models, actresses and Miss Worlds such as Mary Stavin and Marji Wallace – for the sake of a one-night stand with some leggy blonde he'd just met. He got into fights with astonishing regularity, once pronouncing: 'I'll go into the toilet with anyone.' This, after all, is a man who opened his autobiography with the immortal words, 'I punched Michael Caine to the floor in Tramp one night.'

Worst, he wasted the God-given talent that had made him famous, walking out on United and top-class football in 1974 at the criminally early age of twenty-seven. By then, the 'scrapes' of childhood memory had become a lot more serious than mere juvenile pranks.

The rest of the seventies and the whole of the eighties were not good to George Best. After taking more early retirements than Frank Sinatra, he finally turned his back on Old Trafford after all Busby's

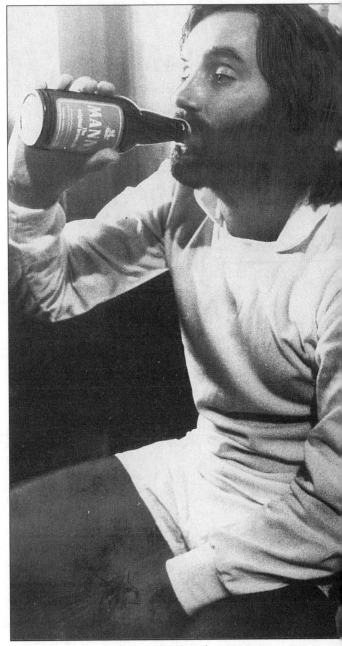

GEORGE BEST FINDS OUT ABOUT MANN'S INHUMANITY TO MAN.

successors – Wilf McGuinness, Frank O'Farrell, Dave Sexton and Tommy Docherty – proved unable to calm him down. Best had gone badly off the rails, and no one knew how to help. He made

AND THERE'S THIS IRISHMAN LYING ON THE BEACH RECKONS HE'S THE GREATEST FOOTBALLER WHO EVER LIVED . . . .

the front pages more often than the back ones, as his and the Reds' fortunes faltered in a way unimaginable for both parties just a few years earlier. The player himself refers to his latter period at United as 'alcohol-inspired madness that led to the lost years of George Best'. After quitting the club that made him, he became a high-profile, highly paid striker with small clubs like Stockport County, Fulham (where he teamed up with another rogue, Rodney Marsh) and Hibernian – recruited, always temporarily, to boost their gates. Another, Cork Celtic, sacked him after three games for

showing 'lack of enthusiasm'. Bored with Britain, Best headed across the Atlantic and had spells with Los Angeles Aztecs, Fort Lauderdale Strikers and San Jose Earthquakes in the nascent North American Soccer League. He loved the money, climate and opportunities for bedding women in the States, but it was an undeniably sad way for the greatest player ever produced in the British Isles to end what could, perhaps should, have been the most illustrious career of all time.

Best became a rebel without a cause, a legend in his own drinking-time. He began having regular run-ins with the forces of law and order. He was convicted of assaulting a girl he had slapped in a night-club. Arrested for drink-driving along London's Pall Mall, he failed to turn up in court. When a policeman was sent to bring him in, Best first tried to escape and then ended this latest débâcle by punching one of a posse of boys in blue determined to capture him. That was in December 1984, and earned him a three-month jail sentence. In court, his counsel told the magistrate that his client was a bankrupt alcoholic who had tried repeatedly since 1979 to beat his drink problem. The rot had set in long before that, however. Best certainly did try to conquer 'the demon who keeps beating me'. He dried out in clinics, went to Alcoholics Anonymous and took alcohol deterrent drugs. He even twice went to Norway to have implant operations meant to curb his thirst. Sadly, nothing worked. Who knows what magic we would have seen if one of those treatments had succeeded?

Nobody could offer a convincing explanation for Best's descent into alcoholic oblivion, least of all Best himself. Had fame simply become too much? Or was he belatedly rebelling against his strict Free Presbyterian upbringing in Belfast? Was he somehow trying to let us know that, although Northern Ireland produces more than its fair share of tortured souls – in music (Van Morrison) and snooker (Alex 'Hurricane' Higgins, the Best of the baize) – he, George Best, was the most extrovert, most cantankerous, most troubled of them all? After all, as he admitted: 'I was so used to being Number One in football, I had to be Number One in everything – even drinking.' Or, more likely, was it all connected to his mother Anne's own (unsuccessful)

battle with, and early death from, the booze? Did he perhaps blame himself for driving her to the bottle by his behaviour and, perversely, react to his guilt by going the same way?

Best himself would have us believe that the dismantling of United's great team of the sixties, and the club's failure to replace legends with men of similar calibre, was the only reason. 'It had nothing to do with women and booze, car crashes or court cases. It was purely and simply football,' he insisted. 'Losing wasn't in my vocabulary. I had been conditioned from boyhood to win, to go out and dominate the opposition. When the wonderful players I had been brought up with – Charlton, Law, Crerand, Stiles – went into decline, United made no real attempt to buy the best replacements available.' Thus Best was left, in his own words, 'struggling among fellas who should not have been allowed through the door at Old Trafford. I was doing it on my own and I was just a kid. It sickened me to the heart that we ended up being just about the worst team in the First Division and went on to drop into the Second.' It is an unconvincing explanation.

Whatever the truth, booze nearly killed Best. It led him to disgrace himself on countless occasions, for example at a golf club dinner in Cheshire in 1993 where guests had paid £30 each to hear him and Marsh reminisce about the good old days. Who was the dirtiest player you ever played against, someone asked. 'Marjorie Wallace,' was the by-now drunken bum's reply, an answer which was soon followed by him branding Alex Ferguson's title winners as 'fucking crap' and Bobby Charlton 'a miserable bastard'. Invited onto the *Wogan* chatshow, he demonstrated the generous nature of BBC hospitality by appearing in front of millions of viewers sozzled and shameless. One of the most excruciatingly embarrassing sequences in modern television finally ended when the hapless host pulled the plug after the following sequence.

Best (talking about women): 'I like screwing, all right.' Wogan (flustered, trying to change the subject): 'So what do you do with your time these days?'

Best: 'Screw.' Wogan: 'Ladies and gentlemen, George Best.'

Ladies and gentlemen, George Best. It was an adulatory phrase Bestie had heard a million times. Yet this time, he was too far gone either to know what a pathetic fool he was being – or to care. Soon after, ITV's *This Is Your Life* scrapped plans, already well-advanced, to give the Belfast boy the full red-book life-story treatment. Pele was among those booked to appear. A hat-trick of TV disasters was concluded in May 1994 when he failed to turn up for *This Morning*, the breakfast telly show; the programme-makers drafted in a suitable replacement – a bottle of champagne. Best enjoyed a brief renaissance after that, actually turning up when he toured the country with Marsh, telling the world he was 'too busy to drink' and appearing more in control of himself than he had been since the early, early days. He even had the love of a good woman, his live-in lover, organizer and long-suffering partner Mary Shatila.

But then he demonstrated the sort of behaviour that, when it comes to bad boy footballers, really puts him in a class of his own. The ever-stoical Shatila told one newspaper that 'I can honestly say that if George fell in love with someone else, whether she's eighteen or forty,

we'd still be friends.' That was in June 1994. Two months later, he did fall in love with someone else. She was twenty-two, a blonde air hostess called Alex Pursey; Bestie was heading towards his fiftieth birthday. Not only that, he went and made her his latest wife, in the process destroying the love of the person who some friends thought was the best thing that had ever happened to him.

That was Best all over. From destroying defences, he had fallen to destroying the people who cared for him most. When he tells the 'where did it all go wrong?' story, as he often does, he seems to be positively revelling in his own downfall. That's the one about the night a hotel porter brought a bottle of vintage bubbly up to George's room, where the legend had £25,000 casino winnings spread out on a bed and Mary Stavin, having slipped into something more comfortable, waiting for him. As he went to leave, the Belfast-born porter stopped. 'George, can I ask you something that's been on my mind for a long time?' he inquired.

'What is it?' the great man replied.

'George, where did it all go wrong for you?'

For some reason, Best laughs when he tells this story.

On and off the pitch, George was both original and the best. He even had the surname to prove it. But in shaking up football, in the process of dragging it into the modern era, he perhaps inflicted too much punishment on himself. He was the first and most spectacularly misbehaved soccer bad boy.

Many spiritual successors to Georgie-boy have tried hard to follow in his footsteps. It's a perverse tribute to the man's genius that none has ever succeeded.

'WELL, IT CERTAINLY BEATS MY SATURDAY JOB . . .'

2

Eight Go Mad in Blackpool

**'There's a famous seaside place called Blackpool,
That's noted for fresh air and fun.'**

Marriott Edgar, 'The Lion And Albert'

As any keen chemistry student knows, volatile substances need very careful handling. Mix them wrongly, and they can suddenly erupt into flames without warning. Since the average footballer is rarely among the most dedicated students at school and probably spent science lessons pouring acid into his classmates' pockets, it's no surprise that players and managers are often described as 'mercurial'. After all, mercury is one of the most unpredictable chemicals known to mankind.

When Tommy Docherty was your boss, you lit the blue touchpaper and stood a long way back since the bang, if one came, was sure to be very loud indeed. But kindle the mixture with a bright little spark called Terry Venables, and detonation was guaranteed. When two of the game's most supercharged characters rubbed each other up the wrong way one spring night by the seaside, the resulting explosion coloured Blackpool more vividly than the town's world-famous illuminations had ever managed. What's more, the pair led English football into a scandal conducted in the full glare of Fleet Street's popping flash-bulbs. Even by the more restrained reporting standards of three decades ago, the incident which took place in one of England's premier resorts

genuinely was, as the *Daily Mirror* put it, 'A Soccer Sensation'.

Yet Blackpool was an unlikely setting for such a spectacular sporting conflagration. With row upon row of modest B&Bs and small hotels, and out-of-season nightlife along the famous Golden Mile, it seemed the ideal venue for a group of jaded footballers, up from the Smoke, to recharge their batteries before launching a last bid for the game's greatest honour: the First Division Championship.

It had taken Tommy Docherty three years since his appointment as Chelsea manager in 1961, at the age of just thirty-three, to knit together a side capable of lifting the title. But his band of youthful blades were in danger of letting him down at the last: a squad aged almost entirely under twenty-five had spent much of the 1964–65 season on top of the table, and beat Leicester City over two legs in the League Cup final. But when the Blues lost 2–0 to Liverpool in the FA Cup semi-final, the defeat heralded a disastrous loss of form in the League. Not even Docherty's already celebrated motivational skills could prevent Chelsea turning into that season's April shower as they dropped down to third, with the great Manchester United side in the making, the team of Law, Best and Charlton, leaping into pole position.

Chelsea had two games remaining when the players checked into the Cliffs Hotel for a week of special training before they were due to face Burnley on Saturday, 24 April 1965, and Blackpool forty-eight hours later. They had just lost to Liverpool by the odd goal, this time in the League, a result which meant that the race for the title was almost certainly between the Uniteds of Manchester and Leeds. But Docherty never tired of reminding his men that football can be a cruel and quirky game – and Chelsea were not going to miss any chance to seize back the initiative through lack of preparation.

Whenever there was a match to be played in the North-west, it was the Doc's policy to stay at Blackpool, where the sharp, salty sea air helped to clear heads, steady nerves and focus minds on the task ahead. That was the theory, anyway. Lungfuls of ozone were good for foot-ballers who spent too much time in sooty, smoggy London, he reckoned. But a few days' break also gave the players a chance to relax – after all, a group of lads, mostly single, away from home with a few quid in their pockets, needed some time to themselves. And they were young lads, too: wing-half John Hollins was the baby of the side at just seventeen, while Ron 'Chopper' Harris, already feared for his crunching tackles, was only a year older. Tricky winger Bert Murray, twenty-one, was the same age as inside-forward George Graham, a £5,000 signing from Aston Villa, and Terry Venables, the quick-witted midfielder whom Docherty had made his captain. Goalkeeper Peter 'The Cat' Bonetti and England centre-forward Barry Bridges were almost geriatric at twenty-two and twenty-three respectively.

SITTING ON THE DOC OF THE BAY: TOMMY DOCHERTY PONDERS A POINT OF PRINCIPLE.

The team may have been full of brash kids, many of them typical products of swinging sixties London, but they still had to be treated like adults rather than a bunch of troublesome infants. That meant instilling the high moral principles which their manager believed in. In a footballing sense, it meant acting like true professionals.

Born into the harsh realities of a tenement slum in Glasgow's Gorbals, Docherty had spent most of his playing days at Preston North End, where the legendary Tom Finney described him as 'the juggernaut behind me'. He also won twenty-five caps for Scotland as the sort of half-back you'd think more than twice about challenging for a fifty-fifty ball. His uncompromising approach to discipline revealed itself soon after the Doc had slipped into the manager's chair at Stamford Bridge: when four players refused to sign new contracts in the summer of 1962, there were no negotiations. Docherty simply kicked three of them out there and then, and the other after just one more game.

However, the Doc was not a martinet where alcohol was concerned. He liked a drink as much as anyone, and had no problems with his players going for a quiet pint, provided they behaved themselves. But he was disappointed after losing to Liverpool, and the Championship which seemed so certain only two months before had almost slipped away. On the way up to Blackpool, he had agreed that the players could have a night out on the Tuesday, but now he changed his mind.

They went anyway.

'They were very boisterous,' Docherty recalled. 'So I got them together and said if anything else happens, you're on your bikes.'

Little could the likely lads have known that it was only the mode of conveyance which would differ as the saga of shame by the seaside started to unfold.

The following night, the Doc put the players under curfew. They could go out, but he wanted them back in the hotel before midnight – and preferably closer to eleven o'clock than the witching hour. Sure enough, as the nearest church clock sounded its eleventh chime, in they trooped. To a man they said no to a cup of coffee, and instead bid goodnight to Docherty, who was sharing a bottle of champagne with trainer Harry Medhurst. 'What a smashing bunch of boys,' chorused the other guests as soccer's band of angels dutifully disappeared to their rooms.

Or so everyone thought. Just half an hour later, the angels had dirty faces. Head porter George Honeyman interrupted the Doc's drink to whisper in his ear: 'Mr Docherty, your players have just gone out again.' Honeyman had found the hotel's fire escape open – a serious breach of insurance and safety rules – and, in true comic-book fashion, had spotted the last of eight pairs of trouser-legs disappearing through the door and down the steps.

'I never spied on the players. I always trusted them. Always,' insisted Docherty. 'There was a rugby team staying at the Cliffs at the same time, and I said, "It'll be that lot. You know what they're like."' But Honeyman was adamant. 'I told him to get a master key, and we'd go up to their rooms and prove him wrong.'

But an inspection only proved him right. As Docherty and Honeyman peered round door after door, they found more empty beds than snoring bodies. Docherty returned to the hotel lounge and told the porter to let him know the minute the players returned.

He had a long wait.

It was after three o'clock when Honeyman shook Docherty out of a drowse. 'They're in,' he hissed. The errant eight had crept back up the fire escape, trying to keep as quiet as possible but, in the way that people do when they've had a few, managing to make more noise than if they'd simply strolled through the front door. The Doc had spent three hours brooding on this blatant breach of discipline, and it was no surprise when he stormed back up to the players' rooms in a fury.

He flung open the first door to find John Hollins and Barry Bridges giving a passable impression of nocturnal bliss, looking for all the world as though they'd been tucked up with a hot-water bottle for hours. 'Have you been sleeping all right?' he barked.

No answer.

'Did you hear me, lads?'

'Yes, thanks, boss,' replied two mock-sleepy voices, adding a couple of theatrical yawns for effect. But Docherty was not convinced. He whipped back the bed-clothes, and there were Hollins and Bridges still in their suits and ties. They hadn't even had time to take off their shoes before diving under the sheets. It was a scene which only needed a peroxide blonde in bra and frilly knickers to emerge from the wardrobe to be straight out of a Brian Rix farce.

But this was no time for levity. The Doc was on the warpath, and Terry Venables' room was next. Surely his captain had not let him down as well? He had, since the bed was clearly devoid of its slumbering skipper. 'I might have known I would most trouble with Venables,' said Docherty. 'He was always the ringleader, they all looked up to him. He told me he had been in Eddie McCreadie's room all the time. I knew this was not true because I had already checked earlier and McCreadie's room was empty.'

Venables, however, had good reason for trying to keep his nose clean. Not only

because he was captain and should have set an example, but because he'd had a run-in with Docherty over breaking curfew once before.

It was Venables' fatal attraction to the stage and an audience which did for him on the previous occasion. The Chelsea squad was staying in Kensington before a game, and the word from on high was that they had to be in their rooms by nine o'clock. But the players knew that the Doc was himself going out for the evening. They all met up in the hotel ballroom to listen to the band. Inevitably, listening soon turned into singing for the player who had crooned with the Joe Loss Orchestra at the Hammersmith Palais when he was just seventeen, resplendent in his England Youth blazer. When Venables was half-way through 'Winter

'HONEST, BOSS, WE DIDN'T GO NEAR THE LADIES ALL NIGHT. . .' TOMMY DOCHERTY FLUSHES OUT THE TRUTH FROM BARRY BRIDGES.

Wonderland' one of the lads spotted Docherty in the lobby and tipped off his team-mates, who quickly scarpered back to bed. The Doc glanced round the ball-room to check that his command had been followed. Then he noticed who was holding the microphone . . .

Dictatorial Docherty had no doubts about Venables' ability and influence on the pitch. So much so, in fact, that he had started to involve his midfield mover and shaker in tactical planning, and even took him on recce to Roma before a Fairs Cup tie later in 1965. But it was the escapade in Kensington which began to sow the first seeds of doubt in the Doc's mind about whether Venables' behaviour was suitably subservient. He might have asked for his opinion on occasions, but it was still a manager–player relationship after all. As he put it later, this was when Docherty started to wonder if Stamford Bridge was big enough for the both of them.

Back in Blackpool, the Doc was disap-pointed. So disappointed, in fact, that his last act before hitting the sack was to hand the eight their rail tickets, and order them to be on the first train back to London the next morning. They even misunderstood this instruction, since they trooped into the hotel reception, suitcases packed and ready to leave at 4 a.m.

Who, then, were the guilty men? Only as fine a collection of footballing talent as it would be possible to round up at such an ungodly hour. There was Terry Venables, the future Tottenham and England coach; George Graham, who would become the most successful Arsenal manager of the modern era until brought down by a scandal far more serious than this one; John Hollins, a Stamford Bridge supremo himself in the 1980s; Barry Bridges, then the England centre-forward; plus Scottish international defender Eddie McCreadie; full-back Marvin Hinton; winger Bert Murray; and reserve forward Joe Fascione. All would miss the crucial clashes with Burnley and Blackpool, games which could yet win Chelsea the Championship. But Docherty no longer cared about trophies. How could he even contemplate working with players who clearly had no respect for him, let alone lead them in celebrating a League title? 'It was them or me,' he admitted recently, his eyes dark with foreboding even thirty years on.

Since no footballer can ever be expect-ed to hit the town without a girl on his arm, it was a stroke of luck – for the reporters now on the case, at least – that there was female interest in this tale, too. Nineteen-year-old brunette Pauline Monk from nearby Cleveleys, photographed by the *Daily Mirror* with her hair back-combed into a spectacular beehive, willingly admitted that she and her friend Shirley Clarkson, a year younger, had met up with the players on their evening's escapade. Nor was it just a chance encounter – Pauline declared that she was no stranger to Venables in particular. 'I have known Terry since October,' she confessed, 'when I met him at a dance.' But it was her next comment which might have helped convince Docherty that his charges were not as irresponsible as he imagined: 'We went to a bar. The players didn't have a lot to drink – just a few lagers. The lads said they would have to be back early because of a curfew.' He might have sought corroboration from the parents of both girls, too, if he suspected that late-night nookie had been the inten-tion: all vouched that their daughters were at home shortly after 11 p.m., and that they never went near the Cliffs hotel all day.

TEL TALES: THE BLACKPOOL EIGHT GIVE THEIR SIDE OF THE STORY.

Back in London, the eight could have lain low and waited for the Doc's storm to subside. But they didn't. And it was a fatal error. If Terry Venables wanted to trace the date when his relationship with Docherty was finally blasted apart, then Friday, 23 April 1965 would be a good place to start.

Venables, Graham, Hollins and the rest were understandably subdued on the train back to Euston, but they were not idle. Not for them a few aimless hands of cards or a collective attempt at the crossword; with Venables to the fore, they cobbled together a statement giving their own version of what had happened in Blackpool. It began in notably combative style, too: 'We have done nothing to be ashamed of.' But after admitting that they had breached club discipline by staying out late, the players went on to issue what must, to Docherty at least, have read as a direct challenge to his authority: 'We are shocked by the punishment, which we believe is out of all proportion. It has not been in our nature to misbehave, and

ELEVEN MINUS EIGHT EQUALS . . . 'HEY, LUV, WANT A GAME?' NOT WHAT THE DOC ORDERED.

anyone who has seen us play should know that we are dedicated to fitness and to the game. We are too professional to do anything that would ruin our reputations.'

Their version of the incident was that after getting back to the Cliffs hotel and chatting in one of the rooms, the players decided to adjourn to the bowling alley where they 'sat around one table, drinking lager and talking in general'. Innocent enough – and besides, Docherty's curfew was not yet in force, as it was still before midnight. 'But some of the lads were hungry,' the statement continued, 'so we decided to have a meal. We left the restaurant and returned to the hotel, arriving there at 2 a.m. Mr Docherty was waiting for us. None of us was drunk, nor was there any disturbance. All this time the eight of us were together, and there were no girls in our company.'

The truth? It certainly sounded plausible, though remarkably innocent. Docherty, however, was steadfast in his belief that despatching them back to London on the first available train was the right way to treat the miscreants. He won the backing of Chelsea chairman Joe Mears, who announced, with masterly understatement: 'If the boys have misbehaved in any way, I am sure Tommy has done right. He is a strict disciplinarian.' But the Doc earned rather less support from the public at large: 'I got murdered,' he readily admitted. 'People started calling me "sergeant-major" – and I had very short hair at the time, too.'

The eight were now 200 miles away, yet even Docherty had no power to keep them at that distance once they had determined to fight back. On Friday afternoon, the disgraced players regrouped at a club in Soho and agreed that, even if they couldn't be on the Turf Moor pitch, the least they could do was back their team – crammed with hastily summoned reserves – from the stands. 'We have been together for forty games this season,' began a bulletin from their London bolt-hole. 'Why should we be out of it when there are only two to go? We don't want any favours. We don't want any tickets. We shall make no contact with Tommy Docherty, or with anyone else connected with the club. But we want to be there. If we aren't allowed to play, at least we can cheer.'

And cheer they did, though there was nothing to celebrate. Chelsea's lingering chance of the Championship was utterly destroyed inside twenty minutes as Burnley stormed into an unassailable 3–0 lead against Docherty's makeshift side. It was 4–1 at half-time, 6–2 at the final whistle.

After seeing his dream shattered over a point of principle, the Doc summoned the eight from their seats. At the end of a meeting which lasted almost twice as long as the game itself, Eddie McCreadie read a statement saying that the players were willing to accept whatever punishment the club decided to fling at them. In return, Docherty considered the slate wiped clean. All eight would be in the line-up for the last match of the season, at Blackpool the next afternoon. They were. But how could they possibly concentrate on football after the traumas of the last five days? The Blues lost again, 3–2 this time.

Docherty spent a whole year reflecting on the night that eight went mad in Blackpool before deciding that Terry Venables' tenure at Stamford Bridge was at an end. 'He started to challenge my authority in training. He would make sar-castic comments about what I was trying to put across. He wanted to be Mr Big in front of the lads,' was the Doc's verdict. 'He was a thorn in my side and too cheeky for my well-being.' After a 'him or me' showdown with chairman Mears, Docherty stripped Venables of the captaincy and in April 1966 put him on the transfer-list. He was gone to White Hart Lane in a matter of weeks.

Three decades on from what is still one of football's most sensational sagas, a head-to-head collision between two immovable objects, both protagonists are willing to shoulder the blame. 'When I look back now at why Tommy Docherty and I fell out, it all seems so irrelevant,' wrote Venables in his autobiography. 'The split may have been mostly my fault; I did not like losing at anything, and I used to get really annoyed if we were having a bad run. Perhaps we were both too young then, doing and saying silly things, which we would regret later.'

Docherty concurred. 'I was disappointed in Terry because he was captain of the team. Looking back, I was too severe. But if I hadn't done what I did, if I had only fined them, they would have had no respect for me.' Docherty admitted that the incident broke up a side which was on the verge of greatness. And considering Venables' belief that the team could indeed have gone on to be as dominant in that era as Leeds or Liverpool, it makes the Chelsea manager's reaction appear all the more intemperate.

But it's the Doc, with the benefit of five decades of experience, who best puts the Blackpool scandal into an overall footballing perspective: 'They'd been out on the piss, in a nutshell. One or two of them may have seen a bird. But by today's standards, that's nothing, is it?'

1. Terence Frederick Venables was a true East End war baby, born in his grandparents' house in Dagenham, Essex on 6 January 1943. He is a Capricorn – which in astrology points to 'an ambitious go-getter, attracted to the biggest challenges'. Capricorns 'seek drama but need dependability' – which makes football management a perverse choice of career.

2. Venables' love of showbiz started early. At the age of four, he was a member of a song-and-dance troupe called the Happy Tappers. Later, he was banned by his manager at Chelsea, Tommy Docherty, from entering the final of a Butlin's talent contest after he had won all the heats. He was also censured by the Doc when caught singing with Joe Loss at the Hammersmith Palais wearing his England Youth blazer.

3. Venables registered himself as a limited company when he turned professional at the age of eighteen – after he had already made his first-team debut for Chelsea. He told his dad Fred that no shark in a camel-hair overcoat would ever pocket twenty per cent of his earnings, and formed the company 'to exploit the talents of Terence Venables'. He enhanced his business credentials eight years later when, in between games and training, he learned to type at a West End secretarial school.

4. Despite his legendary status as a manager at White Hart Lane, Venables was never popular as a player at Tottenham. He resented terrace talk that he was merely a replacement for John White, the Spurs hero killed by lightning while playing golf.

5. Venables won two caps for England in 1964, and became the first and only player to represent his country at all six levels: schoolboy, youth, under-21, under-23, amateur and full international.

6. Venables married Christine McCann in 1966, with the service conducted by a West Ham-supporting vicar – who appeared in the wedding pictures wearing his Hammers scarf and bobble hat. They had two daughters, Nancy and Tracey, before separating in 1985 while Venables was managing Barcelona. He married Yvette, known as 'Toots', in December 1991, announcing their nuptials at Venables' club Scribes West. Expecting a drinks party rather than a full-blown wedding reception, the normally impeccably dressed George Graham arrived wearing jeans.

7. Among Venables' burgeoning business interests in the mid-1960s were Thingummywigs, hats with a wig fixed inside – blonde or brunette – so women could disguise their hair curlers when venturing out of doors. They didn't catch on.

8. The Hazell series of detective stories, co-written with Gordon Williams, was Venables' best-known foray into literature. However, his first attempt at story-writing was called 'The World of Sammy Small'. Williams praised it as a pastiche of Damon Runyon. Venables had never heard of him.

9. One of Venables' first signings when he took charge at Crystal Palace in 1976 was Rachid Harkouk, whom he plucked from non-league Feltham at a cost of £1,500. The following year, Harkouk and team-mate Barry Silkman were arrested for involvement in a forged currency racket, after being stopped by police with a car boot full of cash. The pair made a bizarre claim to police that they were running an 'errand' for their manager. Venables was not implicated, but he stood £2,000 bail for Silkman. Both players were found guilty and fined.

10. Venables could have owned a football club long before Spurs. Queens Park Rangers chairman Jim Gregory offered his then manager the chance of a buy-out in

1984. Venables turned it down to move to Barcelona.

11. Venables clinched the manager's job at the Nou Camp in 1984 when the Spanish club's president, Josip-Luis Nuñez, went to offer Venables a cigar but found his box empty. Venables produced one from his sock, telling the supremo: 'It's the only place to keep them to make sure they don't bend.'

12. For someone so closely associated with Tottenham, Venables was twice on the point of taking the manager's job at north London rivals Arsenal. The Gunners tried unsuccessfully to lure him from Crystal Palace in 1976, and Venables signed an agreement to move to Highbury at the end of his second season in Barcelona. It was the break-up of his marriage which led Venables to stay another year in Spain. His

'WEST HAM 2 CHELSEA 0, HALLELUJAH . . .'

close friend and former team-mate George Graham was installed in the Arsenal hot-seat instead.

13. The Channel 4 *Dispatches* programme and two BBC *Panorama* specials claimed financial malpractice by Venables when obtaining a loan to help finance his takeover of Spurs in 1991. No criminal proceedings followed, however. Ray Needham, the police officer who investigated the claims at Venables' request, stated: 'I am satisfied that Mr Venables has not been up to any mischief.' Venables issued a libel writ against *Panorama*, and threw down a £250,000 challenge: 'Prove I'm guilty or pay up!' There were no takers.

14. Far from being devastated by *Panorama*'s interest, Venables began to joke about it. When he heard of the second programme, he quipped: 'Not even serial killers get two *Panoramas*. I am only a football manager.' Instead of watching it, he went to see Queens Park Rangers play Liverpool.

15. At the height of his battle with Alan Sugar, Venables appeared in a TV advertisement promoting Virgin Airlines. He was reading a book entitled *How to Succeed in Business*.

16. Venables' photograph appeared in newspaper advertisements endorsing a series of business seminars run by the Financial Freedom Forum. He was quoted as saying: 'In only three hours I learnt more about money than in the last thirty years – I can't recommend it enough.' However, in June 1994, the seminars were criticized by the Consumers Association for being 'worrying and misleading'. One disgruntled customer said of the information contained in manuals offered as part of a £599 membership package: 'I got the impression most of it was taken from newspapers.'

17. In April 1993, Venables was convicted of driving at 100 m.p.h. on the M11. He was banned for seven days, and fined £700 with £25 costs.

18. In September 1994, Venables' autobiography was launched at a party held at his Scribes West club. Unusually, every guest was required to buy a copy. However, for a man whose literary talents had been amply demonstrated in the past, he seemed reluctant to acknowledge that this was all his own work. When a journalist asked him if he was pleased with the book, he replied: 'Yes, what I've read of it, I think it's great.'

19. Venables' interview for the post of national coach was interrupted half-way through when a woman threatened to jump from a roof opposite and kill herself.

20. In 1975, Crystal Palace supremo Malcolm Allison said of his chipper young coach: 'I am forging a partnership with Terry Venables. I believe he is the first in a new generation of key football people. Venables is assured of a brilliant future.' Big Mal was right.

3

Seventies Sinners

'From the first time I kicked a ball as a professional, I began to learn what the game was all about. It's about the drunken parties that go on for days. The orgies, the birds and the fabulous money. Football is just a distraction, but you're so fit you can carry on with all the high living in secret and still play the game at the highest level.'

Peter Storey

Peter Shilton, England's cool custodian, knew he was in for perhaps the toughest game of his life. A veteran of cup ties, championship deciders and tense World Cup matches, the away fixture at Highbury in September 1980 was going to be a test of his legendary powers of concentration, and indeed his sense of humour.

Within seconds of his appearance, the chant went up from the Arsenal North Bank: 'Peter Shilton, Peter Shilton, does your missus know you're here? Does your missus know you're here?' There were cries of 'Tina! Tina!', and 'Shilton, Shilton, where's your wife?' When he warmed up by touching his toes, there were more taunts of 'Haven't you done enough press-ups?', followed by 'Super stud!', 'Sexy boy!' and plenty more unprintable remarks.

He was embarrassed, but not surprised. For, a few days before, Shilts, as he is known to his fellow professionals, had been caught in what, for the fans at least, was one of the most hilarious soccer incidents of all time. Nottingham Forest's married shot-stopper had been discovered in his Jaguar with married mother of three Tina Street, at 5 a.m. in a country lane. Tina's husband had arrived, and Shilton had hurriedly driven off and hit a lamppost. He then failed a police breath-test. It was the 1980 prototype for many later footballing scandals, managing to encompass late-night boozing, a married woman, an irate husband, drink-driving and a car accident, all in one seminal moment.

Shilton had met Tina in a Nottingham night-club and then taken her for a meal at an Indian restaurant. Tina's husband, antique-restorer Colin Street, said he had become anxious after Tina phoned at 2.25 a.m. to say she was going for a meal with a girlfriend. He went to look for her and saw her leave the restaurant with Shilton in his Jaguar. Street followed the Jag to a dirt road near Nottingham race-course.

'I put my headlights full on. Both of them were partly clothed. They were definitely making love,' was Colin's version of events. 'I knocked on the window and said, "I know you Shilton, I've got you!" I heard Tina say, "It's my husband!" and Shilton slid back on to the driving seat and roared off.' The car swerved straight into a lamppost and Street called the police. He claimed that when the boys in blue arrived Shilton was doing up his trousers and Tina was struggling to get back into her clothes. Shilton failed a breath-test and later had stitches put in his cut jaw.

Shilton admitted 'taking a lady for a meal' and giving her a lift home, but insisted 'nothing untoward took place', adding 'I don't even know her name – I'm terrible with names, you know.' Tina Street also insisted that 'there was no question of any hanky-panky between me and Peter Shilton'.

But husband Colin disagreed, and immediately started divorce proceedings, claiming, 'I have a burning hatred for Peter Shilton.' Tina went to stay with her mother after the accident, taking her three children with her, while Shilton's wife Sue stood by him. But on the Sunday after the Arsenal match Shilton was besieged by reporters at his mock-Tudor house. He and his wife had had a long lie-in after celebrating their tenth wedding anniversary. Interrupting a late breakfast, Shilton took a philosophical attitude to the stick from the Arsenal crowd: 'Things happen in life, like in football. You have to accept them, and stand or fall by what you have done.'

The whole furore seemed grossly unfair on the legendary goalie. What could a married man and a married woman parked in a country lane at 5 a.m. be doing – except discussing Nottingham Forest's chances of keeping a clean sheet on Saturday?

Other footballers of the seventies and early eighties were involved in far more risqué escapades than Shilton. In this sexually carefree time before Aids came along and hacks began to watch every night-club move of our Fancy Dans, it was a golden period of both individual footballing and bedroom flair, as the stars took all the gifts on offer in the 'permissive society'. Frank Worthington, during his travels with Huddersfield, Leicester, Bolton, Birmingham and just about everyone else, was never slow to admit his prowess at 'birding'.

While most of the publicity went to George Best, Worthington was probably number one in the pulling stakes. Worthington (or 'Wanky Wanky Wanky Worthington' as was chanted at him by fans throughout the country) was perhaps the greatest role model for the modern footballer. This was, after all, a man who called his autobiography *One Hump or Two*. Just listen to this: 'My bed wasn't for sleeping, it was for birding. I was at it five nights a week with rarely the same woman twice and often the odd quick one before a match.'

Worthington would dance the night away in his flares and fringed leather jacket at discos, often taking a girl back to his flat who would stay for a couple of days before the next one moved in. 'I never really minded who it was. Sometimes, though, I'd wake up in the morning and look at the face next to me and wonder what the hell I was up to.'

No wonder a proposed move from Huddersfield to Liverpool fell through because of Frank's high blood pressure. Still, as Worthington once memorably declared: 'I spent a fortune on birds and booze – but as my old mate Stan Bowles says, it was lucky I didn't waste it.'

'WE USED TO
BE FAMOUS
FOOTBALLERS,
HONEST!'

FRANK WORTHINGTON SHOWS THE STYLE THAT PROVED IRRESISTIBLE TO LEICESTER
LINGERIE MODELS.

FOR A FEW DOLLARS MORE YOU COULD HAVE GOT THE HORSE, FRANK.

After the Liverpool signing was put on hold, Anfield boss Bill Shankly told him to take it easy on holiday and see if his blood pressure came down. Frank's way of relaxing was a three-in-a-bed romp with two Swedish women in Majorca and a fling with a 'magnificently built' Belgian woman from Knokke. Not surprisingly Worthington failed his medical again upon his return and missed out on a possible career as an England regular and Anfield great. 'Given my time again I would have heeded the warning and got my feet up with a good book, lots of early nights, no threesomes and definitely no Knokkers,' is philosopher Worthington's verdict today.

But never let it be said that Frank neglected his football. 'I gave myself Friday night off, plus one other night. I just had to allow myself some time for training with the lads.' What a true pro . . .

By his own admission Worthington's career included making love to a chambermaid before getting on the team bus, being caught hiding two dancers in the wardrobe while with Huddersfield, seducing numerous lingerie models and a now-famous cabaret artiste with a craving for a toothbrush attached to a vibrator at Leicester's Holiday Inn, joining the Mile High Club with a married Frenchwoman while with Leicester, making love to another player's wife who wore nothing but stockings and suspenders under a fur coat, sleeping with a mother and daughter while playing in Sweden, smoking dope with a lady lawyer in the USA before 'the most sexually charged hour of my life', and even sleeping with Mandy Rice-Davies (well, he would say that, wouldn't he?). Worthington clearly thought that Lothario was a player worth imitating.

The Elvis Presley fanatic was also ahead of his time in his choice of long-term partners; only a footballer would wed a Swedish blonde model called Birgitta Egermalm, whom he met in Majorca while on holiday with his pal George Best. The six-year marriage finally ended in 1978 when Birgitta, mother of Worthy's two children, declared: 'I blame football and Frank's boasting about all the women he's had.' Frank is now playing at home, happily married to leopardskin-wearing former page 3 girl Carol Dwyer, whose late father Noel kept goal for Wolves, West Ham, Swansea, Plymouth, Charlton and the Republic of Ireland.

And as for Worthington's England career – at a squad get-together in Manchester, Don Revie had about as much chance of getting Frank Worthington into the sack before eleven o'clock as the Faroe Islands have of winning the next World Cup. Before the hour was out, football's original Teddy Boy had found the fire escape at the back of the hotel. In an echo of Terry Venables and his Chelsea team-mates' exit route from the Cliffs hotel in Blackpool nine years earlier, no sooner was the evening meal over than he, Alan Ball, Allan Clarke and Peter Storey were away down it. The quartet may have wanted to play for England, but a petty rule was not going to stop them drinking for it, too.

They headed for a casino run by a friend of Ball's. Nothing too outrageous: autographs for the punters, a few games of roulette, a couple of bottles of champagne, and a taxi at around 11.30 p.m. Even Revie could not have moaned too much about that. But any thoughts of heading back to the hotel soon disappeared when the foursome were in the cab. Ball told his pals to hold out their hands, and filled them with cash. It was a 'thank you' from the casino owner, who had enjoyed one of his best-ever night's business. Armed with an extra £200 each, there was only one place to be: George Best's club Slack Alice's.

While Revie dozed, dreaming of dossiers, Frank and the gang found they were not alone in preferring booze and birds to bed. Peter Osgood, Stan Bowles, Tony Currie, Alan Hudson and a dozen more players had done a runner from the Piccadilly – and with the much lusted-after blonde actress Susan George turning up at Slack Alice's accompanied by the singer Jack Jones, it was, as Worthington put it, 'one of the great nights out'. When the players finally made it back to base around 3 a.m., none cared who saw them – and instead of sneaking surreptitiously up the back stairs, the cream of English soccer simply strolled in through the main doors.

When Tommy Docherty exposed the antics of his errant eight Chelsea players on their crucial trip to Blackpool, it was train tickets at dawn. Revie preferred pistols. The following day, he called Worthington, Hudson, Currie and Bowles over one by one, told them he knew they'd been out drinking the night before, and announced that they weren't the sort of players he wanted. 'You've all got great skill,' he intoned while metaphorically loading the gun, 'but there's just something missing in your game.' Bang.

One man who took his interest in what Frank Worthington delighted in calling 'birding' a little too far was the ex-Arsenal player Peter Storey. As he was about to go to jail in 1980, Storey revealed that ever since he became a pro, he'd started to learn that the game was about drunken parties, orgies, birds and fabulous money.

Storey described a three-in-a-bed sex romp with an air hostess and a team-mate after a tour of Austria, and while on the same tour even making love to one woman while a team-mate watched hidden in the wardrobe. (Is that what they mean by doing the double?)

Storey was a manager's nightmare: 'A young rising star soon learns that as his plane touches down for a foreign tour, or the train pulls in for an away match, the idea is to give the manager the slip, find a willing bird, and settle down for the night.' For Storey it was always a team game, however: 'If there aren't enough birds to go round, well we're all good mates, so let's share.'

Storey was a tough-tackling, hard-running part of Arsenal's Double-winning side, starring at full-back and as a midfield ball-winner alongside the likes of Bob Wilson, Frank McLintock, George Graham, Ray Kennedy and Charlie George. Despite his off-the-field antics he played nineteen times for England.

After big games there were usually drunken parties, revealed the Arsenal bird-bandit. Sex queen Mary Millington was a regular and so was sister Doreen, editor of a porn magazine. Storey's best ever party was after his testimonial game against Feyenoord. His pub, the Jolly Farmers in Islington, was packed and didn't close for two days. Alan Ball, Bob McNab, Olivia Newton-John and Mary and Doreen Millington were all there.

'At 5 a.m. a famous Dutch player was stark naked chasing a girl round the bar. She was wearing nothing but a tiny bra, suspenders and stockings. He eventually caught one of her friends and carried her upstairs,' Storey recalled of his pub's conversion to total football.

Midfield enforcer Storey used to terrorize the opposition with tackles that some regarded as less than legal. That was nothing to his post-Arsenal career, however, which has left a legacy that even current lads done bad Tony Adams and Paul Merson will surely never match.

Moving into the area of sexual healing, Storey was fined £700 and given a six-month suspended jail sentence in 1979 for operating a brothel. Like many players hanging up their boots, Storey had decided to go into management – by running his own team of prostitutes. In 1979 three women sold their bodies from Storey's rented flat in Leyton High Street, a less-than-glamorous part of London's East End. Storey showed a footballer's sense of style by naming the flat 'The Calypso Massage Parlour'.

There was then an interlude from the sex trade, as Storey continued to amass what surely must be a record number of convictions for a retired footballer. He was jailed for three years for financing a plot to counterfeit gold coins in 1980, and given two six-month jail sentences in 1982 for stealing cars, before he was again jailed for four weeks in 1990 for smuggling twenty obscene videos into Britain – no, not tapes of Arsenal winning 1–0, these had titles like *Caught In The Act* and *Big Bust*. The porn films were stashed inside the spare wheel of his car.

When Storey was declared bankrupt in 1983, he was at least, for once, honest: 'I blew it all on birds and booze,' he told the London Bankruptcy Court. After another twenty-eight-day suspended jail sentence in 1991 for swearing at a traffic warden who booked him twice in twenty minutes,

Mr Storey was last seen selling plaid from a London market stall.

At least most seventies stars were caught out for offences that, for the impressionable, might be considered glamorous. Not so Chelsea's Clive Walker – surely the spiritual mentor of Sheffield United's Don Hutchison, of whom more later. In 1978 the recently married Blues' flankman admitted indecently exposing himself to two schoolgirls as they bicycled past his home, and was fined £50. (And to think, this was years before the Full Members Cup had even been thought of.) The prosecution lawyer said that 'as one girl rode past he stood on the doorstep, undid his trousers and exposed himself and smiled at another girl'. Walker's solicitor said that his client was in a daydream (Chelsea fans might have recognized this state) when the incidents happened, and that 'the offences have devastated my client. He cannot explain why he did it.'

Poor Walker had to suffer rather less good-humoured terrace taunts than Peter Shilton, culminating in the massed legions of the West Ham North Bank chorusing 'Walker, Walker, show us yer c**k!'. It was enough to make any player feel a right plonker.

But don't fret, Clive, for today's heroes certainly owe a debt of honour to the stars of yesteryear. Without Worthington, Storey, Shilton, Walker and, of course, George Best, where would the likes of Tony Adams, Mickey Thomas, Duncan Ferguson, Eric Cantona and Jan Molby be today? (Probably still awaiting social workers' reports before sentencing.) They might now be the oldest swingers in town, but yesterday's heroes could surely have today's young pretenders under the table by the end of the first orgy.

4

Faking the Mickey

'You should have been setting young apprentices an example of how a true professional conducts himself. Instead, largely I think because it fitted in with your self-image of a flash and daring adventurer, you betrayed the trust of your employers. And you failed in your duty as a distinguished international sportsman.'

Judge Gareth Edwards sentencing Mickey Thomas to eighteen months in jail for counterfeit currency fraud

In a darkened corner of a Welsh field, Mickey Thomas's buttocks were heaving up and down. There, beneath him in his Volkswagen, was a dusky brunette called Erica Dean. She wasn't just any other woman, though. Dean was none other than the sister of Thomas's ex-wife. And she was also a married woman herself. Not for the first time the midfield maestro had contrived to find himself in a very dodgy situation. Sprawled across the front seat of the car, Thomas was nevertheless enjoying his dangerous liaison. He was about to shoot and score with his companion in lust when suddenly the window was smashed, sending glass everywhere. Two men, one armed with a hammer and the other with a screwdriver, began attacking the football legend as he lay helpless. 'They ripped my clothes off and started stabbing me,' Thomas recalls. 'They were trying to break my legs. I was on my side, so they pulled me over by my hair and banged fuck out of me.' Scars still disfigure the player's wrists and hands – proof of how he tried to protect himself from the blows, cuts and punches that rained down in what police called 'a prolonged attack'. Life had been cruel before to Mickey Thomas, but this was the first time he had suffered the indignity, not to say pain, of a beating while indulging in some nocturnal nookie in a lovers' lane. 'One minute we were just messing around,' the player explains, 'and the next minute the window came in – crash!'

The incident perfectly summed up both Thomas's life and his erratically successful football career: one minute everything was fine, the next disaster had struck. He was a player whose goals, antics and habit of going AWOL enlivened and infuriated the many, many clubs – thirteen at the last count – for whom he turned out in a career stretching from the early 1970s to the mid-1990s. He wore the colours of some of the game's biggest names – the Uniteds of Manchester and

MAD, BAD AND DANGEROUS TO SIGN: MICKEY THOMAS TIES THE KNOT.

Leeds, and Everton and Chelsea among them – yet refused to change his wild ways for any.

But back to that field. The full story of what had led to the brutal assault emerged later when Dean and her two co-conspirators – who turned out to be her husband Geoffrey and an equally sadistic pal of his called Mark Gorevan – were brought to trial. It was an extraordinary tale of infidelity, revenge and loathing. The real villain turned out to be Geoffrey Dean. He hated Thomas with a vengeance. Dean blamed Thomas for allegedly ruining Debbie's (Thomas's former wife's) life and then shagging her sister – Dean's wife – into the bargain. Erica and Mickey had been sweethearts at school and she still had 'a soft spot' for him. Determined to get even, Dean pressured his wife to lure the famous footballer to that secluded spot near Prestatyn where, his mind on other things, Thomas would be easy meat. Sentencing the trio, Judge Elgan Edwards was particularly scathing about Erica's conduct. 'You were the bait, and you lured Mr Thomas into what can only be described as a most vulnerable position. You allowed him to have sexual relations with you while knowing he was about to be attacked seriously.'

It had indeed been a devious plot. Erica Dean had rung Thomas asking to meet that night to give him information about her sister, his ex-missus, from whom he had become estranged and embittered. They had been having an affair for several months so Thomas knew he was going to get not only some useful details for his pending divorce battle but also some Thursday-night sex. In the careful words of the prosecution counsel, they 'drove to the entrance of a field, reversed the car down the track and commenced lovemaking. Three to four minutes later the driver's window was smashed, Mr Thomas looked around and saw a shape lurch through the door and grab him by the hair. This person started punching him in the face and shouted, "Run, Erica, run." As the cheating, deceiving wife got out of the VW, the light came on and revealed Thomas's attacker to be her thug of a husband. He grabbed Thomas by his curly hair and began punching him. Meanwhile Gorevan got to work with the hammer. Then Dean began stabbing their helpless prey with a screwdriver in the stomach, body and buttocks. Terrified Thomas cried out, 'You're going to kill me!' to which Dean replied: 'That's exactly what we're trying to do.' At another point Gorevan threatened to cut off Thomas's penis and ear, mark his face and break his legs. In a desperate attempt to end his ordeal, the player pretended to be unconscious. But Dean and Gorevan kept assaulting him, then ran off. Justice was done, though. The judge rejected the men's argument that the Wrexham captain had simply received 'fair retribution' for his affair with scheming Erica. They got two years each in jail for the horrible, cowardly and bloody attack; she escaped with community service for her part in the set-up.

That was in July 1993. Just eight days later, however, Thomas ended up behind bars himself. He got eighteen months for a counterfeit currency scam which had been going fine until some of the Wrexham YTS lads, who had bought some of the funny money from their club captain, had gone for a night out at the Tivoli night-club in Buckley, near Chester. The next day Thomas was enjoying a restful Sunday at home with his beloved mum when two detectives knocked at the door. Before he could say, 'You must be taking the Mickey,' Thomas was arrested and taken to Deeside police station. The Wrexham trainees had named him as the source of their dud notes. Thomas was charged with distributing the high-quality dodgy tenners that the Tivoli had found in its tills. He was kept in custody overnight, brought to Wrexham magistrates court the next morning and freed on bail protesting: 'I still want to play. I'm innocent.' The magistrates were taking no chances, though. They ordered Thomas to surrender his passport, report to the police twice a week and not contact any of Wrexham's apprentices.

Banned from training with his teammates, Thomas kept in shape by pounding the beach alone near his seaside home in Colwyn Bay. Wrexham's next game was a biggie: away to West Ham in the fourth round of the FA Cup. The plum draw was the Fourth Division side's reward for creating one of the tournament's greatest-ever shocks in the previous round by disposing of the reigning League champions, Arsenal, 2–1 at the Racecourse Ground. It was an even more impressive result because the Welsh outfit had gone 1–0 down, only to be rescued by a magnificent Thomas free-kick and a winner minutes from the end. If the veteran campaigner was worried about the attitude of the Upton Park crowd, he soon realized he needn't have been. When he ran out at five to three, dozens of Hammers diehards in the Chicken Run shelf terrace began gesturing furiously and shouting at him. Intrigued, Thomas strolled cautiously over. He found rows and rows of the claret-and-blue faithful waving handfuls of photocopied tenners and chanting, 'Loadsamoney, Thomas, we've got loads of money!' The player appreciated the jovial display of that famous Cockney humour and a broad grin creased his face.

That smile quickly disappeared, though,

when it was time for Thomas to stand trial. He denied the charges but was found guilty on three counts of selling around £800 worth of fake twenties and tens to Wrexham trainees for a few quid each in real, honest money. The Knutsford Crown Court jury declined to believe the player's defence that the seven apprentices caught with the dud notes had only named the club's senior professional as their supplier in a bid to save their own skins. David Thompson, Thomas's barrister, claimed they had jumped on the bandwagon because they had been told that somebody wanted Thomas implicated in the scam. Three weeks later, the player returned to court to hear his fate. At first he appeared his usual relaxed, jokey self. 'Has anyone got change of ten quid for the phone?' he quipped with waiting newsmen. He knew he couldn't get away with just a fine, 'because everyone will suspect I'll print my own money to pay'. Such humour died in his throat, though, when he heard Judge Gareth Edwards pass sentence. His Honour didn't think the offences a laughing matter and ignored a plea from Thomas's lawyer for a non-custodial sentence. In his speech the solicitor, with memorable understatement, described his client as a 'foolish man [whose] judgement is at its best on the field, not in his private affairs'. The judge gave Thomas eighteen months at Her Majesty's pleasure and sent him away with this scathing indictment ringing in his ears: 'You are admired by youngsters throughout Wales and much further afield, a man who many times had the honour of wearing the Welsh shirt.'

With that, the disgraced 'distinguished international sportsman', father-of-two and footballer who had played over 700 League games and won fifty-one caps for

'A FLASH AND DARING ADVENTURER'? MICKEY THOMAS TAKES THE RAP.

his country, was carried off to the slammer.

Her boy's conviction and jailing broke Mary Thomas's heart. But one woman was happy. Debbie, the ex-wife who had divorced Thomas back in 1989, spoke bitterly about her husband's womanizing while they had been married. 'I knew he was cheating, so it was no surprise to find out about Erica. Mickey was always a bit of a fly-guy,' she said. 'After all that wild living, I suppose he's finally getting his just rewards.' Erica Dean also spoke to the newspapers. She claimed that Thomas had begged her to don a Wrexham strip before they made love. Worse, she revealed that she 'wasn't that impressed with him as a lover. He wasn't that energetic for a footballer.'

To this day Thomas still insists he was not involved in the dodgy dinero racket. 'Nobody ever said I gave them any fake money,' he says. 'All they said was that I knew about it. I got eighteen months for that.' The real brains behind the scheme, he alleges, was Liverpool businessman Alex Roache, a friend and 'hanger-on' who had pleaded guilty to the charges. 'I got guilty and I got jail because of my name. If I'd been anyone else, I wouldn't have gone to jail.' Given the small sum involved – this wasn't exactly a multi-million pound serious fraud – he probably has a point. And the player still boils with anger at Judge Edwards's comments. 'He was enjoying it, with all the media there. He made an example of me, of course he did. I thought, "He doesn't know me so how can he judge me?" *He* should have got eighteen months for what he said about me.'

The prison sentence finally ended Mickey Thomas's colourful, incident-strewn career. It was a very long way from the glory of turning out for Manchester United, who had signed him from Wrexham in 1978 for £300,000. The short-arsed, long-haired midfield dynamo was soon burdened with the stunningly unoriginal nickname of 'the Welsh George Best' – which turned out to be a fair comparison. United were determined to prise the skilful, tough-tackling number eleven from Wrexham, where he'd played since he was seventeen. Entering Old Trafford, Thomas was certainly in awe of his new surroundings. He vividly recalls standing butt-naked for his medical, being watched by manager Dave Sexton and starting to tremble with nerves at the prospect of his big move. A thought suddenly flashed through his mind. 'What the hell am I doing here?' It was to prove prophetic.

At first the 24-year-old from the tiny north Wales seaside town of Colwyn Bay could hardly believe his luck. He was earning £450 a week, three times his wages at Wrexham. His new team-mates were all household names: Martin Buchan, Steve Coppell, Lou Macari, Garry Birtles, Gordon McQueen, Joe Jordan, Mike Duxbury and, er, Ashley Grimes. Thomas's first appearance for United introduced him to a new phenomenon: travelling to away games by train – in first class. The Red hordes liked their first sight of their new signing, especially when he set up the only goal of the match for Jimmy Greenhoff. The fans took instantly to the little Welshman whose industry and aggression they recognized as essential if the team was to show the flair for which it was famous. Thomas the tank engine seemed to be a star in the making.

Before long, though, things began going wrong. Although the club rules at United forbade players from touching the hard stuff in the build-up to a game, Thomas started drinking regularly and heavily on a Friday night. Drinking, and drinking, and drinking. Bottles of wine, pint after pint of Guinness, it didn't really matter. While the rest of his team-mates were following the boss's orders by going to bed soon after *News At Ten*, Thomas was busy getting pissed. 'I was drinking until three, four, five and sometimes six in the morning on a Friday night,' he admits. Why? The Welshman blames it on the pressure of playing for such a big club. 'I used to get pissed on a Friday so I could still be pissed on a Saturday so I could play. I was getting myself drunk so I was so tired I wouldn't be uptight and I'd be relaxed, because when you relax you're sometimes a better player than when you're nervous. Or I am anyway.' Come 3 p.m. the next day, Thomas would still be pissed. 'I was playing really well because I was so relaxed, see? I don't know why I got into it. I just thought, "It'll help me" – and it did. I only missed a couple of games, and only those because I was injured. I had so much energy because I was so fit.' Amazingly, nobody at Old Trafford rumbled what was going on, so no one disturbed what became a Friday-night ritual for Thomas at United and many of the other clubs he played for.

Forever a law unto himself, Thomas at least kept his pre-match boozing private. In 1981, however, his wayward nature led to a very public dispute with United. It involved the club's close-season summer tour to Malaysia. In theory it offered a free trip to a dream location in return for playing a few exhibition-standard matches. Despite that, Thomas didn't fancy it at all. His idea of a holiday was two weeks in his back garden in Colwyn Bay. But like the rest of the Old Trafford stars, he

assembled at Manchester Airport, bags reluctantly packed for this involuntary break in the Far East. As the players milled around, he told team-mate Sammy McIlroy that he was going to do a bunk. The Ulsterman sympathized: he wasn't keen to go either. The dissident duo nevertheless trooped dutifully on to the plane. Then, with take-off approaching, McIlroy suddenly changed his mind, headed for the exit and scarpered.

Given the restlessness in the ranks, the United management could thank their lucky stars that they were only one down by the time they reached London, where they had to change flights. At Heathrow, Thomas was walking towards the terminal when Jimmy Nicholl sidled over. 'I'm not going,' he confided, then shot off. To misquote Oscar Wilde: 'To lose one player may be regarded as a misfortune. To lose two seems like carelessness.'

For Thomas, that was it. An impulsive creature at the best of times, he decided that he would join the refuseniks. Spying Lou Macari and Gordon McQueen sitting playing cards, he moved across and revealed his plan. The Caledonian card-sharps didn't believe him. 'Bet me a tenner I'm not going,' challenged the little Welshman. Out came two brown ones. His team-mates' wagers collected, Thomas too joined the mini-exodus – in the direction of a ticket desk to book himself on to the next shuttle back to Manchester. As the depleted United party jetted off to the balmy beauty of Kuala Lumpur, their midfield general headed for the slightly cooler climes of north Wales, the refrain of Peters and Lee's 'Welcome Home' playing sweetly in his head. It was a hell of a way to win a bet.

The three truants were fined two weeks' wages and warned to start behaving themselves. But only mad Mickey was asked to come and have a chat with chairman Martin Edwards in his big office. Sensing his player's unhappiness, Edwards decided not to condemn Thomas's vanishing act and tried flattery instead. 'Everybody likes you here, Mickey. You're doing very well,' he soothed. Thomas's reply left the chairman open-mouthed. 'I told him, "I don't like the pressure of playing for Manchester United, it's too much for me. I just want to enjoy myself."' The wandering Welshman explained that he couldn't cope with the much higher profile he'd had since swopping the Racecourse Ground for Old Trafford. For Thomas, being a Red Devil was something to endure, not enjoy. It was 'pressure', something he didn't like. Edwards offered him more money to stay; Thomas refused. Eyeball to eyeball he told the astonished chairman that he wanted to leave. Players are usually desperate to join, not quit, United. With Mickey Thomas, though, it paid to expect the unexpected.

He admits now that, 'If I went through my life again I'd probably be all right, but at the time I couldn't handle it.' Thomas insists that being at United turned him into a heavy boozer. 'Everybody recognizing you everywhere you go, it was horrible. I didn't like that. Your life's not the same once you've become somebody. You go from being a normal person walking down the street to a situation where everybody points at you.' Though it's hard to imagine Thomas as a stay-at-home type, he insists that the price of footballing fame was so high that he became afraid to go out, either in Manchester or even at home in north Wales. He didn't want to risk suffering one of the game's occupational hazards: some pissed-up fan of another team having a go, offering the big-name player a fight outside.

Edwards was surprised by Thomas going AWOL pre-Malaysia; Dave Sexton wasn't. He had lost count of the times his player had been late for training or missed it altogether. One time madcap Mickey stayed at home in Wales for a week after missing a penalty against Ipswich at the Stretford End. On another occasion United were due to play Celtic in a testimonial for the Glasgow club's legendary full-back Danny McGrain. Thomas finally turned up half an hour before kick-off. The manager's answer, though, was not to go running to Edwards or tell the press, but to keep under wraps the personal problems bubbling away in his midfield maestro's increasingly chaotic life. In a throwback to Matt Busby's handling of George Best, Sexton opted for one-to-one management of a guy who had both a special talent and his fair share of problems.

Thomas's marriage was in trouble, for example. Although Mickey and Debbie Thomas had walked up the aisle in 1979, a year after he joined United, their rows began soon after. Debbie was an ex-beauty queen seven years younger than Thomas – a classic footballer's wife. She also had a temper as fierce as one of her husband's tackles. After one argument, she threw his video gear on to the lawn of their house in Rhyl. During another, the former Miss Wales finalist kicked a glass door and had to have a dozen stitches put in her foot, which she had neglected to put a shoe on first. Part of her trouble was post-natal depression following the birth of their first child, Aaron. Thomas, too, had his own run of bad luck. 'Apart from recurring injuries and illness, I wrapped my car around a tree and had my 1979 Cup Final medal stolen.'

Ask Thomas now how he got away with so much rule-breaking for so long at Old Trafford and he answers with the name of Dave Sexton. 'He was a great guy. He knew I was a shy, nervous person. I don't come over like that, but I was like that in those days.' It is a startling confession from one of football's most gregarious, larger-than-life characters. Remind him that his image is of a wild, high-living extrovert and he comes out with this immortal line: 'The public think I'm nuts. [Pause] I probably am.'

Despite Edwards's best efforts, Thomas insisted on leaving Old Trafford. It was probably the worst mistake of the many he made in his long career. He jumped at the chance of joining Howard Kendall at Everton, the team he had supported since boyhood. But his time at Goodison would simply confirm the pattern he had already established at United: at first things were fine and then somehow he would screw them up – and always blame someone else. After playing thirteen games for the Toffees, he pulled a thigh muscle. After a characteristically quick recovery, he looked forward to getting back into the starting line-up to face Manchester City. Kendall, though, wanted Thomas to play for the reserves at Newcastle in order to regain his sharpness for the Merseyside derby the next weekend. This time the player at least warned his manager in advance that he wouldn't be gracing the reserves with his presence. 'I'm not going to turn up. I want to play for the first team,' he explained. Kendall, foolishly, thought mercurial Mickey was only joking. Sure enough, come match-day, Thomas didn't show for the reserve team coach to the north-east. Instead he spent the afternoon in the bar of a Liverpool hotel, wishing he was at Maine Road with the rest of the lads. Punishment was inevitable: fined two weeks' wages and told to train with the reserves on the Monday. 'Kendall loved me,' insists the Welsh rarebit. So why provoke a bust-up with him? 'On principle. I stick to my guns. If I believed I was right, I wouldn't back down, even though I knew I could get into trouble.' The bizarre logic of the pub drunk cut no ice with the Goodison boss, who reluctantly but quickly concluded that Thomas had to go in case he undermined his authority and caused dressing-room discontent by being seen to get his own way. That latest moment of stupidity ended Thomas's brief liaison with the club he had supported for years.

The 1980s would undoubtedly have been a much duller football era without Mickey Thomas's antics. Wherever he went, he brought talent, charisma, a strong sense of mischief – and a shocking attitude problem. That, however, did not deter a host of clubs from investing in this most peripatetic of players. Perhaps each thought it would be the one finally to persuade him to settle down. Brighton and Hove Albion – then, incredibly, in the First Division – were next. The south coast club paid £500,000 for him. Manager Mike Bailey hoped that Thomas, plus players such as Jimmy Case, could help keep the Seagulls in the top flight. Thomas, though, recalls that 'half an hour after I signed, in front of all the media, I was back in my hotel and I thought, "Fuck me, what have I done here?"'

It was a disastrous move for both club and player. Brighton had spent half a million on someone who quickly decided he had made a mistake. From the very start Thomas just wanted to get away. He knew he would never settle there – it was too far from Colwyn Bay – so why bother

'HEY, PAL, LEND US A TENNER FOR SOME PETROL?'

trying? An incident just twenty-four hours after he signed set the tone for his stormy relations with the Seagulls. Thomas was more than happy to oblige when he was asked to present some prizes at a local night-club. With drinks on the house, trouble was almost inevitable. By the end of an evening spent clutching two glasses of wine at once, he was absolutely paralytic. Somehow he got back to his luxury hotel suite where he proceeded to throw up in each of its seven rooms. Next day, he didn't surface until lunchtime. He was so hung-over it was even beyond him to reach the phone beside his bed to take any of the calls from an increasingly frantic Mike Bailey. At least his drinking buddies, new team-mates like Case, Steve Foster and Mike Robinson, made it to training. The Welsh wino finally turned up at 3 p.m. 'Bailey asked me where the hell I'd been for first day's training. I was dead honest and told him I couldn't help it. I was pissed. He fined me £50, which was nothing to me because I was earning big money.'

After only a few games, Thomas had had enough. Instead of playing for Brighton against Everton, he went to watch his old Wrexham mates in action. Then he returned to the seaside, told a horrified Bailey he wanted to leave and headed off to Marbella for a break. After his return he still went missing. And again. And again. Even the arrival in Colwyn Bay of Bailey and his assistant John Collins begging him to return made no difference to Thomas. The player says now he feels guilty about messing Brighton around – 'They were really nice people and I caused them all sorts of problems' – but admits that his misbehaviour had a certain perverse logic to it too. 'I wanted to do so many bad things that they'd say, "Hey, we've got to get rid of him, he's nuts." And I fucking did. I was bad.'

Mad, bad and dangerous to sign: that was Thomas to a tee. However, even his by-now atrocious reputation for unreliability, unprofessionalism and generally taking the piss did not deter clubs from hiring him. Joining Stoke City at least helped satisfy his wife Debbie's ultimatum that he either move to a club nearer home or he'd lose both her and Aaron. Moving to the Midlands did little to calm him

down, though. In Spain on a midwinter break, for example, Thomas threw his bed out of the hotel window – 'a bit of fun', he called it – and had to cough up £750 damages. Why did he keep doing such stupid things? 'Boredom,' he answers at once. 'I get bored easily. Not everyone's the same.' Yes, quite. After wearing City's red and white stripes for eighteen months, he left the Victoria Ground and headed for the much more glamorous surroundings of Stamford Bridge.

Thomas recalls playing for Chelsea as the happiest, most fulfilling time of his career. Certainly his debut home performance – two goals in a vital win over Sheffield Wednesday in front of 38,000 fans – helped ensure his popularity with the blue faithful. In fact the footballing gypsy turned out to be a lucky mascot for a Chelsea side chasing promotion from the Second Division. Of the fifteen games they had left to play when Thomas joined, they won twelve and drew the other three, pipping odds-on favourites Wednesday to the title. No wonder Bridge boss John Neal described signing Thomas as like finding 'the last piece of a jigsaw'. Neal helped Thomas settle in quickly. They were old buddies, Neal having nurtured the player while Wrexham manager. Like Dave Sexton, he appreciated that special talents require special handling. The presence of Joey Jones, his original partner-in-crime from their days as trainees together at Wrexham, also encouraged Thomas to feel settled at a club for the first time in years. Neal handled Thomas superbly, often turning a blind eye to indiscretions. Sometimes, though, he issued his midfield marauder with a non-refusable invitation to enjoy some Friday night, Saturday morning B&B chez Neal – to ensure he actually turned up for the game the next day. It was a tactic Neal had used at Wrexham with both Thomas and Jones, the Laurel and Hardy of football mayhem.

Ask Thomas about his blue period and he recalls it as a time of bliss and security in a usually turbulent career. For once, he seemed cured of his wanderlust. He insists that if things had worked out differently, he would have stayed at Chelsea for a long time. But the replacement of John Neal by John Hollins, a strict disciplinarian in the Tommy Docherty tradition, changed all that. The new boss told Thomas to come and live in London and stop all this travelling to and from north Wales several times a week. Rather than move home, Thomas moved on. His heavy-hearted departure from Stamford Bridge began a frantic period in which he played for a whole series of clubs in quick succession, but none for very long. West Bromwich Albion. Loaned out to Derby County. America, with Wichita Wings in the indoor league. Then a return to Britain, yearning for 'the real thing' football-wise, with lowly Shrewsbury. Then, amazingly, a move to Leeds United at the ripe old age of thirty-five. After just three games, back to Stoke. Despite scoring seven goals and winning the club's Player of the Year award, he was shown the door once more. After that, the critics wrote Thomas off yet again. Too old; too lazy; too unreliable; too slow; too crazy. Not for the first time, the critics were wrong.

Unknown to both them and Thomas himself, the most illustrious moment of his long career was just around the corner. A return to Wrexham, where he had begun as a schoolboy, gave no hint of what was to come. When the draw was made for the third round of the FA Cup,

few thought the Racecourse Ground would provide one of the tournament's famous upsets. And when Arsenal, the reigning League champions, went ahead, it looked as if Goliath would overcome David with ease. Then up stepped Mickey Thomas with a stunning free-kick, over the top of the Gunners' wall and past David Seaman's struggling dive, to level matters in dramatic fashion. The goal ripped the heart out of the Highbury outfit and sent shockwaves around the country: Chelsea followers watching their team at Hull, for instance, immediately began chanting their former player's name. FA Cup folklore was completed a few minutes from the end when the previously unknown Steve Watkin concluded a memorable afternoon's work for Wrexham by knocking in the winner. That was in January 1992, but soon after things began to go wrong: arrested for the funny money scam, then stabbed and finally convicted and jailed. Doing time was easy enough, admits Thomas. 'I got plenty of Guinness regularly, I had the best food, I had my own car there and I got home quite often. I can have a good laugh at the criminal justice system now because they took the piss out of me and I took the piss out of them.'

Freed after serving half his eighteen-month stretch, Thomas found that nobody in football would touch him. Well, almost nobody. Brymbo Steelworks in the Cymru Alliance League signed him up and relished the prospect of having such an illustrious veteran in their ranks. However, they had reckoned without a truly amazing transfer swoop from Inter, those footballing giants, for the services of a by-now forty-year-old player. Inter Cardiff, that is, not Inter Milan. This move by a side which had begun life as a

Sunday parks team still had a fairy-tale element about it, though. They wanted the little man to bolster their unlikely campaign to win the UEFA Cup. A first-round, first-leg 2–0 home defeat to GKS Katowice of Poland did not inspire confidence, but, with Thomas in the side, manager Lyn Jones spoke manfully about trying to overcome the deficit, and Thomas talked enthusiastically about having to dust down his passport so he could travel to play in the away leg. Jones went to great lengths to ensure that Thomas, having recently been released from jail, would be allowed to leave Britain. But he needn't have bothered. While the rest of the Inter squad reported to Cardiff airport, Thomas failed to appear. When a furious Jones accused him of using the club for 'a European jaunt', wags wondered if the real reason was because Thomas hadn't been able to print off any Polish currency for himself and the lads.

Little has been heard of Welsh football's most notorious son since that last disappearing act. In 1995 he was still deceiving old father time by turning out as player-manager of Port Madoc in the Konica League of Wales aged almost forty-one and was also starting to do some after-dinner speaking based on his riotous life and times. It's hard to disagree when he argues that all the drinking did him no harm at all, and that his big mistake was to admit that he liked a good slurp. It is alarming, though, to hear that even in his boozing heyday, 'I wouldn't say I was a heavy drinker, I don't think I'd have got in the football drinkers XI.'

These days Mickey Thomas is as confused as ever. One moment he's playing up his bad boy image. 'I'm just completely crazy, I just don't know what I'm going to do from one minute to the next,' he almost boasts. Then he claims that he's now mellower, more easy-going. Football, he says, was both the making and the breaking of him. 'I came from a council estate. I never had much as a youngster but when I became a footballer I had the trappings of everything. I had money, everything I wanted, travel first class, fly everywhere. I went to United at twenty-four and trebled my wages and it fucking spoiled me. I'd been happy at Wrexham on a few hundred quid.'

He accepts that most people will recall not his goals, not the terrier-like performances for United, Chelsea or Wales, and not that strike against Arsenal, but the fact that he kept going AWOL. Yes, he admits, he is unreliable. 'But I'd never be unreliable on the pitch. I always gave 100 per cent there. I'd die for my team on the pitch. I wouldn't let anyone down.' He constantly points out his undoubted on-field commitment. What he doesn't say is that he could only give 100 per cent if he turned up – which he often couldn't be bothered to do.

The depressing truth about mad, maverick, missing-from-the-action Mickey Thomas is that deep down he probably knows that he squandered his enormous talent. At least he has his memories: fifty-one Welsh caps, playing at Wembley against England and 'murdering' German full-back Bertie Vogts on his Welsh debut.

'I love the game,' says Thomas. 'But I just wanted to play on Saturday for a local team in north Wales where there was no pressure. I didn't like the big-time. A lot of times in my career I just wanted to pack up.' And in a simple line which could well serve as Mickey's epitaph: 'I just wanted to enjoy myself.'

5

Fighting Fit
(Handbags at Ten Paces)

'It was blown up out of all proportion, just the kind of thing that happens often enough at all clubs. When David Webb was Bournemouth manager he never thought training was any good unless there had been a punch-up.'

Harry Redknapp

I**t all began** during a typical day at training. Wimbledon's 'Crazy Gang' were doing warm-up exercises in preparation for the forthcoming League campaign. The session was being taken by captain John Fashanu, a man known as 'Fash the Bash' thanks to his rugged playing style – a misplaced Fashanu elbow nearly cost Spurs' captain Gary Mabbutt his sight after an aerial challenge in the 1993–94 season. Fashanu felt that Lawrie Sanchez, the man who scored the winning goal for Wimbledon in the club's greatest ever triumph at the 1988 FA Cup Final, wasn't putting everything into his stretches.

The Wimbledon warm-up became seriously overheated. Fash believed that Sanchez was refusing to do any of the warm-up exercises because of his dislike of him. He placed his face close to Sanchez. Something snapped and the pair squared up, as the other players tried to separate them. Fashanu shouted that he wanted to get it sorted. Sanchez agreed – 'Let's do it then!'

Showing admirable awareness of their responsibilities to the juniors, Fashanu and Sanchez asked the younger players to leave the area before they began their fight. Fashanu, the presenter of *Gladiators*, the TV show where hulks called Saracen, Panther and Zodiac battle it out on indoor walls and ceilings, prepared to enter a less public arena for his own private battle.

A fight followed, and things rapidly turned very ugly. Fashanu aimed a kick at Sanchez, who later accused the second dan martial arts expert of trying to end his career with a kung-fu-style blow. Both parties lashed out and finally Terry Burton, Wimbledon's assistant manager, dived between the two Dons of war and battled to keep them apart. Eventually they were separated.

The quarrel between Fashanu and Sanchez had been festering ever since Fash joined Wimbledon in 1985; the two Dons stars got on about as well as Ian Paisley and the Vatican. There had been years of antagonism and their ya-boo dispute over the captaincy could have come straight from any school fourth-form side.

'We are two people who just don't get on. I got the captaincy and he, the senior player, didn't. He was also passed over in the contracts stakes when other players arrived at the club,' Fashanu claimed.

Sanchez countered that Fashanu thought he could ride roughshod over the other players and was instrumental in taking the club captaincy away from John Scales: 'On a pre-season tour of Scotland he constantly moaned and sniped that John was having a nightmare on the pitch and wasn't organizing bonuses for the rest of the players. That was crap.'

The two players' versions of events contained more contradictions and conspiracy theories than the death of President Kennedy.

'I just stood there and put my fists up, thinking that we'd go for it like it was handbags at ten paces and it would be all over,' recalled Sanchez. 'He used a series of kicks with predetermined intentions to break or severely injure my legs, particularly my left knee, which he knows I had an operation on.'

Fashanu emphatically denied this, arguing that he was defending himself after Sanchez had thrown the first punch and then 'used the most cowardly form of attack imaginable, the head-butt'. Fash claimed he had X-rays on a cheekbone and was unable to play for Wimbledon in a friendly that weekend. 'If I had used martial arts on him he would have been seriously hurt.' But Sanchez later declared that it was Fashanu who had head-butted him, and that Fashanu had cut his own head doing it.

The day after the fight became public knowledge, Fashanu tried to pour cold water on the rumours. 'Fash the Splash' threw a bucket of water over a reporter and photographer, before encouraging Vinny Jones to aim even more at the hapless hacks.

Meanwhile, manager Joe Kinnear, who fined Fash £4,000 for his role in the Sanchez incident, was asked by a journalist for his version of events. 'Why don't you just **** off' he said, before adding, 'You're an a***hole, print that if you like!'

Once the Dons' boss had calmed down, he came up with a watertight solution. Kinnear said that both players had hit each other and had black eyes. They had been fined two weeks' wages each and would both miss a friendly match at St Albans because of their injuries.

It didn't end there though. On the first day of the new season Sanchez received a letter from Fashanu's solicitors saying he was going to be charged with common assault, a few hours before they were set to play in the same side. (A few weeks later Wandsworth police said they had no intention of pursuing the charge, but that the two Wimbledon pugilists should set a better example to the rest of the players.)

Perhaps the incident did have its benefits – despite Fashanu's solicitors' letter, both players scored in that season's opening-day victory at West Ham. Only Wimbledon being Wimbledon there was an inevitable row over obscene graffiti being left in the visitors' dressing-room. Chairman Sam Hammam took the blame, although some observers did wonder if it might have been the only way that Fashanu and Sanchez were now communicating.

Do such incidents heal with time? Er, no. The whole affair emerged again in August 1994 when Fashanu was sold to Aston Villa. Never one to hold a grudge,

Sanchez released pictures of his leg injuries and fulminated: 'He was just a disruptive prima donna . . . You could say we hated each other. I can never forget or forgive him for what he tried to do to me.' So you're not a regular viewer of *Gladiators* on a Saturday night then, Lawrie?

In the year 2525 there won't be sport, but there will be Wimbledon training sessions. Anyone who has seen the film *Rollerball* will identify with the Dons' attitude to competitive activities.

Take the time when, for once, Fashanu and Sanchez were actually on the same side, sorting out Robbie Turner, another giant centre-forward. After 'getting fresh' with John Fashanu in training, Turner returned to the changing-room, followed by Fashanu, Sanchez, Dennis Wise and Vinny Jones, and the door locked behind them.

Turner later described how the players went for it in a peculiarly Plough Lane-style rite – or should that be riot – of passage: 'We threw each other all over the place, but in the end Fash beat me fair and square. It was then I realized he was top man. Funnily enough we got on like a house on fire after that.'

When at Wimbledon, goalkeeper Dave Beasant nearly ended winger Wally Downes's career after a training flash-point. In a one-on-one exercise, Downes was meant to take the ball round Beasant, but instead, encouraged by manager and wind-up merchant Dave Bassett, kept shooting or nutmegging the keeper. Finally he blasted the ball straight at Beasant.

'I threatened to do him and accused him of not having the bottle to go round me,' remembers Beasant. The next time Downes did try to round the goalie, nick-named 'Lurch' after the character in *The Addams Family*, 'I took him out with a flying, two-footed tackle about knee-height. I wasn't even looking at the ball, only at Wally. He went down like a sack of spuds.'

In the dressing-room, after Beasant had calmed down, Downes showed the keeper the spot where he'd caught him, just above the place where he'd had a major cartilage operation at sixteen. 'To this day he reckons that if I'd hit him a couple of inches lower I could have written his career off,' says Beasant. 'All I could think to say at the time was: "Well, it serves you right, you shouldn't push me so far." I don't recall him taking me to the edge again.'

And quiet flow the Dons? Most certainly not. Manager Bobby Gould liked nothing better than a punch-up to solve any inter-club tensions among the Dirty Dons, and was even once injured by cabbies' friend Dennis Wise. 'At Wimbledon we have what we call a rough and tumble where anything goes and soon after I arrived he [Dennis] cracked my ribs.'

Charles Bronson in *The Streetfighter* might have baulked at the Dons' 'rough and tumbles'. In January 1990 Gould said that there had been a few problems in the dressing-room. 'There was a big punch-up and I was involved. We get as far away from the training ground as possible and get in a circle. We say: "What's the problem, come on, let's get in there and sort it out. You want a piece of the action? OK."' Gould added that this had long been the custom at Wimbledon and that he thought it good 'because it gets rid of a lot of tension'. As, no doubt, did the Vietnam War.

A match between the first team and reserves at Roehampton seemed to create the kind of tension these rough and tumbles were meant to alleviate. In October 1989 skipper Keith Curle (later transferred to Manchester City for a hefty £2.5 million) finished up in hospital after a fight with hardman centre-forward John Gayle.

Curle was winding up Gayle in training. Gayle, all 6 feet 4 inches and 14 stones of him, started throwing punches and kicking Curle and had to be dragged off by his team-mates, in what Curle later described as a 'minor' fracas, before pleading with then manager Ray Harford not to fine the errant striker.

Gayle, a raw, brawny forward, was fed up with the taunts he had received since he joined Wimbledon from non-league Burton Albion. Gayle, it seemed, was only following his father's advice: 'My dad always told me to make your mark early. If you don't, people will walk all over you.'

Despite an FA probe, Ray Harford adopted the classic managerial line: 'It was a scuffle. These sort of things happen in football. It will be dealt with internally.'

After a few weeks of relative calm in the Wimbledon camp – although Gayle still had time to attain the dubious distinction of being sent off for an over-the-top tackle and elbowing incident *against* Vinny Jones (then at Sheffield United) – Gayle claimed in an unprecedented outburst that he had wanted to kill his skipper.

He said that Curle had driven him mad with taunts and that, 'Every time I was anywhere near him he would call me a big useless so-and-so and a waste of time. I wanted to kill him, and would have done if seven of my team-mates hadn't dragged me off him.' Ray Harford got tough, and Gayle left the club, having definitely made his mark early.

Perhaps all these incidents only added to the mystique of the 'Crazy Gang'. For if they behave like that with each other, imagine what they must do to the opposition.

The 'training ground incident' (that's a soccerspeak euphemism for giving one of your work-mates a good thumping) is a ubiquitous part of English footballing life. Tommy Tynan, who's been around at clubs as diverse as Liverpool, Swansea, Sheffield Wednesday, Plymouth, Rotherham, Lincoln and Torquay, has this to say on the subject:

'If you ask footballers, I bet you they'd say there's a fight once or twice a week at most clubs. It's a flashpoint, someone might go over the top not really meaning it, someone might turn round and punch them. The players split it up and it's all forgotten about. Nine times out of ten it's handbags at ten paces. Football is a physical game. Especially when it's muddy, one or two tackles are flying about and you've got out of bed on the wrong side that morning.'

Tynan himself was involved in a fight with another player at Rotherham. 'The manager, Norman Hunter, tried to keep it quiet so he said that it was between me and him. That made it worse because the press then thought I'd had a go at the manager!' And who, except a complete psycho, would pick a scrap with old Norman Bites Yer Legs Hunter?

Ex-England striker Frank Worthington recalls a flashpoint at Leicester when centre-half Jeff Blockley went in a little too hard on tough Bristolian Chris Garland: 'He just lashed out with the almightiest of right-handers and broke Jeff's jaw in two.' At Huddersfield, Worthington had seen Jimmy Lawson split Jimmy McGill's eye with a head-butt following a similar training ground incident, 'but it paled into insignificance compared to this'.

Yes, the training ground incident is a national ritual. Even the normally placid

Alvin Martin, then aged thirty-six and West Ham's senior professional, couldn't resist one final punch-up with his teammate Matthew Rush before quitting Upton Park for Leyton Orient.

West Ham had just lost 2–1 away to Walsall in a Coca-Cola Cup first-leg humiliation in September 1994. At training they'd had a 'clear the air' talk after the defeat; and, as inevitably happens in football, the players liked to clear the air with their fists. Winger Rush had been critical of the defensive system employed by the Hammers. The lads then played five-a-side in training. Near the end of the game there was a tackle, resulting in a shouting match.

Then Martin went for the 22-year-old Rush. 'Martin was like a man possessed and was shouting, "I want blood!"' said a shocked observer. But should Alvin have picked on a man fourteen years younger? He was caught by several punches and left with a cut above his eye before players moved in to stop the bout.

The fighting Hammers were separated and the players thought Scouser Martin had calmed down. Then he suddenly went for Rush again, only to receive another upper-cut and be told to leave the match by manager Harry Redknapp. But Martin seemed to have an almost Frank Bruno-esque penchant for receiving endless punches. As he was walking off the pitch he suddenly came charging back as if he wanted another go, as the soccer Academy began to look more like a borstal. This time assistant manager Frank Lampard had to lead his belligerent centre-half away.

'It was nothing more than a wrestling match on the ground after a tackle,' pleaded manager Harry Redknapp, with commendable understatement, two days later, announcing that he would not be taking any disciplinary action.

Midfielder Peter Butler backed up Redknapp: 'It was the usual handbags at ten paces that erupts on every training ground at times.' (The uninitiated might like to note that every incident that doesn't result in fatal injury is usually dismissed as 'handbags at ten paces' by the soccer fraternity.) 'I've been involved in a few in my time, and you end up knowing that kind of passion is a good sign, but has to be channelled in the right direction,' continued Butler.

Perhaps Redknapp was lenient on his boxing charges because as a player he'd been in a few behind-the-scenes scraps himself. His ex-team-mate Billy Bonds remembers him throwing a beer bottle at the former West Ham boss Ron Greenwood.

'H', as he was known to his fellow pros, was criticized by Greenwood in the dressing-room following a home defeat by Newcastle. Redknapp yelled, 'You're always picking on me!', snatched up a bottle of beer and hurled it across the room, just missing physiotherapist Rob Jenkins' head as it smashed against the wall. 'There was broken glass and foaming brown ale all over the place and a very startled Rob Jenkins!' recalled Bonzo. (Which begs the question, did West Ham always have beer in the dressing-room after games, and was it only tea they drank at half-time?)

Perhaps the reason why West Ham have so long been regarded a soft touch on the pitch is because they expend all their energy fighting each other in training. Even Redknapp's assistant manager and brother-in-law Frank Lampard has been in trouble. Billy Bonds remembers the time Lampard chinned his fellow

Top 10 Training Ground Excuses

1. 'It was just a scuffle' – Ray Harford
2. 'These things happen in football' – Joe Kinnear
3. 'It was handbags at ten paces' – Peter Butler et al.
4. 'It was just a wrestling match after a tackle' – Harry Redknapp
5. 'He was seeing what I was made of' – Terry Venables
6. 'It was just one of those things' – Jesper Olsen
7. 'He shouldn't have pushed me to the edge' – Dave Beasant
8. 'My dad always told me to make my mark early' – John Gayle
9. 'Stan Collymore's apologies were so profuse I didn't fine him' – Frank Clark
10. 'Lawrie wasn't taking his warm-up exercises seriously' – John Fashanu

GLADIATOR FASH LIMBERS UP WITH PAULA HAMILTON: 'GO ON, SANCHEZ, COME AT ME WITH THAT HANDBAG!'

full-back John McDowell during a training session in the 1970s.

McDowell had been mouthing off in training and Lampard advised him to be quiet. 'Go on then, put it there!' said McDowell, thrusting his chin out at Frankie. This was not a wise move, as Lampard, a man still fondly remembered at West Ham for the tackle that deposited Orient's John Chiedozie several rows back in the West Side terrace, did exactly that. 'John trailed away to the dressing-room, nose streaming blood, definitely a sadder but wiser man. Frank was duly fined pretty stiffly by John Lyall, but seemed to think it worth it!'

The manager's alternative to dismissing the training ground incident as 'just a scuffle' is to sack the miscreant. It seems fair to speculate that David Webb, Mickey Bennett and Joe Allon no longer exchange Christmas cards.

The Brentford lads were on a routine day's training in November 1993, when an apprentice put in a couple of over-enthusiastic tackles on £275,000 record signing Joe Allon, and as the two players exchanged words Bennett stepped in. He was pushed away by Allon, but Bennett then threw a punch that broke Allon's jaw in three places – resulting in Geordie Joe being hospitalized and missing three months of the season. Definitely a case of being left Home Allon, as the Brentford fanzine *Beesotted* put it.

By far the most mysterious aspect of the affair was that everyone connected with the club remarked how mild-mannered Bennett was – in fact he was even a born-again Christian. *Beesotted* devoted its front cover to a picture of Joe Allon falling down accompanied by the headline: 'Now I know why they call them Bible bashers!' Perhaps Bennett had

decided that if Jesus saved, he'd make sure that Joe Allon was in no fit state to get the rebound.

Manager David Webb, on this occasion a less-keen follower of pugilism than Harry Redknapp remembers at Bournemouth, favoured Old Testament revenge over New Testament mercy. He terminated Bennett's contract and waived the club's right to any fee, saying he was making a stand against violent conduct.

A month later Bennett was still at the centre of controversy when, after PFA representations, there came a less than divine intervention from the Football League, which issued a directive ordering Brentford to reinstate Bennett and instead fine him two weeks' wages. David Webb was so incensed that he decided to – no, not chin someone – quit in protest. The club refused his resignation as Webb fumed: 'They ruled that we were not right to dismiss Bennett for a serious breach of contract – serious misconduct. If punching somebody and breaking their jaw doesn't constitute serious misconduct, then I don't know what does.'

But what ye sow, so ye shall reap. A compromise between Brentford and the League was reached, and ultimately the wayward winger was on his way and atoning for his sins amid the purgatory of playing for Charlton.

After training ground fights, sackings and potential court cases are often more likely than Wimbledon-style respect for the 'top man'. In September 1993 Bristol City dropped their attempt to sack midfielder Ray Atteveld and transfer-listed him instead, after a training ground incident in which a young player was hurt. Even the managers sometimes get involved. In November 1992 Bournemouth's Shaun Brooks decided not to take legal action against his boss Tony Pulis after an alleged fight. After a club probe, Pulis was reprimanded and Brooks, who had stitches in a face wound, was warned about his future conduct.

Even former Arsenal manager Bruce Rioch, normally a tough disciplinarian, was once in trouble on the training ground. Rioch was player manager at Torquay in 1984. His first signing had been Colin Anderson from Burnley. Anderson was a gifted player, who later performed for WBA, Walsall, Hereford and Exeter. Torquay were in deep financial trouble at the time, and a big name club was rumoured to be interested in buying Anderson. Unfortunately, when Anderson was watched by the club's scouts, he had a terrible match.

During the following week's training Rioch had his charges playing five-a-side on a tennis court. Anderson began to show his Fancy Dan skills and nutmegged his player-manager. It was too much for Rioch, who punched the youngster on the jaw.

Anderson threatened to go to the PFA and Rioch was placed in an untenable position. If the PFA had insisted on Anderson pressing assault charges Torquay would have been involved with more unwelcome headlines. Rioch quit, and Anderson let the matter drop.

Today Rioch admits: 'I was wrong and I resigned. It's a period of my life I often reflect upon because I knew I was out of order.'

From Bournemouth to Manchester United, the training ground is home to one long catalogue of incidents. Paul McGrath remembers Remi Moses in action in 1986: 'I haven't seen many people go down harder than Jesper [Olsen] did when he crossed Moses in a training match.

Suddenly the tackles were flying, something was said and Remi threw a punch. Jesper went down like a sack of potatoes.'

Olsen was left with a black eye and eleven stitches, but today he has forgiven Moses for breaking the first football commandment – 'thou shalt not belt thy teammates': 'I haven't seen Remi since I left United and if we did meet there would be no problem. What happened was just one of those things. For one or two weeks after the incident it was a bit difficult.'

It's not just in training, though, that brawls happen. Even a sparsely attended reserve match can cause feelings to surface that would probably be concealed in a first team game. In 1991 Tottenham's Paul Walsh was upset at being substituted in a reserve match against Charlton at White Hart Lane. Coach Ray Clemence, the former England and Spurs goalkeeper, was only taking him off to preserve him for a European Cup Winners Cup game against Sparkasse Stockerau later that week. But Walsh showed some reluctance to leave the field, and an exasperated Clemence shouted, 'Just f***ing get yourself off!'

The stoic Walsh, showing almost Cantona-like restraint, threw his shirt in Clemence's face. Big Ray, still a fine keeper, caught it and threw it back at him, clipping Walsh's head and tousling his golden locks. Walsh then did what every subbed footballer fantasizes about, but seldom actually achieves – he punched his coach in the face, resulting in a massive black eye for Clemence the next day.

It was the end of Walshy's Spurs career. He was fined £3,000, ordered to apologize personally to Clemence and transfer-listed, eventually joining Portsmouth. 'The Ray Clemence thing was stupid really. I just lost my temper,' is Walshy's verdict on the incident today. 'I thought he was wrong but you can't go around taking pokes at the coaching staff.'

And, of course, 'Old Big 'Ead' Brian Clough has long been a one-man training ground incident waiting to happen. Cloughie was once unhappy with the contribution of his Nottingham Forest striker Nigel Jemson in a reserve match. Ex-Forest forward Lee Chapman recalls the moment at half-time when Clough told Jemson to stand up and asked the young man if he had ever been punched in the stomach: 'As soon as Nigel said no, a forceful blow was delivered to his midriff. Nigel doubled up in pain and let out an agonized groan. "Now you have, son," said Clough and turned away.'

And when the swellings and cuts have eased, what is the errant player's best way of pacifying both manager and media? A grovelling apology after a training ground incident seems to be the best approach for those involved – it certainly helped Stan Collymore when he was at Forest.

He was set to be fined £4,000 after decking team-mate Alf Inge Haaland with a right-hander in training, in November 1994. But the next day manager Frank Clark told the press that it paid to be a sorry Colly: 'Yes, I was going to fine him. But Stan's apologies were so profuse and genuine that I decided against it.' Colly repaid his boss's touching faith by going AWOL later that week, missing a day's training, but somehow finding the time to turn on Nottingham's Christmas lights. 'His studs must have gone down my achilles tendons half-a-dozen times,' Stan was later to recall. 'I turned round and said: "What the ****ing hell did you do that for?" And he said something and he said it again. What did he say? Eff off. So I just hit him once and he went down.'

Punch-ups don't only occur on the training ground. The post-match inquisition is a fertile ground for belligerence. After a defeat at Luton in February 1996 Grimsby player-manager Brian Laws cried fowl. He spotted star Italian midfielder and supporters' hero Ivano Bonetti (the fans had raised £50,000 to keep him at the club until the end of the season) eating a chicken leg. This was the wrong response to defeat, thought Laws, telling Bonetti to put it down. The irate Italian threw the chicken leg at his manager. Feathers flew. The pair squared up and according to contrasting accounts, either Laws punched Bonetti, or he threw a plate of food at him. Whatever, the result was that the Grimsby manager fractured his best player's cheekbone and Bonetti was taken to hospital. After surgery on the fractured cheekbone and a trapped nerve Bonetti was unable to play for six weeks.

Laws – apparently as unpredictable as his old Forest manager Brian Clough – described it as a 'regrettable incident' and said he would go if it was in the best interests of the club. Meanwhile, Bonetti's self-confessed 'love affair' with Grimsby was surely heading for divorce. But the pair eventually staged a rather tacky reunion, shaking hands on the pitch before Grimsby's FA Cup tie with West Ham.

Laws' powers of motivation worked, as Grimsby walloped Premiership West Ham 3–0. Clearly the threat of hospitalization reaches the parts other team talks don't. The Grimsby chairman said, rather unfortunately bearing in mind Bonetti's swollen face, the incident 'had been blown out of all proportion.' Without a trace of irony West Ham manager Harry Redknapp added after the game: 'We just have to

'SO THERE'S NO ANIMOSITY BETWEEN THE LADS AT ALL . . .' IVANO BONETTI AND BRIAN LAWS SHARE A JOKE AFTER THEIR DRESSING-ROOM DUST UP.

take it on the chin.' It didn't end there, though. Bonetti was transferred to Tranmere and issued a writ for £67,000 worth of damages against Laws.

The lure of the training ground incident goes right to the very top of the game. Immediately after he joined Tottenham, one young pro made the mistake of going past Dave Mackay in a training match in the gym. Mackay was having none of this and punched him in the testicles as he went by.

The next time the youngster got the ball he slid it past Mackay again and once more he was whacked in the Buster Gonads by the Tottenham ball-player. 'This time I was sure it was no accident; I turned round and punched him in the face. Unfortunately I had a ring on my middle finger and it sliced his cheek open and damaged my knuckle.'

Mackay had a scar on his face for a few days, but in the best all-lads-together tradition of English football the youngster and Mackay went to the pub for a shandy after training and resolved their differences. 'Honours were about even – he had belted me in the balls, but I had punched his face . . . He was obviously determined to sort me out and find out what I was made of.'

That young professional in question was Terry Venables. Did he later find out what his England players were made of with a strategic jab at their wedding tackle? And was Vinny Jones employed in a specific advisory role? No wonder Euro '96 was a whole new ball game.

6

Spot the Brawl

'Don't you know who I am? I can make more money in an hour than you can make in a week.'

Jason Dozzell

Night-clubs, hotels and wine bars are a footballer's familiar habitat. Indeed if it were not for the nocturnal antics of our soccer aces, such venues as Coco Savannas in Stockport, The Boardwalk in Ipswich, Zen's in Dartford and Bumbles in Hertfordshire might never have attained national fame and a place in football folklore.

Ah, the smell of after-shave and cheap perfume, the lure of tight Lycra stretching across inviting expanses of bottle-tanned thigh, white stilettos, peroxide blonde hair and, most importantly, late-night quaffing of rum and blacks. Football is a sociable game and, after training, with all afternoon and evening to drink in, the local night-spot sees our players at their finest.

However, the average fan must wonder why they go anywhere near the places. They are a soccer warzone – the problems of negotiating bouncers, have-a-go merchants and the prospect of Gazza-style injuries in the toilet should logically make players opt for Marks and Spencer pyjamas, hot chocolate and *Match of the Day*. Only, our soccer stars are mysteriously drawn to night-clubs like eels to the Sargasso Sea, they just keep coming back for more.

Even an impending court case can't keep footballers out of clubland. In March 1995, Manchester United's Eric Cantona and Paul Ince were both facing possible jail sentences, after Cantona's infamous kung-fu kick on a Crystal Palace fan and Ince's follow-up intervention. Clearly they took this threat seriously. The two Red Devils prepared for an early-morning appearance in front of Croydon magistrates by clubbing until 4.30 a.m. at trendy London nightspots Brown's and the Emporium, where the artist formerly known as Prince was playing a secret gig.

Even when there are no arguments over the entrance fee, and cries of 'Don't you know who I am?', footballers still have to negotiate the delicate sexual mores of their fellow punters. In April 1993 the Welsh squad were training near Epping, Essex, before flying out for a World Cup fixture against the RCS. As part of their preparation, a group of Welsh internationals (Dean Saunders, Gary Speed, Ian Rush, Mark Hughes, Clayton Blackmore and, for some reason, West Ham's Scottish star David Speedie) decided to visit the nearby Epping Forest Country Club. And, of course, the evening ended in a drunken brawl.

Builder Wayne Manley was punched in the eye by Aston Villa's Dean Saunders, after he had hit Saunders' team-mate Gary Speed, in a flare-up over a woman. Both Manley and Saunders were taken to Loughton police station, where they agreed to drop charges of assault on each other, and were cautioned by the police after admitting disorderly words and behaviour.

Trouble flared when remarks were made to Wayne Manley's girlfriend, Nicola. 'One or two players were behaving like prats,' said witness Jake Canning. Manley claimed that one of the players said, 'Don't worry lads, she's with that wanker!' He then punched Speed, who required stitches. He was dragged out by bouncers, but then felt a 'punch from nowhere' come from Saunders, giving him a black eye.

The players' manager Terry Yorath helped resolve the situation at the police station with a bit of Welsh rabbit. The Welsh boss's verdict was: 'It was a totally unprovoked attack on Speed by someone who thought he was eyeing up his girlfriend. That wasn't the case . . . The players were not to blame, I am convinced of that . . . Dean Saunders went to Gary's defence.'

Occasionally the lads do behave during a night out, but there can still be aggravation at breakfast. In November 1996 a court was shown a security video of Leeds' Lee Bowyer throwing chairs at staff at that most salubrious of venues, the drive-in McDonald's at the Isle of Dogs. Maybe he was just trying to get a part in David Cronenberg's *Crash*, another film that caused moral outrage. At around six a.m. Lee and two friends had popped in for a McBreakfast – and the result was the mother of all McPunch-ups and an estimated £450 worth of damage to the restaurant.

In court Bowyer admitted affray and said that he deeply regretted his actions. After the footballer's dawn raid two of McDonald's staff suffered cuts and bruises, one of them needing stitches to his head. Chairs, tables and a plant pot were all thrown. (It wasn't the first time Bowyer had been in trouble with pot: he failed a drugs test with Charlton after testing positive for cannabis in 1995.) Lee and pals then burgered off, but were stopped by police on anti-terrorist duty at a Canary Wharf checkpoint. Bowyer, at £3.5 million the most expensive teenage player in the country, was done up like a Fillet o' Fish. His two companions were also charged with affray and other offences.

The attack took place in September, while Bowyer was recovering from injury. The bizarre fracas was apparently all the result of a dispute over their order. We can only imagine the scene at the Big Mac attack: 'I tell you I ordered large fries, not regular!'

The contrite Leeds midfielder admitted throwing the chairs in a police interview and volunteered the description of his behaviour as 'disgraceful'. 'It all started from a minor argument and should never have happened. I just wish we had gone somewhere else for breakfast,' he later sighed. Well, if you play silly burgers, Lee . . .

We might assume that a footballer would be pleased to see a familiar face from his club. But no, in March 1990 Oxford's John Durnin was fined £300 and ordered to pay £500 compensation for attacking a former club physiotherapist in a night-club in Witney, Oxfordshire.

Football's Top Nightspots

Coco Savannas in Stockport (shiner for Lee Sharpe)

Drive-in McDonald's in the Isle of Dogs (breakfast burger brawl with Lee Bowyer)

Haçienda in Manchester (Hughesie decked by bouncer)

Tramp in London (Waddle, Woods, Palmer on eve-of-game walkabout)

Hy's in Norwich (Chris Sutton damages car, hides in toilet)

Zen's in Dartford (Paul Walsh in Jacuzzi shocker)

Epping Forest Country Club in Essex (Speed hit, Saunders wallops assailant)

The Boardwalk in Ipswich (scene of Jason Dozzell pavlova assault)

Butlin's in Bognor Regis (Ray Parlour glassed)

Joe Bananas in Croydon (Geoff Thomas punches thug)

Harper Louie's in Windsor (drinking for England)

007 Club in Blackpool (Bobby Moore booze-up on eve of FA Cup tie)

In November 1989 Durnin had been fined £1,000 and ordered to pay £550 compensation for attacking two teenagers after drinking eight pints of lager (only eight pints?) at a Witney night-club. Magistrates heard that Durnin had been taunted and after a scuffle he was hit over the head.

After cleaning himself up Durnin returned to confront those he believed to be the culprits, head-butting an innocent eighteen-year-old. Durnin then left the night-club and passed a gang of youths who he thought were taunting him, head-butting a sixteen-year-old, causing him to fall through a plate glass window. In his defence, Durnin claimed that Witney was a very rough place to live in and he was always being picked on by 'kids' and others.

Every part of a night-club has more hidden traps than were ever encountered in the Pyramids. You wouldn't think that the toilets would hold too much terror for soccer aces. The routine should be simple: walk in, point Percy at the porcelain, and then walk out. But no, incredibly, Paul Gascoigne managed to injure himself in the gents' at a club in Newcastle and was afterwards required to take several days off in lieu.

Most footballers would probably consider a Jacuzzi to be an Italian babe on the dancefloor, so when night-clubs such as Zen's in Dartford, Kent, run to such exotic features, you know there can only be one result. Perhaps in January 1992 Tottenham's Paul Walsh was unaware of Zen's and the art of swimming-pool maintenance when he noticed the inviting Jacuzzi in the club's VIP lounge. Deciding to forget about the recent furore over his punching of Spurs' coach Ray Clemence, Walsh took an early bath.

Naturally enough he stripped to his boxer shorts (ignoring the costumes provided by the club) and leapt in. Not too much wrong with that, but then Walshy spied a brunette on the dancefloor and pulled her into the Jacuzzi fully clothed. No one knows if the DJ was playing Wet Wet Wet at the time. The staff were not best pleased – knowing that the chemicals in the Jacuzzi couldn't cope with the acids from dry-cleaned clothes. (Who knows what effect the chemicals in Walsh's hair must have had.) 'It cost us a hell of a lot of money to have the Jacuzzi emptied and refilled,' moaned manager Tom Holland. Walsh was immediately shown the red card, being asked to leave the club by bouncers unimpressed with his liquid assets.

Even the best-behaved of clubbers run the risk of an embarrassing police raid. When police raided Ferdenzis club in London's West End in November 1992, who should they find still clubbing it at 5 a.m. but that arch-disciplinarian known as 'Colonel Gadaffi' to his players, ex-Arsenal manager George Graham? There was no question of Graham or his then girlfriend Arianne Accristo being implicated in the bust, but eight people were arrested after being found with drugs, including cocaine. The manager of the club (opening hours 2 a.m. to 7 a.m.) offered to invite Graham back and buy him a bottle of champagne to make up for his embarrassment – for what kind of an example was this to set to such true professionals as Paul Merson, Tony Adams and Ray Parlour?

Footballers can't even leave a night-club without getting into trouble. Look at what happened to Paul Ince and Mark Hughes when they left Manchester's Haçienda at 2.30 a.m. in December 1994. The lads were on a trip out following United's Christmas party. It was only a few days after Nottingham Forest's Stuart Pearce had apologized to Ince for a racial remark made in the heat of a 1–2 home defeat to Forest at Old Trafford, and Mark Hughes decided to have a 'joke' at Incey's expense.

'Right you black c***, take me home,' cried Hughes, clearly as diplomatic off the field as he is on it. 'Sparky' was promptly punched in the face by a 20-stone bouncer, who raged, 'No one calls my mate a black c***!'

An onlooker revealed: 'It was a really hard punch and Hughes went down like a ton of bricks . . .' Ince was furious with the bouncer as he knew Hughes was only joking, and shouted at the doorman, 'What did you do that for? He's my best mate. He can call me what he likes!'

A groggy Hughes then staggered to his feet and moved towards the bouncer, but was restrained and advised to go home in a cab. Hughes, who didn't even win a free kick, later played down his flooring: 'We were just having a joke and the bouncer got the wrong end of the stick,' was his verdict – and pass that steak please, Mr Physio.

Another hazard for players leaving clubs is the tendency of those nasty paparazzi photographers lurking outside to snap them in the act. Sheffield Wednesday's Chris Waddle, Chris Woods and Carlton Palmer must have thought it a clever wheeze to go clubbing at Tramp, a top London nightspot that attracts the likes of Jack Nicholson, Rod Stewart, Joan Collins and Mick Jagger, on New Year's Eve, 1993 – the only problem being that Wednesday had a match at QPR the next day.

The trio were photographed leaving Tramp at 3.30 a.m. on New Year's Day – just eleven hours before the kick-off at Loftus Road. Even worse for the disgraced threesome was the fact that a bemused populace now had photographic evidence of the footballer's idea of what to wear to a classy club – Waddle and Woods were in jeans and Palmer wore a shellsuit top and trainers.

Let's hope they enjoyed their drinks (champagne is £40 a bottle), because disciplinarian boss Trevor Francis, a man who once fined midfielder Martin Allen for attending the birth of his child instead of playing, docked them two weeks' wages each for breaking a club curfew – a staggering total of £42,000 (£20,000 Waddle, £12,000 Palmer, £10,000 Woods). Still, perhaps their preparation wasn't that bad; Wednesday won 2–1 the next day, with Palmer playing and Woods on the bench (Waddle was injured – and no, the injury wasn't caused by picking up a glass).

Crystal Palace's Geoff Thomas also had problems when leaving another memorably named club, Joe Bananas revue bar in Croydon, in September 1992. A group of men on a Bananas bender had earlier been thrown out of the club for taunting Palace players. As Thomas's party left they found the gang waiting for them, and a Palace youth player was hit. Thomas went Joe Bananas, punching the assailant in the face and leaving him bleeding.

After a scuffle and much shouting the doorman separated the warring parties and the Palace players went back inside. Police were called, but by the time they arrived all was quiet. 'He [Geoff] tells me he did punch the man in self-defence,' explained Thomas's agent Geoff Berlin. Thankfully for Thomas, he was free to spend many further fruity nights at Joe Bananas, as the club said there was no question of his being banned as he had not started the incident.

The footballer also faces the problem of his manager waiting outside his chosen nightspot. In 1988 manager Ian McNeill revealed that he had to 'turn private detective' to catch players Victor Kasule and Alan Irvine out in the fleshpots of Shrewsbury. Kasule, a Glaswegian/Ugandan arrest-prone winger who was later to set some kind of record by playing in four different countries in one season, went on to gain soccer immortality when he received the dubious accolade of having the fanzine *A Large Scotch* named in his honour. McNeill might have needed a large Scotch too, after tracking down Kasule and Irvine. 'I had to do my own investigating, because people would tell me stories, but they don't want to be involved and to be the stool pigeon,' explained the Shrewsbury Town supremo.

Perhaps, every Friday night, throughout the land of footballing Babylon known as Great Britain, there are lonely soccer bosses sitting in cars outside nightclubs, eating takeaway pizzas and imagining they are Spender, Columbo, Philip Marlowe, or any other of their favourite fictional detectives. What McNeill witnessed while doing his Taggart impression did not please him – he promptly fined and transfer-listed Kasule and Irvine for breaking a club curfew.

McNeill's explanation of Kasule's behaviour was managerial psychology at its finest: 'He came down here when he was twenty-two and got hit with a bit of hero-worship and from a maturity point of view he couldn't handle it.' Hero-worship – in Shrewsbury? Just imagine the effect on poor old Victor if he'd made it big and been subjected to the temptations of the nightlife in Scunthorpe, Grimsby, Carlisle, or even John Durnin's Witney?

And then there's the evidence that suddenly appears the next morning. In July 1993 Manchester United's Lee Sharpe had to try to explain the two black eyes, split

(ABOVE) PRE-MATCH
TRAINING AT TRAMP
WITH THE STYLISH
CHRIS WOODS AND
CARLTON PALMER.
(LEFT) CHRIS WADDLE:
'I DO HAVE A TIE
SOMEWHERE . . .'

nose and cut face he sported after an incident at a venue sounding more like a Barry Manilow out-take than a night-club, Coco Savannas in exotic Stockport. Despite a dressing-down from manager Alex Ferguson and witnesses at the club insisting that Lee had been involved in an altercation with local yobs as he left, resulting in the police being called, Sharpe opted for a less controversial explanation: 'I got whacked with a pal's golf club while we were fooling around' – becoming the only footballer ever to have fought in the golf war.

Sharpe later admitted there was a fight. An initially friendly customer turned nasty after several drinks. 'He was giving it loads to his mates, saying, "I'm going to sort him out,"' remembers Lee. 'I said, "I've got a lot more to lose than you, I'm not going to fight."' Sharpe got in a car to leave the club. 'He took a step back and volleyed me in the face with his left foot. It was very painful. I just wish I'd got out of the car and put one on him before he managed to kick me. It was a dodgy club and we shouldn't have been there really.'

Even when they're safely away from the club, players can be shopped by fans the following Monday. Heroic England captain Bobby Moore was not immune to the lure of clubland and his peerless record was blemished by one 1971 incident on the eve of an important FA Cup tie against Blackpool.

The 007 Club, owned by the boxer Jack London, had its share of football spies, and the late West Ham captain was suspended for two weeks and fined a week's wages after a Hammers fan spotted him drinking there on the night before the cup-tie. Moore was accompanied by team-mates Jimmy Greaves (soon to admit he was an alcoholic), Brian Dear (who also liked a drink) and teetotal Clyde Best. They stayed out till 1 a.m. and the Hammers did not play like men with golden guns, losing 4–0. The irate fans reported the incident to manager Ron Greenwood and, although Moore had only had a few lagers, the West Ham manager had to be talked out of sacking all four players (in fact only Dear departed).

Apart from night-clubs, some footballers frequent venues that make Coco Savannas and Bumbles look positively classy. Where did Arsenal's Ray Parlour choose to go for a cultured night out? Butlin's in Bognor Regis.

Parlour – previously involved in amusing pranks with Tony Adams such as letting off a fire extinguisher over customers at the Hornchurch Pizza Hut – was in the Manhattan revue bar (Bognor Regis that is, not New York). Someone bumped into Parlour, people squared up to each other, and a witness said Parlour came out with that perennial line, 'Don't you know who I am?' Hi-de-ho. An almighty brawl ensued. Parlour ended up needing four stitches in a wound just above his eye after he was glassed in the face. He consequently had to pull out of the England Under-21 squad, as well as give up all hopes of ever becoming a holiday camp Redcoat.

Perhaps one of the greatest and most ill-timed night-club offences of recent years was performed by Sunderland's John Kay. Celebrating his team's hardly inspiring 2–2 draw away to Exeter he went to a local night-club and downed five or six pints of lager. Waiting for a taxi outside the club, Kay suddenly developed a manic hatred for all forms of automobile, perhaps in a drunken haze mistaking them for opposition wingers.

He jumped up and down on the roof of a Vauxhall Chevette, causing £123 worth of damage, and then ran up a £607 bill when he ripped a windscreen wiper and mirror off a Mini Metro and hurled the mirror at the Chevette. When police arrived he was described as 'abusive'. Another Sunderland player, nineteen-year-old Paul Williams, was with Kay, but charges against him were dropped.

'Before, during and after the match the behaviour of Sunderland fans was exemplary. Unfortunately the same cannot be said of Mr Kay,' prosecutor Neil Lawson declared.

To make things worse for Kay, not only was the court case held on his twenty-sixth birthday, it also coincided with the publication of the Taylor Report detailing ways of changing the face of football and countering the scourge of hooliganism – among fans though, not players.

Kay apologized for his behaviour and was fined £500 and ordered to pay £765 in compensation and costs. And what was the Sunderland defender's excuse for his impersonation of a one-man car-breakers' yard? 'It was just high spirits.'

Most of these incidents have a humorous side, but one incident that sadly didn't was when Wolves midfielder James Kelly helped kick a man to death outside a hotel in Liverpool. Kelly, his brother John and a third person had all taken part in the attack after Peter Dunphy and others had refused them re-entry to a party in the hotel. While Dunphy was doubled up after the other two had hit him, James Kelly was said to have kicked Dunphy's head 'like a football'. Justice was done, and in February 1996, Kelly was jailed for five years after admitting to manslaughter. The judge told Kelly that although his soccer career was ruined, 'You will be able to rebuild your life. The deceased is denied that opportunity.'

Red Red Wine

When not in night-clubs our soccer stars cause similar mayhem in wine bars, hotels and pubs. Only a drunken footballer could start a pavlova war in Ipswich.

In 1993 Tottenham's Jason Dozzell and his former team-mate, Ipswich's Chris Kiwomya, were thrown out of the Boardwalk wine bar three times by police, after the cunning duo kept walking around the block to return to the trendy venue. At one point the self-effacing Dozzell (on £5,000 a week) said to a policeman (on £20,000 a year): 'Don't you know who I am? I can make more money in an hour than you can make in a week.'

Dozzell and Kiwomya had been annoying customers in the bar by behaving 'obnoxiously', pestering women and calling a barmaid 'pancake features'. 'They were like arrogant idiots trying to throw their money around,' said the bar's manageress. Things really turned sour when they pelted off-duty waiter Gary McCarthy with a cake. Never mind Paul Merson's coke abuse, it seems that cake abuse is an even bigger problem in East Anglia.

McCarthy was quietly sipping a drink on his own, when Dozzell shoved the pavlova into his face: 'They laughed their heads off and said, "Don't you think that's funny? Where's your sense of humour?"' fumed the splattered but unamused McCarthy. After this bunfight in the Boardwalk, Kiwomya gave McCarthy £10 to cover his cleaning bill, as staff decided to throw out the juvenile stars. To compound their pavlova felony, Kiwomya then asked the cake victim for his £10 back.

After three red cards from the police and Dozzell's wages taunt, the same officers no doubt took great delight later that evening in seeing Dozzell in his BMW and pulling him over for a breath-test, which, most surprisingly, he failed, being nearly double the legal limit. Dozzell admitted drink-driving at Ipswich Magistrates Court and was fined £500 and banned for a year.

After the manageress complained to Ipswich manager John Lyall, both Kiwomya and Dozzell returned the next day with flowers for her – 'John Lyall was like a headmaster with Chris looking very sheepish, like a naughty schoolboy.' Dozzell was dropped by Spurs soon after his court appearance – rumour had it that he was likely to be replaced by a foreign import called Pavlova.

Hotel Matches

Away trips are a manager's nightmare. The combination of night-clubbing and a hotel in a strange city can prove irre-sistible to soccer lads. What more could the footballer want: other guests to dis-turb, night porters to wind up, corridors to rampage down and a complete squad of fellow professionals to conspire with? Dave Watson, the former Sunderland, Manchester City, Southampton and England centre-half, has a memorable tale from his early days in the 1970s at Rotherham. After his side had won at Plymouth the lads decided to celebrate before travelling north the next day. Watson was safely in bed in their hotel when he was woken by a desperate night porter hoping that he could control his drunken team-mates.

Feeling hungry, the Rotherham lads had decided to raid what they thought was a huge refrigerator. It was in fact a giant oven, roasting ducks on spits. In true medieval banquet style, two ravenous senior professionals grabbed the ducklings in their bare hands, only to find them too hot to handle.

After this duck surprise, they dropped the birds on the floor, with grease spilling everywhere. Then, using what might be referred to as their 'football brains', the quick-thinking duck-pilferers found a collection of telephone directories to hold the by now battered ducks in, and retreat-ed to their rooms with their prey. After devouring the ducklings they threw their leftovers out of the window and on to another guest's car.

Meanwhile, in what would have made a wonderful plot for an episode of *Fawlty Towers*, other players had taken over the hotel switchboard and were attempting to phone their team-mates who had retired early – usually getting the wrong rooms and waking up other furious guests.

Rotherham's bird-brained players cer-tainly got a result – a ban from the hotel (which meant the team had to stay in Basil Fawlty's home town of Torquay for future Plymouth games) and each of the players had to contribute £40 in damages – a sizeable sum in those days.

Footballers can knock a couple of AA stars from a hotel's rating in a matter of minutes – fellow guests would surely rather be left alone in the hotel with Jack Nicholson in *The Shining*. Wimbledon were banned from Sheffield's Moat House hotel after their late-night boozy antics in March 1993. After a hard-fought mid-week game at Sheffield Wednesday the players went out clubbing and returned at 2 a.m. Guests accused the Wimbledon

The Premier League of Lethal Weapons

1. Kettle – used by Torquay's Tommy Tynan to attack his captain.

2. Prawn crackers – thrown in a Hong Kong taxi's open bonnet by Ray Parlour, resulting in Parlour going prawn crackers himself, punching the cabbie and being fined in a Hong Kong court.

3. Budweiser label – used by flash Don Hutchison to conceal his wedding tackle and alarm innocent holidaymakers.

4. Pavlova cream cake – thrust into a wine bar customer's face by Jason Dozzell.

5. Kitchen knife – stab wounds after a domestic incident involving his wife left Trevor Morley in a pool of blood on his driveway.

6. Fire extinguisher – let off by Ray Parlour and Tony Adams over the customers of the Hornchurch Pizza Hut.

7. Ashtray – used by brawling Southampton players on a tour of Jersey.

8. Brick – thrown at a bus-driver's groin by Fulham's Ronnie Mauge.

9. Screwdriver – embedded in Mickey Thomas's buttocks by an irate husband.

10. Paper cup – utilized by furniture-climbing England coach Steve Harrison in an infamous piece of toilet humour that resulted in Millwall giving him the sack.

---

lads of sexy canoodling in public, running naked in the corridors, swearing and smashing glasses – so it was quite a routine evening for the Dons.

Wimbledon's chairman Sam Hammam took an eminently practical view of their antics, seeing nothing wrong with a little post-match sexual healing: 'If Wimbledon players have women with them that's great – what's wrong with that? It depends what players were with what women. If young eligible bachelors are with young eligible females, I think that's great.'

While at Sheffield United, Vinny Jones remembered his Wimbledon days fondly: 'When I was there you knew that if you lost your hotel key the room would get wrecked and someone would wee in your washbag. At Leeds, they'd all help you look for it.'

Part of the Dons' folklore is Dave Bassett's final game in charge away to Sheffield Wednesday. On the eve of the match the Wimbledon players went out to bars and clubs all over Sheffield.

Bassett himself returned to the hotel in the early hours, pressed the lift button and found his room's bed, linen, and bedside table neatly laid out in front of him. The incident left Bassett floored, even if the prank was perhaps just a case of elevated spirits.

Would you trust footballers on New Year's Eve? Lou Macari's departure as West Ham manager was hastened after 2 a.m. 'high-jinks' on New Year's Eve, 1989 – the Hammers had a match against Barnsley the next day. The Hammers lads were shopped by Hartlepool chairman Gary Gibson, whose side happened to be staying in the same hotel. There was much late-night revelry, and women were involved too. Indeed, a female member of West Ham's staff left the club after the incident.

The Hammers seemed to respond to such preparation, though: 'The irony is that our lads were in bed early and we lost to Colchester, while the next day West Ham beat Barnsley 4–1,' mused a puzzled Gibson.

The West Ham lads were in trouble again after a damages bill was taken from Harry Redknapp's desk and leaked to the press in 1995. The happy Hammers had wrecked a hotel room in Bournemouth in March. Redknapp had been billed £210 for a ruined pool table and £270 for the room damages, specifically alcohol spilled over a bedroom carpet and mattress, smashed glass, food scattered over walls and carpets and bedspreads fouled with food and alcohol. 'High-spirited footballers are bound to be boisterous,' explained Harry, who has never expected his lads to keep clean sheets.

Manchester City didn't do much better while preparing for a game at Southampton, in January 1996. They were chucked out of the upmarket Meon Valley Golf and Country Club in Dorset after a drinking session in local pubs and then the hotel. Customers saw City stars shouting and swearing and then stagger about the hotel in their socks, claiming that their footwear had been stolen. Then one sozzled City ace went up to a stranger in the restaurant and cut off his tie with a pair of scissors. It proved the final cut – the whole City party was booted out.

And they're even worse at Christmas. Manchester City's Terry Phelan almost missed the 1994 World Cup after a disgraceful eye-gouging incident at a Manchester hotel during a 1992 Christmas party. Phelan was celebrating with his City team-mates and some other guests asked the players to quieten down. It was then that Phelan decided to show the true Christmas spirit by grabbing victim Andrew Holland and digging his fingers and thumb into his eye, before he was restrained.

The prosecution described Phelan as 'being wild with anger, like a madman – growling, screaming and spitting'. (Objection! Perhaps he thought he was still playing for Wimbledon, your honour.) Holland collapsed with blood pouring from his eye and it took him three months to recover. Phelan admitted actual bodily harm and affray in November 1993. He was told to pay Holland £1,750 damages plus £200 costs. Phelan received a twelve-month conditional discharge, and could have missed the World Cup finals if the US authorities had refused him an entry visa because of the conviction.

If it isn't eye-gouging then it's nose-biting. What Vinny Jones had to celebrate after mindless English fans caused their country's friendly with the Republic of Ireland to be abandoned, we'll never know. But after drinking champagne all day, the lovable Dons Rottweiler greeted *Daily Mirror* photographer Ted Oliver's entrance to the Jury's hotel bar in Dublin by clamping his teeth around his nose: 'Vinny fixed me with his teeth and shook me like a dog with a dead rabbit.' Vinny said to Oliver, 'I always do that to people I like.' He later claimed that it was 'a joke' that backfired and pleaded with Oliver, left mopping blood from his wounds with a napkin, not to publicize the story.

Even the prospect of promotion can't stop hotel pranks. Not many players could manage to attack their captain with a kettle just before a promotion play-off at Wembley – but Torquay's Tommy Tynan somehow achieved this feat.

Was Tynan's Gold Blend below standard? No, the kettle attack began after a drinking game called 'buzz' during Torquay's Wembley preparations at the Gloucester Hotel and Country Club. The game involved players shouting out 'buzz' instead of certain numbers, and if they said the wrong number the penalty was to down a drink.

By midnight the players were rather tired and emotional – or, as they say in the pro business, completely pissed. Captain Wes Saunders had an argument with player-coach Russell Musker, who was running the game (so that's what they teach them at coaching school). Tommy Tynan then tried to defend Musker from Saunders. In the words of Torquay chairman Mike Bateson: 'He [Tynan] was sort of leaning on Wes when Wes just turned round and punched him in the face.' The 35-year-old Tynan was left with a cut by his right eye, but after he and Saunders were separated, things seemed to calm down. But at around 2 a.m. Tynan decided to make his own late tackle.

Tynan went to Wes Saunders' room, and barged his way in. 'Unfortunately he picked up the nearest thing handy, which was a kettle, and hit Wes with it,' said Bateson. The kettle clattering left Saunders with facial cuts and bruises and a reprimand from the club.

Torquay's reaction was to pull the plug on Tynan, by cancelling his contract. Tynan was no longer full of beans: 'I was the injured party and I went to his room to get things sorted out. I bitterly regret what happened . . .'

Tommy Tynan, now a publican in Hillsborough, Sheffield, is still haunted by the incident. 'It was handled all wrong, it should never have come out. No one ever remembers that I had a black eye and a cut over my eye, but because I was the big name in Plymouth it was all about me. Wes hit me first and all I was trying to do

TOMMY, WE TAKE IT ALL BACK. NOW KEEP AWAY FROM THAT KETTLE . . .

was stop the fight.' No one dares ask Tynan if he sells Kettle Chips in his pub.

The most notorious hotel incident in recent soccer history concerns Millwall coach Steve Harrison. As the Lions were preparing for a game at Ipswich in October 1991, Harrison was sacked on the spot for what was euphemistically described as a 'lavatorial prank'. His chairman Reg Burr described the joker Harrison's act as 'too revolting for words'.

And what was the 'unacceptable conduct' that Harrison was dismissed for? It took place on a Friday night in a hotel room and did at least keep his charges out of night-clubs. To amuse the bored players Harrison had climbed on a chest-of-drawers and defecated into a paper cup on the floor. The players were roaring with laughter but then in walked coach Ian McNeill. The incident revolted manager Bruce Rioch and Reg Burr, the shit hit the fan, or indeed the cup, and Harrison's job went down the toilet.

Even more embarrassing for the FA was the fact that Harrison was the third man (or should that be turd man?) in the England set-up, having been brought in by Graham Taylor and Laurie McMenemy to boost the players' morale with his japes. After a few days' deliberation Harrison resigned from his England post.

Harrison was soon given another job, however. Within days Steve Coppell offered him a coaching position at Crystal Palace. Harrison was much-loved in football circles for his Brian Clough and Norman Wisdom impersonations (why is it always Norman Wisdom footballers impersonate?), his practical jokes and his crucial ability to relax players.

Harrison vowed to keep up his pranks. His father was a comedian in the working men's clubs of Lancashire. 'Our house was full of fun. It was always plastic fried eggs in the morning and plastic biscuits later.' And who knows what plastic imitations were in the bathroom?

The lovable prankster rejoined Graham Taylor at Wolves – although it's best not to speculate what he got up to with any stray turnips.

Ale House Brawlers

The late Bill Shankly once described Southampton as a team of 'ale house brawlers' and it was an apt metaphor, as pubs are yet another source of footballing mayhem. Our old friend Paul Merson was involved in a pub fight over a game of pool at the Green Man in Hertfordshire in 1989. Merson angrily broke his cue in two when he was heckled by other customers, who were making such provocative taunts as 'Arsenal 0 Green Man 2!'. His friend also became involved and in five minutes of madness glasses and stools were thrown and another drinker had a stool smashed over his head, before the landlord bundled Merson and mate out and called the police. Merson was questioned by the police, but no charges were made. Let's hope he never plays Hurricane Higgins at snooker.

Tony Coton (then at Watford) and Mick Harford (then at Luton) were once involved in a memorable pub brawl with some lippy workmen in Hemel Hempstead. Coton remembers that after he nutted a workman who called him a c***, Harford arrived, 'flying through the air like he's going for a diving header. He's come out of the blocks faster than Linford Christie, head-butted one and decked another three. At the end of it, five or six of them were flat out and two needed hospital treatment.' Then the landlord hit Coton with a cosh. 'He was coshed on the head but his knees didn't buckle.' Harford asked Coton to take him to hospital. 'He then told the landlord that when he came back he'd be in a fair amount of trouble. You should have seen the look on the landlord's face.'

Perhaps Nottingham Forest's goalkeeper Mark Crossley was too quick off his line after a visit to a Sheffield pub. A judge rapped his 'appalling behaviour' when he was fined £1,500 following a punch-up, and his less-than-perfect cousin Andrew Crossley was jailed for six months in July 1994. Mark Crossley had earlier been in trouble with manager Brian Clough after breaking a club curfew on the eve of an FA Cup tie.

Both Mark and Andrew Crossley admitted unlawfully wounding nineteen-year-old Daniel Drury. After the pub argument the Crossleys went to Drury's house, where Andrew threw milk bottles (was he only throwing them because he feared Mark Crossley would drop them?) until Drury came out holding a cricket stump.

In the fight that followed, Drury suffered injuries to his arms and chest caused by Andrew before the Crossleys were carted off by police to spend a night in the cells. 'By his presence Mark Crossley was encouraging him,' argued the prosecution. Judge Trevor Barber, unusually optimistic about the behaviour of footballers, told the errant custodian: 'You should be setting a better example to youngsters.'

Even the most innocent of pub evenings can end in controversy. Tommy Tynan recalls that when he was a Sheffield Wednesday player the lads were all invited to stay at Jack Charlton's mother's farm. After a quiet Sunday night drinking in the village pub, they found themselves caught short. 'We were in this strange village in the middle of the night having a pee in the pitch dark, totally oblivious to the fact that we were peeing on this highly regarded war memorial. There were a few broken glasses too, all the result of accidents.' Jack Charlton knew exactly what had happened the next day, and wasn't too pleased when the incident made the local paper. A case of wee who also serve, perhaps.

Party Animals

We've seen what footballers get up to in public nightspots – imagine the scenes of misbehaviour at club functions. In December 1989 West Ham's legendary lad done bad Frank McAvennie, recovering from a broken leg, tried to gatecrash the forty-eighth birthday party of West Ham's commercial manager Brian Blower.

It was a private party and only members of West Ham's commercial department had been invited to the celebrations at an Essex country club. Brain Blower refused to allow Frank's party in and McAvennie, as a page 3 girl-dating, coke-snorting striker does in these situations, promptly punched Blower in the face, in front of Blower's wife and three children.

It was another stunning Blower to Lou Macari's troubled reign at the Hammers. Blower sent a solicitor's letter to McAvennie and threatened to prosecute him, but after an apology from McAvennie the matter was allowed to rest.

And who invited David Speedie into the VIP suite at Coventry? In front of supporters and their families, Speedie became involved in an infamous racism row and brawl with Asian night-club owner Mo Kandola after a Rumbelows Cup tie against Bolton in 1990. First punches were thrown in the VIP suite, and then the pair began brawling again in the reception area in full view of guests leaving the club. Kandola – who paid £1,000 a year to be Coventry vice-president – later revealed that this was the second fight between him and the fiery Speedie.

A few months earlier they had come to blows in Coventry's Styvechale Arms pub, when Kandola was drinking there with his model friend, 26-year-old Katherine Dale. Kandola alleged that Speedie had asked Katherine, 'What's a girl like you doing with a black bastard like that?' The pair exchanged punches before being separated by two doormen – only then the Sky Boozers tangled again in the pub car park, with Kandola claiming that he floored Speedie, who vowed revenge.

Speedie later broke his silence on the affair and said that he was provoked by Kandola in the clubhouse brawl: 'I deny any suggestion that the incident arose as a result of my feelings towards black people.' The affair did neither party much good. Speedie was fined £3,000 and transfer-listed by manager John Sillett, while Kandola was sent from Coventry – being banned for life by City.

The footballer's capacity for misbehaviour in all situations is infinite. In 1989 Derby's Geraint Williams spent seven hours in a cell before being freed without charge after a row in a Chinese restaurant, Wong's takeaway. Perhaps it was a Wong order. And Orient's Steve Castle managed to be fined for doing a runner from a Pizza Hut restaurant in London's Leicester Square in 1990, leaving his £20 bill unpaid.

No wonder football managers sit ashen-faced outside dodgy, neon-emblazoned night-clubs and are so keen to see their players married (although that doesn't necessarily stop them misbehaving), anything that might give them less time for drinking in night-clubs, wine bars, and pubs. Perhaps a thrusting entrepreneur will soon set up a football-related chain of theme clubs – with such titles as Rumbles, McAvennie's revue bar, Night-Club Incident, Night-Club Brawl, Club Curfew, Club Fine, Club Suspension and Club Pavlova. They'd be overflowing with booze and footballers, seven nights a week. Late licence guaranteed. And, of course, entrance would be free to all those who came out with the line: 'Don't you know who I am?'

1. Before he became a pro, Vinny worked as a hod-carrier on a building site earning £100 a week. Since then, the Dons' hod-man out has played for Wealdstone, Wimbledon, Leeds, Sheffield United, Chelsea and Wimbledon again. His combined moves total more than £2.6 million – a lot of money for a player primarily noted for his long throw. 'None of Jones' managers has yet stated that the prime and obvious reason for having him in their teams is to intimidate the opposition,' commented the *Guardian*'s David Lacey in 1992.

2. After signing from non-league Wealdstone for £10,000, Vinny gave away a penalty on his league debut for Wimbledon against Nottingham Forest. In his second game he scored the winner against Manchester United, but was sent off for elbowing Arsenal's Graham Rix a few outings later. He has continued to fall foul of referees ever since. He once received a record-breaking booking after five seconds in a game at Manchester City and was sent off on his home debut after returning to Wimbledon.

3. In 1987, after a late tackle by Kenny Dalglish, Vinny told the Liverpool maestro that if he did it again, 'I'll tear off your ear and spit straight in the hole.' This is believed to have inspired Quentin Tarantino to include a similar scene involving Michael Madson and a kidnapped cop in his 1992 film *Reservoir Dogs*.

4. When he first joined Wimbledon, after watching the film *The Untouchables* and seeing Al Capone lay into one of his mob with a baseball bat because he was a mole, Vinny took a baseball bat into training the next day to gee-up his teammates. Let's hope he never watches *The Krays*.

5. In a now-legendary picture taken during the 1987–88 season, Vinny was photographed grappling with Paul Gascoigne's testicles. Never mind the crunching tackles, Vincent always really wanted to be a ball-player. 'I squeezed his ego,' Vinny declared. 'You can do that against the big players.' After this move, known as the 'wedding tackle', a tearful Gazza no doubt felt like kicking Vinny in the ego, and a few other places besides.

6. In Wimbledon's 1988 FA Cup Final victory against Liverpool, Vinny's first act was to clatter the Reds' hardman Steve McMahon. He recalled: 'I hammered him and he went about on tiptoes after that . . . If I was on my own and a gang of lads started on me, I would whack the biggest and toughest straight away – and that's what happened.' This man could yet make it as a community policeman. Team-mate John Fashanu said the tackle 'started at his [McMahon's] neck and finished at his ankle, and that put him out. We knew after that, because everybody had seen what a tackle it was, that they didn't want to play.'

7. When Liverpool's Jan Molby was jailed for motoring offences in October 1988, Vinny sent him a letter telling him to keep his chin up, even though he had only met Molby once. 'Away from the action he is one hell of a nice guy,' Jan said of pen-pal Vinny. Perhaps he will find a new career presenting *Hearts of Gold* when he finally retires.

8. When Vinny was at Chelsea (1991–92), he was introduced to their most famous fan, John Major, at a pre-match meal. Jones shouted, 'Sort out the fucking interest rates, will you?' and Major, perhaps fearing a good clumping, replied, 'I'm trying, I'm trying!'

9. After the furore over Vinny's September 1992 video, *Soccer's Hard Men*, Wimbledon chairman Sam Hammam labelled Jones a 'stupid mosquito-brain who talks with diarrhoea in his mouth'. Vinny was 'gutted with myself' after being fined a record £20,000 by the FA. On the video, narrated by Vinny, he listed a number of ways of on-pitch intimidation, including elbowing behind the ear, poking in the eye, raking studs down the achilles and calf, pulling armpit hair, treading on toes, grabbing testicles and giving out verbals about players' wives leaving them.

10. To psyche out the opposition Vinny likes to play his ghetto blaster at full volume in the Wimbledon dressing-room before kick-off. Everton once disconnected the dressing-room plugs to stop this, but Vinny had brought along emergency batteries. After Wimbledon won at Manchester United in October 1992, Vinny turned up the blaster to full volume and danced naked in the corridor with a cigar in his mouth.

11. Vinny once made a record, a 1993 cover of 'Woolly Bully' with his local pub band the Soul Survivors. On the CD version of the single, Vinny claimed in an interview that the then-England manager Graham Taylor had tried to sign him for Aston Villa.

12. When calling up Vinny Jones in December 1994, Wales manager Mike Smith admitted that 'some of his tackles are rash and dreadful'. And that was just while describing Vinny's good points . . .

13. On the eve of his international debut for Wales (having discovered he had a Welsh grandmother after previously courting Ireland and even England), Watford-born Vinny was determined to prove he was a player of international stature. So he promptly became involved in a four-letter-word bust-up in a row over a table in a Cardiff restaurant with businessman David Willis, who labelled Jones a 'foul-mouthed yob'.

14. After Vinny's international debut for Wales (a 0–3 home defeat to Bulgaria) another row erupted after he called some of his team-mates 'crap'. Of course, Vinny should certainly know a crap player when he sees one.

15. In February 1995, after England fans had rioted at the Ireland v. England friendly, bloodied *Daily Mirror* photographer Ted Oliver claimed that Vinny tried to bite off his nose in a Dublin hotel. Vinny, fast becoming an ear, nose and throat specialist, claimed it was 'a joke', but later apologized, saying, 'I behaved like a prat on too much champagne.' Again, Quentin Tarantino was said to be interested in the film rights.

16. 'Vinny has a job for life as captain with us. We are proud of him because he sets such a good example to the young men of England,' declared a faithful Vinny fan, Wimbledon chairman Sam Hammam, three days after the nose-biting incident.

17. Vinny has a tattoo on each leg, one celebrating Leeds' Second Division Championship, the other Wimbledon's FA Cup win, and a Welsh dragon tattooed close to his heart. If Vinny wins any more honours then he'll soon have enough tattoos to marry *Baywatch* babe Pamela Anderson.

18. In March 1995, Vinny denied the story that never was, believing he was about to be accused of match-fixing in a Sunday newspaper. 'Me fix a game? There is more chance of me being involved with the Great Train Robbery,' fumed Vinny. 'I go out to die for my team. If I knew I was playing with a crooked team-mate, someone not with us, then someone else would have to die.'

19. In October 1995, Vinny had to play in goal for the final thirty-five minutes of Wimbledon's game at Newcastle, after Paul Heald was sent off. He was greeted by chants of 'Dodgy keeper!'. He bowed to the crowd and, according to the *Guardian*, 'punched like a fishmonger slapping down half a pound of cod'. However, despite conceding three goals, Vinny pulled off a superb double save and was then regaled by the Newcastle fans with cries of 'Super keeper!'. When Neville Southall retires, he might yet play between the sticks for Wales.

20. In February 1996, Vinny was fined £2,000 for calling Chelsea's Ruud Gullit a money-grabbing cockroach. Jones had been sent off for fouling Gullit on Boxing Day. In his newspaper column, Jones ranted that Gullit had dived: 'I own two pot-bellied pigs yet they don't yelp as much as Gullit.' He went on subtly to state his verdict on the Bosman ruling: 'There's a new noise in football – money-grabbing imports dying on a bed of cash. Beautiful game? What's beautiful about lying in mud like a cockroach on its back?' A bit much coming from old Mosquito Brain himself. Vinny received a Ruud awakening at his FA hearing. It was Jones' fifth fine, meaning he had been docked an astonishing £26,250 in three years by Lancaster Gate.

'OI! WHO ARE YOU CALLING MOSQUITO BRAIN?'

7

Tour de Farce

'Every pre-season we would tour Holland. We invariably found the right place to quench our thirst. We would regularly roll back way after curfew, sneaking in the back entrance or climbing up the drainpipe to avoid the manager's spies.'

Terry Butcher

Any footballer wanting to live up to his job description attempts to be involved in a night-club incident, training ground fight, domestic fracas or romance with a page 3 stunner at least once in a season. So imagine how the soccer ace behaves on a close-season tour of foreign lands, when, freed from the pressures of the domestic campaign, he can really unwind – with no wife or girl-friend to restrict his fun. True, there's the odd slow-paced match against often feeble opposition, but nothing too strenuous to affect the routine of sunshine, sand, sex, soccer and high-jinks.

Everyone in football looks forward to the club tour. Managers use them to encourage a good dressing-room spirit, chairmen like them even more if some local Sheikh is paying a fortune for the lads to perform in a friendly, and for the players there's no real pressure to win from fans or press.

However, with the players in the mood for an end-of-season beano, embarrassing accidents will occur. Winger Peter Beagrie is full of beguiling trickery, from his dribbling to that famous double somer-sault when he scores. But one stunt he surely now regrets involved a motorbike and a hotel's plate glass doors on a 1991 pre-season tour of Spain, when he was playing for Everton.

After a match against Real Sociedad, the hopelessly lost Beagrie, following a night out sampling the local Spanish hospitality, emerged from the darkness to flag down a motorcyclist in the early hours of the morning. The rider took Beagrie to the San Sebastian Hotel, where he tried unsuccessfully to rouse the sleeping night porter.

The only way in was up ten steps and through the windows to the cafeteria. Perhaps Beagrie thought he was in Germany and not Spain. For some strange reason he seemed to imagine he was Steve McQueen in *The Great Escape*. He promptly commandeered the bemused Spaniard's motorbike, and rode up the hotel steps – straight through the plate glass window. And to make the situation worse for the hapless Beagrie, clearly a student of the Mark Thatcher school of navigation, it was the wrong hotel. No one knows if Beagrie did an aerial somersault on the bike before falling to earth.

Beagrie was left nursing around fifty stitches and a new nickname of 'Evil Knievel'. Manager Howard Kendall, certainly not in stitches, was left to pick up many shards of glass and a large bill, although he promptly denied that Beagrie would be 'on his bike'.

A shattered Beagrie later said of the incident: 'I deserved to take the flak because it was a daft thing to do . . . People probably think I'm a prankster and a practical joker but I'm not a nutcase. Even my best mates know I wasn't capable of *deliberately* doing that.' As Ray Wilkins would no doubt say: 'Smashing, Peter, smashing.'

Even today's model pro Gareth Southgate nearly threw up over chairman Ron Noades on a Crystal Palace under-21 tour of Italy. After several tequila slammers with his team-mates Southgate staggered back to his hotel and found himself sharing a small lift with Noades. Then came the technicolor yawn. 'At least he had the presence of mind to be sick in the corner. We were probably all a bit pissed. He was only a young lad and I never thought anything more of it,' Noades says today.

No tour is complete without the odd bar-room brawl. A typical scenario was described by striker George Reilly after West Brom, then under manager Ron Atkinson, had played a friendly in Portugal in 1988.

'It was supposed to be a nice break but there were more black eyes than you get at an average Albert Hall fight night.' Such was the life of Reilly abroad with the Albion. Don Goodman was larking about in a club when he managed to hit hardman winger Robert Hopkins on the head with an ice cube. 'The next thing we knew they were throwing punches and our coach Stuart Pearson became involved,' recalled Reilly. The lanky striker managed to guide the party to another club, where the owner told him that if there was any trouble he would shoot them, and produced a gun from under the counter to back up his threat.

Of course, a mere shotgun is no deterrent to the footballer on tour. Reilly was at the bar with Tony Morley when Tony Kelly started giving the barman some 'verbals' – 'Morley told him to quieten down and Kelly let go with a right hand which split his lip.' With one eye on the owner Reilly got the players back to the hotel. But the lads were only warming up – Don Goodman and Darren Bradley then came to blows over some perceived insult. By this stage the exasperated hotel manager decided to kick out the whole West Brom party a day early, and Big Ron Atkinson eventually fined Kelly and Goodman for their roles in the shenanigans.

On tour the relaxing holiday mood can prove to be contagious. On a 1993 pre-season jaunt to Holland, seven Manchester City players were fined £500 each for breaking a curfew. Manager Peter Reid must have been thinking that at last his disciplinary nightmares were over when he boarded the KLM flight back to England – only to find that four of the Man City party were missing.

The jet's captain then had to put out a message asking Reid to identify himself so that a search could be made. Take-off was delayed for twenty-five minutes until the four – players Steve McMahon, Keith Curle and Rick Holden, plus curfew-maker turned curfew-breaker, assistant manager Sam Ellis – were found at the

PANTS FOR THE MEMORY: DAVE BASSETT FINALLY PROVES THAT HE DOES APPRECIATE BALL CONTROL.

airport bar – at nine o'clock in the morning! It seems that liquid lunches had been superseded by beery breakfasts. Reid, who must have half expected Leslie Nielsen and the cast of *Airplane* to turn up, then had to carpet the three players and his own deputy.

Imagine what the players get up to when the boss isn't around. In 1992 Sheffield United manager Dave Bassett made the mistake of not travelling with his players to the Conquistador hotel at Playa de Las Americas, Tenerife, on a trip to celebrate United finishing eighth in the old First Division.

'They were like lager louts, shouting and swearing day and night. It was chaos,' said one fellow guest. Fourteen boozy players were booted out of the hotel after 'mooning' in front of mothers and children at the hotel pool. The Sheffield United players showed a respect for hotel fixtures and fittings that would have made the late Keith Moon proud. They were accused of swearing in front of other families, smashing furniture in their rooms, dropping a table from a fifth-floor balcony, throwing sunbeds and tables into the pool and breaking a woman guest's camera. The club agreed to pay the hotel for the damage.

Bassett should have known better. Forewarned is forearmed, and in 1990 United's David Barnes and Billy Whitehurst were thrown off a plane just before it took off for the Costa del Sol, after allegedly causing £10,000 worth of damage. Passengers saw the players draw diagrams and team tactics all over the plane's in-flight film screen and ridicule Dave Bassett. A BA spokesperson described the incident as 'wanton vandalism. If soccer fans had been involved they would rightly have been condemned,' although BA eventually agreed not to press charges.

Mind you, at Wimbledon Bassett would sometimes use the odd scuffle abroad to help engender team spirit. *Sun* reporter Steven Howard recalled seeing Wimbledon at work in a bar in Torremolinos (Bassett must have been unaware of the Monty Python sketch) while they were preparing for a cup tie with Spurs. 'Bassett issued the command, "OK, lads, let's rumble . . ." With that, a dozen players launched into each other before collapsing in a heap on the floor. Bassett, at the bottom of the pile, emerged with a torn shirt, cut lip . . . and went straight back to the bar to order the next round.'

The curfew-shunning footballer on tour can often find himself charged with containing similar rowdiness when he becomes the gaffer. Some of the worst offenders as players end up as strict disciplinarians when managers.

In his autobiography, ex-England, Ipswich and Rangers centre-half Terry Butcher wrote of Ipswich pre-season tours to Holland where he and his curfew-breaking chums would shin up the drainpipes to avoid Bobby Robson's spies. 'But the following morning the boss was always able to single out the night-clubbers. In four pre-season tours I was fined every year,' reminisced the big man.

Could this Terry Butcher be any relation to the Terry Butcher who, as manager of Coventry in 1991, transfer-listed a 'Sky Booze' trio of his star players – Kenny Sansom, Trevor Peake and Lloyd McGrath – for staying out drinking on a pre-season tour? Yes, it was the same Butch, who argued: 'It wasn't just that the players went out drinking before a game, it was that they challenged my authority when we were back at the hotel.'

Even a short trip to Jersey can result in mayhem, and turn Saints into sinners. In September 1992, prior to a Southampton 'friendly' match in Jersey, eight players were found brawling in a hotel lounge, the hotel manageress was hit by a flying ashtray and striker David Speedie spent a night in a police cell after being charged with disorderly behaviour.

Eight players, including hardman midfielder Terry Hurlock, had been out for the night and returned to the Grand Hotel in St Helier at 1.40 a.m. They asked for drinks but the bar was shut. Then, it seems that, deprived of alcohol and dance-floor entertainment, they decided to fight each other – all in a 'friendly' spirit, of course.

Duncan Fisher, the hotel's general manager, directed the players to the residents' lounge, where a confrontation developed between the Saints stars. 'There were punches thrown between one of the party who was picking a fight with somebody else. There was a fist fight and eventually someone got injured. When the manageress went into the room she was hit by an ashtray that was flying through the air.'

Manageress and ashtray-victim Samantha Chatham had a ringside view: 'The main fight was between David Speedie and this other guy. I found a lot of Terry Hurlock's long hair on the floor.'

A mere twenty-three police officers were required to restore order. David Speedie was taken to hospital and given fifteen stitches in a face cut, before being taken by police to the cells. Another player had a head injury. A fitting final comment on this surreal display of Saints' brawl skills was provided by Terry Hurlock, who was quoted as telling a reporter, 'If you say anything about me I'm going to have you!'

There must be something in the

normally sedate Jersey air that attracts scandal and football. Blackburn's multi-millionaire benefactor Jack Walker might have spent his money more wisely in the summer of 1994, when he paid for a team trip to Jersey to celebrate finishing second in the Premiership. The Blackburn lads managed to fit lesbian strippers and an alleged blackmail plot into just one night out at the Raffles night-club in St Helier.

Manager Kenny Dalglish, Alan Shearer, David Batty and Tim Flowers drank Grolsch and watched four saucy strippers called the UK Centrefolds frolic on stage – although their broad-minded wives and girlfriends were also reportedly present. A barman at the club said: 'The girls were inches from the players and were thrusting their boobs at them and bending over to wiggle their bottoms.'

The strippers wore wearing stockings and suspenders and lacy basques, and one had a schoolgirl uniform on. After they stripped two of the strippers 'did a lesbian act that drove everyone wild', and then one of them pulled down the trousers of a member of the audience (not a Blackburn player) and sprayed an aerosol can of whipped cream over his privates.

Only the Blackburn whipped cream frenzy turned sour when Raffles bouncer Adrian Hakes was arrested and charged with blackmail. He had allegedly threatened to sell pictures taken at the show unless night-club owner Colin Brown paid him £10,000, and tried to link goalkeeper Tim Flowers with blonde barmaid Mary Innes when she was invited back to the players' hotel for drinks after leaving Raffles. However, at his trial in February 1995 Hakes was cleared of demanding money with menaces on a majority verdict. In court Mary Innes testified that she was invited back to the Pomme D'Or hotel with at least a dozen other Raffles girls, and that there was certainly no Flowers of romance or any improper activity.

But at least Sharon, Karen, Jane and Jan, the strippers dubbed the 'Blackburn Ravers', had happy memories of the evening. Who says football people can't behave in night-clubs? 'Alan Shearer approached me afterwards to make sure we all had a drink. He was really nice,' said stripper Jane Kearns. Another player asked Jane for a date, while Jan Francis even received a kiss on both cheeks from Jack Walker.

And still on the subject of sex, ex-England star Frank Worthington was a star who always enjoyed his trips abroad. 'One of the great things about being a professional footballer is the end-of-season trip. It's the ultimate perk,' is Frankie's opinion, and he should know. This is, after all, a man who once allowed a Leicester team-mate to hide in his wardrobe and watch him make love to a Eurasian woman while Leicester were playing a friendly in Kuwait.

Frank's best tour was in Barbados with Leicester, where he scored with, among others, Miss Barbados (he managed to spot her in the crowd while he was actually playing in a match, which says something about the standard of the game).

But when it comes to behaving badly abroad, the greatest, most surreal incident ever involved Arsenal tourist Ray Parlour. The midfielder with the Shirley Temple hairdo had already made his reputation as a bad boy: he had joined his captain Tony Adams in letting off a fire extinguisher over customers in the Hornchurch Pizza Hut, and been glassed after a fight at Butlin's in Bognor Regis.

But it required a degree of recidivist brilliance to combine all-night drinking with an arrest, a punch-up, a red light district and a packet of prawn crackers.

Parlour, on Arsenal's end-of-season tour of Hong Kong in the summer of 1995, had decided to celebrate the conclusion of the outing. Nothing wrong with that, you might say. But this being an Arsenal tour, it meant going out for a mere twelve pints of lager with team-mates Tony Adams and Chris Kiwomya. Parlour was boozing in the Big Apple night-club in the sleazy Wan Chai red light area and then the Hard Rock Café – the footballer's idea of exploring the local Hong Kong culture – until eight in the morning. So it was quite a moderate night out by Arsenal standards.

Hailing a cab back to the team hotel from Wan Chai, an argument with sixty-five-year-old driver Lai Pak-Yan ensued. The Gunners' midfielder tossed a packet of prawn crackers into the taxi's open bonnet. (What if he'd been holding a packet of corn flakes – would Ray have become a cereal killer?) When the elderly driver objected to the prawn crackers, Parlour punched him on the nose, before being held back by Adams. Yes – this man was so wild he had to be restrained by Tony Adams.

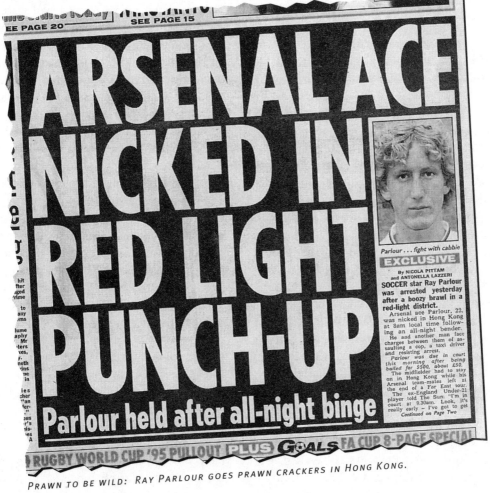

SEE PAGE 15

EE PAGE 20

EE PAGE 16

ARSENAL ACE NICKED IN RED LIGHT PUNCH-UP

Parlour held after all-night binge

Parlour ... fight with cabbie

EXCLUSIVE

By NICOLA PITTAM
and ANTONELLA LAZZERI

SOCCER star Ray Parlour was arrested yesterday after a boozy brawl in a red-light district.

Arsenal ace Parlour, 22, was nicked in Hong Kong at 8am local time following an all-night bender.

He and another man face charges between them of assaulting a cop, a taxi driver and resisting arrest.

Parlour was due in court this morning after being bailed for $500, about £50.

The midfielder had to stay on in Hong Kong while his Arsenal team-mates left at the end of a Far East tour.

The ex-England Under-21 player told The Sun: "I'm in court at 9.30am. Look, it's really early – I've got to get

Continued on Page Two

RUGBY WORLD CUP '95 PULLOUT PLUS **GOALS** FA CUP 8-PAGE SPECIAL

PRAWN TO BE WILD: RAY PARLOUR GOES PRAWN CRACKERS IN HONG KONG.

In what must have resembled a scene from Benny Hill, the irate cabbie – who later needed five stitches to his nose and forehead – chased prawn-to-be-wild Parlour with a wooden club, accompanied by two Chinese colleagues, until the runaway ace was finally arrested by a motorcycle policeman. Considering that Arsenal's midfield was dominated by John Jensen and Martin Keown, it was surely the best run a Gunners midfielder had made all season.

While his team-mates flew home, Parlour had to stay on to appear in court. But even arriving shame-faced in his club blazer and tie couldn't help him. His defence admitted that 'he has no one to blame but himself. He was very drunk and behaved very badly.' Parlour was fined £165 after admitting the assault. He also had to pay £170 compensation to the driver, was fined two weeks' wages by Arsenal and stripped of his £3,000 tour bonus by caretaker boss Stewart Houston.

Rampaging Ray had little choice but to admit going prawn crackers as – even more embarrassingly for the club – his companions Adams and Kiwomya, although not involved in the fight, both confessed to a lawyer that they were too drunk to remember what had happened. It was the Romford boy's finest moment – a *pièce de résistance* in the art of going prawn crackers after twelve pints.

At thirty-six, you'd expect Lee Chapman to know better than some of his younger colleagues. But no, with his wife Leslie Ash starring in *Men Behaving Badly*, the Ipswich striker decided that a holiday in Ibiza was the perfect chance to outdo even Neil Morrissey and Martin Clunes in the bad behaviour stakes. Not even the presence of his wife – butt of endless terrace innuendo during his time at Leeds – could stop wine connoisseur Lee going on the mother of all benders.

It was the end of the 1994–95 season and Mr and Mrs Chapman had left their two young sons at home for a three-day break in Ibiza. Lee and Leslie had been out clubbing all night, first at Koo and then at the aptly named Amnesia, bearing in mind cheeky Chappy's later conduct. He'd been knocking back wine, beer and vodka and orange. At 6 a.m., apparently early doors by Lee's standards, he decided that he wanted to go to another club called Space.

Leslie realized that it was time to show sozzled Lee the way to go home. 'She kept warning me that I was in a bad state and there were lots of English people around,' Lee remembered. Leslie insisted he return to their hotel room. There was a row and she stormed off. Chapman thus became possibly the only man in Britain capable of turning down the offer of returning to a £250-a-night hotel room with Leslie Ash.

At Space Lee fell in with a group of English tourists, who bought him even more drinks. It was around 7 a.m. and he began chatting up blonde Cheryl Roberts, a 26-year-old former model from Leeds, and her friend Claire Lovatt from Stoke. 'He'd keep coming up to me and saying, "Darling I love you." But I told him, "It's her you want" – pointing to Cheryl,' remembered Claire. Lee wasn't fussy. He turned his attention to Cheryl and was photographed, arm in arm with Cheryl at the disco, his glazed eyes staring intently into hers. The girls bundled Lee into a taxi when they left the club – he still owes them his share of the fare – and he ended up back at their apartment.

It was then that Lee's famous prone-on-sofa to in-bed-in-boxers-with-a-blonde transformation took place. 'It's all a bit hazy,' the disgraced striker recalled. 'I can't even remember the woman's name or how I got to her apartment. I passed out in my clothes on the sofa – and woke in my boxer shorts in bed with a woman beside me.' Sounds like quite a night, Lee.

Chappy was adamant that he hadn't scored with Cheryl: 'I know I didn't have sex with her. It's not something a man forgets.' But Claire Lovatt revealed that Cheryl later boasted she had spent the night with Chapman – 'But Lee was so out of it I don't think he was capable of doing anything about it.'

It seemed that Lee grabbed his chance with more alacrity than he ever showed during his final days at West Ham. Rather embarrassingly for this Chapman behaving badly, a picture of Lee in bed with Cheryl then found its way into a Sunday paper. Lee was caught in bed, with Cheryl underneath rather than beside him, giving her a full-on snog. Chapman insisted he was drunk and incapable – here he looked drunk but capable of performing badly.

When Chapman awoke, he realized he was due to fly home that day and staggered back to his apartment. 'I could barely string two words together. I was still drunk and senseless.' Leslie was more upset than Lee had ever seen her and told him, 'You could have been dead for all I knew.' On the flight home Leslie refused to talk to him. He vomited several times on the plane, presumably declined the duty-frees on offer, and then spent two days at home with a massive hangover.

Chapman told Leslie that he had crashed out on a friend's floor, but she wasn't convinced, believing him to have been unfaithful. When news of the pictures broke, Leslie was in tears and told him she couldn't go on with their marriage. Eventually, after mediation by Leslie's mother Ellie, Leslie decided that she didn't want to throw her eight-year marriage away. Lee was now a man grovelling sadly: 'Leslie and our two boys are the only things in the world I really care about . . . I was such a selfish bastard. I can't believe I risked losing them,' he gushed. Leslie took back her contrite husband, now running a bar in swanky Chelsea – and presumably now hides all her *Men Behaving Badly* videos, lest lusty Lee gets any more ideas.

A few players actually sign for foreign teams in the mistaken belief that life will be just like the pre-season tours. Mike Marsh was so homesick for Merseyside while at West Ham that he signed for Coventry and then Graeme Souness's Galatasaray in Turkey in the summer of 1995. His stay was brief. All it took was one boozy night with Barry Venison.

Marshy was seen hanging out of his hotel window in Van screaming at the top of his voice. The lads were celebrating a 1–0 victory over Vanspor, and after a drinking spree in their room kept guests awake with their shouting. Normal procedure in England really. But not in Turkey. After the players refused to answer knocks on their door the police were called and Galatasaray officials had to calm the situation.

The players' behaviour deeply offended Turks in the conservative east of the country and also Galatasaray's directors. They were fined £3,500 each and vice-president Adnan Polat stormed: 'I have told the manager in the strongest terms that we will not tolerate this indiscipline. This is not England.' You said it, mate.

The directors then banned the Galatasaray players from drinking alcohol at all, except on their day off. Enough to make any English player scarper. In

September 1995, Marsh was released by the club, returning to Britain to join Southend. Venison – who might also have offended the Turks with his Day-Glo jackets – was soon packed off to Southampton.

Footballers are naturally unadventurous souls, pack animals by instinct. Set a player down in any of the world's most exciting locations, and the average professional will opt for group tedium by the poolside to an incognito tour of the sights. As West Brom's John Trewick said while standing in front of the Great Wall of China: 'You've seen one wall, you've seen them all.' A year before the 1986 World Cup finals, the England squad made an acclimatization trip to Mexico. Marooned in the Camino Real, right in the heart of bustling Mexico City, Kenny Sansom and Glenn Hoddle – yes, even God failed to provide on this occasion – were reduced to setting up team-mates with pretend crossed lines on the phone. When Terry Fenwick took a call in his room, the first voice he heard whispered, 'Hey, Tony, have you got the drugs?' Hoddle whipped the phone over to Sansom, who replied in his best Chicago street drawl: 'Hey, man, I've got it, and I'm talking about 100 kilos.' Then suddenly: 'Hey, man, there's someone on the line. I'm splitting.' And he slammed the phone down.

As well as being conservative creatures, footballers must also be among the world's most gullible. At lunch the following day, Fenwick was itching to reveal what he'd overheard: 'You won't believe what happened,' he spluttered. 'There were these two American gangsters dealing in drugs in this very hotel!' Good job Paul Merson wasn't in the party.

After a warm-up game in Hong Kong prior to the 1996 European Championship, some of the England squad chose to prepare for the tournament by celebrating Paul Gascoigne's twenty-ninth birthday in the China Jump Bar. Gazza bought Dom Pérignon champagne at £140 a bottle and cocktails followed, as the bar staff span the drinks like Tom Cruise in *Cocktail*. After that the lads saw a drinking game that really took their fancy. Football ambassadors Gazza and Teddy Sheringham were strapped into a dentist's chair and had tequila poured down their throats.

They followed this up with £8-a-shot Flaming Lamborghini cocktails – sadly not named in honour of the typical footballer's driving skills – which looked more like a chemical experiment than a drink. The Flaming Lamborghinis consisted of Kahlua, Sambuca, Galliano, Cointreau, blue curaçao, Bailey's, crème de menthe and cinnamon, which were then set on fire and drunk through a straw, as the barman topped up the lethal concoction with another shot of Bailey's and blue curaçao. Isotonic it wasn't.

Fired up with the Flaming Lamborghinis, Gazza began tearing the Green Flag-sponsored shirts from team-mates Teddy Sheringham, Steve Howey, Darren Anderton and Steve McManaman. They responded in kind by ripping the drunken Rangers star's shirt leaving it hanging from his neck by just the collar: Gazza reacted by spraying his team-mates with beer. The players were finally rounded up by England's Bryan Robson and staggered back to their hotel to meet a 2.30 a.m. curfew.

The next day the hungover players flew back on a Cathay Pacific flight to London. Some players, apparently believing their business-class seats were dentist's chairs,

TEDDY SHERINGHAM LIES BACK AND THINKS OF ENGLAND.

started drinking heavily. The result was that two TV screens and a table were smashed, damage which reportedly cost Cathay Pacific £5,000 to repair.

No one knows which international stars did the damage. Terry Venables conducted his own investigation and announced that the squad had decided to take collective responsibility and fines were shared among them all. Some commentators suggested that with cover-up skills like these, Venables was in the wrong job and should instead be a government minister.

Consider the offences footballers commit abroad and there is only one conclusion. They should all be sent to the same exotic island, where they can play each other in friendlies, throw objects at each other, drink, fight, take the mickey out of Dave Bassett, but generally avoid offending innocent holidaymakers.

Come to the Costa del Football, a sunshine resort offering all-day bars, ashtray and ice-cube-flinging contests, prize fighting, mooning competitions, flying tables, and 24-hour night-clubs. And on the way over, in-flight entertainment provided by Billy Whitehurst and David Barnes. Plus outdoor activities brought to holidaymakers by your friendly couriers: motorcycle stunts from Peter Beagrie and prawn crackers served by Ray Parlour – while Harry Bassett invites us to join the 'Wimbledon rumble'. And introducing your cabaret for the summer – the Blackburn Ravers! Book now – flights may be delayed if Man City are travelling on your plane. Costa del Football – it's the last resort.

8

Red Devils
(The 26-Year Itch)

'I'm not one of these judges who says: "Who's Gazza?". I know this young man – he is a football player for Manchester United.'

Judge Barry Woodward warning the jury in Nicky Butt's assault trial
not to be influenced by the defendant's fame

CRYING SHAME: FORMER ALTAR BOY TOMMY DOCHERTY, SACKED FROM OLD TRAFFORD LITERALLY FOR HIS SINS.

It became football's equivalent of the quest for the Holy Grail. Year after year after year, Manchester United spent millions trying to capture the League Championship trophy, the one piece of domestic silverware which had somehow not adorned the Old Trafford sideboard since 1967. Year after year after year, however, they failed. The Red faithful needed King Arthur and his valiant knights to take charge of their search for the ultimate prize. Instead, United had to entrust their fate to men with names like low-budget gangsters: Frank and Tommy and Big Ron. They were hired to reunite the self-styled Most Glamorous Football Club on the Planet with an honour which United had once been able to regard as almost as sure a bet as George Best seducing the latest Miss World. Unlike Georgie boy, though, none of them pulled it off.

As the seventies and eighties wore on, the distant memory of their Best, Law and Charlton heyday under Matt Busby began to torment United. The occasional FA Cup was no consolation when teams like Nottingham Forest, Aston Villa and

Liverpool – especially Liverpool, the real enemy – were busy winning the League. In the early eighties, when Yosser Hughes symbolized the new era of three million unemployed, United fans loved cruelly to inquire, 'What's it like to have no job?' any time the Scousers visited Old Trafford. The visitors from Anfield would have been well within their rights to chant back, 'What's it like to have no title?' But that didn't scan right. So instead they filled the away end with choruses of 'What's it like to win fuck all?' and 'You'll win fuck all again, Manchester, Manchester'. Those jibes hurt. First Division championships and European trophies galore left little room for mockery. When Everton began claiming the title too, so threatening to turn the League into a Merseyside swap-shop, United became even more desperate. To them, exorcizing the ghost of '67 was deadly serious, an all-consuming passion. To the rest of football, however, it was a huge joke.

While United's hunt for title glory became increasingly obsessive, their dismal failure to find it turned into an increasingly hilarious farce. Had chairman Martin Edwards, as rumour suggested, really got a hotline to the Samaritans installed in his plush office? Did he indeed sing U2's 'I Still Haven't Found What I'm Looking For' in the bath? Old Trafford fans, brought up believing their idols enjoyed football's equivalent of the divine right of kings, didn't like it. When Terry Waite was released in 1991 after almost five years as a hostage in Beirut, Scouse scallywags produced T-shirts bearing a photograph of the Archbishop of Canterbury's bearded envoy asking incredulously: 'What, Man Utd *still* haven't won the League?' Manchester City supporters visiting Anfield for their annual stuffing gleefully snapped them up. They could not ridicule United's conspicuous under-achievement with quite the same conviction as Liverpool fans, but at least their side had lifted the title more recently than their bigger, flasher, arrogant south Manchester rivals. ''68, '68, '68' was a long time ago, yes – but not as long as '67.

United did eventually end their self-inflicted agony in 1993 – but only after a dramatic last-minute collapse the year before gave rival fans everywhere their biggest laugh in ages. Alex Ferguson's appointment as manager in late 1986 set the Reds on their way. Within eighteen months, the tough-talking Glaswegian guided the Reds to a second-place finish in 1987–88; but not for the first time the Liverpool machine, still functioning with its usual awesome slickness, robbed Old Trafford of its chance of glory. By 1991–92, however, the First Division title was there at last for the taking. But amid frenzied media hype about United finally ending twenty-five years of dismal failure, the weight of history made key players nervous. With only a handful of games to go, Bryan Robson's team bottled it and suddenly began losing games they would normally have won. That allowed a Leeds United side, dull except for the panache of an enigmatic but brilliant Frenchman called Eric Cantona, to steal past them and end the season in top spot. United denied, again – unbelievable, Brian. As eleventh-hour sporting slip-ups went, it was pretty spectacular; like a horse six lengths ahead in the Derby inexplicably veering off with just a furlong to go. As anguished Alex assumed the look of a haunted man, and began thinking that United were fated never ever to win the

League, cynics delighted in this latest evidence that, contrary to Old Trafford mythology, United's players were not untouchables after all.

The joke had to end sometime, though. A year later, it did. Untroubled by that humiliating self-destruction, United swept to the inaugural Premier League title in swashbuckling style. Ironically, this time *they* were helped by a last-minute implosion – by their closest challengers, an Aston Villa team managed by Ferguson's predecessor, Ron Atkinson. So Old Trafford's odyssey was finally over. The Reds had won the League at last. After twenty-six years of searching, they had found their Holy Grail. Nostalgia about '67 could now give way to money-making myth-creation of a more contemporary nature. But as the fans rejoiced, and the players drunkenly celebrated having finally thrown the monkey off United's back, still nobody could answer what became one of the most perplexing football questions of our time: what the hell took them so long?

Now, at last, the truth can be revealed. And it is a sordid truth, involving more sex, alcohol and egomania than a Jackie Collins blockbuster. The explanation for that 26-year title famine lies not in terrible tactics, big-name flop signings or whether Liverpool were secretly a team of laboratory-conceived, Lee Majors-style bionic men. (Answer: very probably.) Though the powers-that-be at Old Trafford have portrayed the club as an upright footballing institution, it is the sad duty of *The Lad Done Bad* to reveal that the real reason United failed to win the Championship for so long was the sheer number of boozers, shaggers and brawlers they employed to arrange their date with destiny.

While Liverpool virtually monopolized the League title thanks to the likes of Tommy Smith, Kevin Keegan and Graeme Souness – men who played hard away from Anfield, but worked even harder on the pitch on Saturday afternoons – their would-be Red rivals opted for a succession of bad boys who were too busy doing their worst in bars, night-clubs and courtrooms to give 100 per cent on the pitch. Mickey Thomas was a classic example of the genre, but he was by no means alone.

In theory, it should have been the other way round, with United players the disciplined professionals and Liverpool stars the yobs, hooligans and hell-raisers. United, after all, was dominated not just by the achievements of Matt Busby – an ex-Liverpool player, ironically – but by his stern morality too. The ex-miner from Lanarkshire was a strict Catholic at a club with a well-earned Roman reputation. Services to the faith had earned him a Papal knighthood to go with the accolade he had received from the Queen. His influence as United's father figure – he had rebuilt the team not once but twice, after both the Second World War and the 1958 Munich air crash, led them to four League titles and made them the first English side to lift the European Cup – pervaded all of Old Trafford. 'Inside Old Trafford he was as big as the Pontiff in the Vatican,' recalled one acquaintance, 'yet he had been known to kneel quite unselfconsciously inside his own boardroom to kiss the hand of a visiting bishop.' At United's ground, Catholic clergy were always treated like VIPs. 'Matt laughed at the way Denis Law once pestered him for an introduction to a priest, a guest of Paddy Crerand,' continued the same Busby-watcher. 'Keeping his face straight, Denis

explained: "I had never met a priest until I joined United and this one will be the hundredth."' Sir Matt's philosophy was simple, if unrealistic: players should settle down early with a nice wife, not sleep around, drink modestly and concentrate on developing their God-given talents. An impossible dream? Perhaps. But it worked. Busby's way brought United success, which in turn gave the club the glamorous aura which endures today. And while Sir Matt failed to persuade George Best to see the wisdom of the quasi-monastic life, he at least coaxed from the wayward Irish genius probably the greatest individual performances ever seen in United's famous red shirt.

But after Busby retired in 1969 to become United's general manager, the club began disintegrating. Its decline as a footballing force was matched by its slide into a moral abyss. Scandal and controversy began to descend regularly on Old Trafford. Coincidence – or the Good Lord's will? Whatever the answer, the erosion of standards of behaviour set by Sir Matt, by many of the club's masters as well as its servants, surely played a part in ushering in the wilderness years. Take, for example, the Edwards dynasty which had run United since 1965. They were hardly paragons of virtue. In 1980, then-chairman Louis Edwards – Big Louis, as he was known – was exposed on television for bribing staff of a local education authority to award meat contracts worth a tidy £1 million to his butchery business. He was also accused of being involved in a tax fiddle, and of offering the parents of talented youngsters money to get their sons to sign for United.

And then there is Louis Edwards' son Martin, who inherited the reins of power from his father in 1980 and remains in charge today. If the *Guinness Book of Records* ever invited entries for the most extra-marital affairs by a football club chairman, Edwards would be a strong contender for that dubious honour.

Mistress number one was exposed in April 1990 by the *People* in a story headlined 'Man Utd: Sex, Cash and Blackmail Sensation', which almost certainly made Edwards choke into his Sunday-morning coffee and cornflakes. An Estée Lauder cosmetics salesgirl called Caroline Wyke had sent the millionaire United chairman a letter demanding £100,000 within the week as a reward for having not talked to the Press about their affair. 'I did not talk to them [because] I did not want to cause you problems and ruin your marriage and position at Manchester United,' wrote 26-year-old Wyke, a grey-eyed auburn-haired temptress. But, she continued, 'I am not financially capable of living away on my own so would be grateful if you could financially help. I have not discussed it with anyone only my friend and realized that it is best for both of us if you could send me £100,000 for a flat for me to get away from home.' The incentive for Old Trafford's resident romeo to comply was obvious: 'We think this is a reasonable amount as I have not confirmed anything with the Press and your marriage and private affairs are secure.' Her business-like approach was in stark contrast to the high passion of their liaison. The former fashion model ended her letter thus: 'Please contact me soon to settle the matter within seven days. Yours sincerely, Caroline Wyke.' The message was clear: pay up, Mr Moneybags, or else.

To compound Edwards' embarrassment, the shopgirl, eighteen years his junior, then spilled the beans on their relationship to a *People* reporter, apparently without

realizing his true identity. 'I spent a couple of nights in hotels with him, but most of the time we just had dinner. He was petrified of being recognized and kept thinking people had spotted him,' recalled Wyke. 'We talked a lot about his wife, Sue, but I didn't really want to know. I think it's fair to say he did most of the chasing.' Then the gold-digging make-up madam revealed why she and a friend had written the blackmail letter. 'We had been reading in the papers about Donald Trump and the vast sums of money he would have to pay if he divorced his wife. It seemed to be the answer to my problems, so I wrote to Martin and asked him for £100,000.' Her none-too-subtle approach seemed to be paying off. 'It clearly worried him because he's been ringing me up being incredibly nice.' And just in case the randy chairman was thinking about denying the affair, Caroline had conveniently remembered to keep a detailed diary of all her meetings with Edwards during their steamy sessions. If the hapless, hormone-driven United boss had not suspected before that he was being set up, then he certainly knew differently now.

Women, not United's results, certainly appear to be Edwards' Achilles' heel. A week later, the same newspaper's splash trumped even that exclusive. It detailed how the Old Trafford supremo had taken sultry BBC TV newsreader Lynette Lithgow to London the night before United played Chelsea at Stamford Bridge, wined and dined her at trendy Langan's brasserie, then spent the night with her at a posh hotel. His Nudes at Ten may only have cost £200, small change to a man of his wealth, but the revelations provoked further problems in his private life. His wife Sue was less than ecstatic.

The secrets of suite 1327 filled four pages of that Sunday's *People*. Coming soon after the chairman had secretly tried to sell his controlling stake in United, and with the club in some danger of getting relegated, scandal was the last thing he needed. At least this time the woman involved was his own age. Lithgow, forty, was a former air stewardess whose charms – 'colourful outfits, radiant smile and deep sexy voice', as the paper put it – had helped make her a rising star of the bitchy world of TV newsreading. She may have used an autocue for the day job, but when she was with the United chairman the headlines they made in bed needed no prompting. While Edwards was playing away from his wife, Trinidad-born Lithgow was already divorced. She was, by the chairman's own admission, very keen. 'I think I've got problems,' he told a friend. 'She's totally in love with me.' In classic naughty lovers style, they registered at the swanky Royal Lancaster hotel as Mr and Mrs Edwards. True love didn't blossom, though. While Lithgow may have wanted Edwards to be her man, the energetic United chairman had no intention of limiting his affections to just one (other) woman.

Before long, mistress number three hit the headlines. Where neither Caroline Wyke nor Lynette Lithgow had kissed and told, this time blonde Debbie Miller certainly did. Her sense of timing was as faultless as a Mark Hughes header. On the Sunday the Reds were due to play Aston Villa in the 1994 Coca-Cola Cup Final at Wembley, she was pictured on the front of the *News of the World*, wearing a United kit and a cheeky smile, beside the headline, 'Cup Final Sensation: My Sex Games With United Boss'. The law firm receptionist – who at twenty-eight was

The Manchester United Bad Boys XI

1. Gary Bailey: Received undeclared payment from United which later formed part of a wide-ranging Inland Revenue investigation into the club's finances.

2. Paul Parker: Pleaded poverty when taken to court in a bitter battle over maintenance payments for the baby daughter he had fathered while married to another woman, for example by offering to pay off £1,200 arrears in instalments of just *five pounds* a week.

3. Norman Whiteside: Belfast-born booze fiend who used to turn up at morning training sessions reeking of the hard stuff.

4. Paul McGrath: If necessary, he could drink as readily as play football for Ireland, and he ended up in court after one spectacular binge.

5. Remi Moses: Left Jesper Olsen needing eleven stitches in an eye wound after a fight during training.

6. Neil Webb: Fined two weeks' wages, £5,000, by Alex Ferguson after a 'drinking incident' – breaching club rules by having a drink with a meal the day before a game.

7. Bryan Robson: Legendary boozer who was once banned from driving after being found wandering round a motorway service station at 3 a.m. while totally pissed.

8. Roy Keane: Has been questioned by police in Manchester, London, Nottingham and Ireland over a variety of incidents, usually involving night-clubs and alcohol.

9. Bobby Charlton: Banned from receiving FA Cup Final tickets for three years after a ticket issued to him fell into the hands of touts.

10. Ryan Giggs: Loved and left a string of blonde beauties, including sixth-form schoolgirl Davinia Murphy and babe TV presenter Dani Behr.

11. Lee Sharpe: Left with two black eyes after being attacked by yobs outside a Stockport night-club, though claimed his injuries were because he'd been 'whacked by a pal's golf club while we were fooling around'.

---

young enough to be 48-year-old Edwards' daughter – told how she and the United chairman had made love in hotels all over England.

Edwards had pursued Miller after meeting her at a party to mark Nigel Benn and Chris Eubank's scrap at Old Trafford. As soon as he saw her, it was a case of gloves at first sight. Initially, she teased him by dressing to thrill and then refusing to sleep with him. Soon after, though, the ex-convent girl succumbed to the married football boss's persistent urgings. 'He may be forty-eight but he has the body of a 30-year-old,' she cooed. 'His legs', she said, were 'hard as steel' – was she not confusing him with Vinny Jones? – 'and he's got lots of body hair.' Edwards liked his latest flame's body beautiful too. 'I slowly peeled off my clothes while he watched. He was shaking and obviously getting very excited,' recalled Miller. 'Eventually I was standing in just my black stockings and suspenders, with a little black choker around my neck. He said, "You drive me potty." Then he just jumped on me and we made love there and then. It was unbelievable.' Doubtless, when Sue Edwards learned of the affair, she found it a choker too.

Afterwards, they drank champagne together in the bath. Edwards got top marks for his performances: 'a wonderful lover,' enthused Miller, 'but very straight. He's definitely not kinky and just likes the missionary position. I wanted him to be a little more rough, but he was always very gentle and considerate.' During their affair, he always picked up the bill. The difference in their backgrounds was stark: Edwards would arrive at their chosen rendezvous in his BMW, Miller in her ancient Honda Civic. She recalled how once in a hotel in Leeds, they were watching Blackburn Rovers on TV when 'Martin said how much he hated their manager, Kenny Dalglish'. On another occasion, Old Trafford's lusty Lothario mischievously asked his mistress 'What's a Gillian Taylforth?' On the way to a French restaurant, she promptly showed him. 'We were driving down a country lane when I leaned over and said, "This is going to blow your mind!"' Somehow Edwards kept control of his car.

Geordie-born Miller revealed elsewhere how Edwards 'was like an animal in bed'. The way she talked about the Red Devils' chairman made him sound like an ideal replacement for Bryan Robson in United's midfield: 'His stamina was terrific. He could make love all night. He told me he played tennis to keep fit.' The blonde bombshell's vivid recollection of Edwards' physique left little doubt just how intimate they had become during a five-month fling. 'He would moan and growl, and that's why I nicknamed him my gorilla. He's also got a tremendous amount of body hair over his back and arms, and is covered with freckles.' She also explained exactly how the married father-of-two cunningly stopped his wife from finding out what he'd been up to.

'After we had made love, Martin would always get his silk pyjamas out of his bag and put them on the floor. As I watched in amazement, he would trample them into the ground and say over and over, "That'll fool her."' Married men thinking about having an affair take note.

Edwards' latest extra-marital fling faltered, however, when the randy receptionist grew more and more possessive of her beau. 'I was falling in love with him,' she said. 'When I was with him, no one else had him.' The final straw for Miller came when she met Edwards at yet another hotel on her twenty-eighth birthday. As a present, he handed her £100 and told her to buy herself something nice. 'I felt so let down,' explained his away-day scoring partner. 'I thought, "You mean bastard. Mr Moneybags, and he can't even get me something nice for my birthday." In my heart of hearts I know I have to finish an affair which can only end in tears.' Which female actually shed those tears, Debbie Miller or Sue Edwards, was never revealed. Confronted just before publication at the top people's Austrian ski resort of Lech, where he was photographed walking hand-in-hand with his wife, Edwards' reply was as frosty as the snow: 'I confirm I know Debbie, but I never talk about my private life.'

The Edwards family's ability to make the headlines for all the wrong reasons shows no signs of waning. In February 1994, the United chairman's 24-year-old son James appeared in court to plead guilty to threatening behaviour. The wild child of the dynasty had terrorized his ex-girlfriend at gunpoint as she cradled their baby son. Sally-Jo Wilde, a former Miss England, had been 'frightened to death' when Edwards junior turned ugly during a 'tense and emotional' doorstep row at her home. He reached into his jacket, produced a pistol, pointed it at her face and threatened to blow her head off. Neither Sally-Jo nor two-year-old Jasper, who had become hysterical, knew it was a plastic toy intended as a gift for his son. It made no difference to her that afterwards James rang her on his carphone and apologized. Hell hath no fury like a woman terrorized, and she reported him to the police anyway.

Macclesfield magistrates handed down a sentence of £45 costs, £400 compensation and a twelve-month conditional discharge. The target of his stupidity was unimpressed. 'I think he got off very lightly,' she said. 'He needs treatment. James' moods can switch at the snap of a finger.' It will be an interesting sign of the times at Old Trafford if, after an indiscretion like that, James Edwards follows his father and grandfather on to the board.

Manchester United's moral values have certainly changed a lot since Matt Busby's reign. These days, carrying on regardless of almost any scandal is Old Trafford's guiding motto, as Eric Cantona found out after he practised his kung-fu on a toerag called Matthew Simmons. But the old morality still held sway back in the summer of 1977 when, despite having just guided his team to a famous FA Cup Final victory that denied Liverpool the treble, Tommy Docherty was sacked after confessing to his affair with Mary Brown, wife of the club's physio, Laurie. Perhaps following the Wembley triumph the Doc felt secure. Whatever his thinking, he rang Louis Edwards at home on the Monday morning after the game to tell him about the turmoil in his private life. Louis was out, but his son Martin enquired: 'What is it, Tom, anything I can do?' When Docherty told him, Edwards junior

paused and replied: 'Tommy, that's a private matter. It's nothing to do with the club. What you do with your private life is your own business.' Given what would later emerge about Edwards junior's high-energy bedroom training sessions, the chairman's son was probably wise not to jump to any moral judgements. Even after the media got wind of the 'love tangle sensation', United seemed to be standing firmly by their man. In a bid to escape the furore, Docherty flew to Portugal, where Louis Edwards had taken the youth squad for a tournament. 'We never spoke about Mary,' recalled the Doc later. 'When I flew back to Manchester, I genuinely thought it had blown over. I looked forward to working normally again and made a vow to myself that I would win United the title and prove that my ability to manage the club had not been affected.'

But Docherty had reckoned without Busby's powerful influence. The club's father figure was very upset that a fellow Catholic had, to his mind, brought shame upon the good name of Manchester United in such an unforgivable manner. To him it did not matter that Laurie Brown had accepted the relationship, allowed the Doc to come and live in what until recently had been his marital home, and even babysat his own children to allow their mother – his wife – to go out with her new love. Such open-mindedness was lost on 'the Pope of Old Trafford'. Busby, deeply upset that the United manager had been seeing another man's wife for two years, went to work. Discreet words of advice here, expressions of disgust there. Docherty was acutely aware of the danger of not having taken Sir Matt into his confidence. 'For my part I believed my only crime was that, although

I was married, I had fallen in love with another woman. But would he see it as simply as that?' the manager wondered. He soon discovered the answer to that question.

During a break in the Lake District, the Doc was suddenly summoned back to Manchester for a showdown meeting with the United directors – including, ominously, Sir Matt. The 'all for one' attitude and talk of a new four-year contract were now forgotten. Louis Edwards came straight to the point. 'Under the circumstances we think it would be in the best interests of everyone concerned if you resign as manager, Tommy.' Though Martin Edwards mentioned that Docherty had sold Cup Final tickets, the real reason was obvious. The Doc faced a simple choice: resign – or be sacked. The normally chirpy Glaswegian was baffled by the board's sudden change of heart. 'One day I was staying, the next I was forced out. I just could not believe that the situation could have turned against me so quickly. Something was not right.'

Speculation was rife about what had gone on behind closed doors. Were those whom the Doc contemptuously called 'the junior board', mischievous 'self-opinionated and self-appointed friends of the directors and players', to blame? Or had the players' outraged wives really threatened to boycott the club if Docherty stayed? Both seem unlikely scenarios. Almost certainly the man who broke both Doc's heart and his career was Busby, who had been away on holiday when the manager plucked up the courage to tell 'Big' Louis Edwards what was going on. It was, after all, during Docherty's fateful weekend in the Lakes that, by his own admission, he finally 'recognized the serious view that Sir Matt must by now

have taken of the whole business'. With considerable understatement, the Doc's biographer Brian Clarke acknowledges that 'some suggested the strong Roman Catholic influence at United had made people concerned about his personal life and that that had been the key factor'. Quite. After all, the Ten Commandments proclaim that 'thou shalt not commit adultery'. Yet a former altar boy had done just that. And so Docherty was sacked by United – literally for his sins.

The Docherty saga was a turning-point for United. Six years later, placed in a very similar dilemma by manager Ron Atkinson, the club's directors abandoned any pretence of occupying the moral high ground. Like the Doc, Big Ron had just won the Cup, albeit on a replay after surviving the infamous last-minute 'and Smith must score' near-miss against Brighton. After two rocky years in charge, that triumph had earned him a temporary reprieve from the criticism that dogs every occupier of the Old Trafford hot-seat. Weeks later, Atko told Martin Edwards, by now chairman, that he was cheating on his wife Margaret with another woman, a glamorous ex-model ten years his junior called Maggie Harrison. Just like when Doc had left his wife for Mary Brown, Edwards told him his private life was a personal matter and his job was safe. Unlike the Docherty episode, though, this time United stuck to their word. Mind you, at least Big Ron wasn't shagging the trainer's missus.

It was almost another year before the affair became public knowledge – when Big Ron left his wife of twenty-three years to live with his mistress. An unrepentant Maggie Harrison uttered exactly the same words as the Doc had done: 'My only crime is to have fallen in love.'

Predictably, the affair became a media circus. The papers pursued the man they called 'football's Mr Flash, known for his extravagant taste in clothes and jewellery' – and, it seemed, women. 'Some might say she's got a tarty image,' bitched the spurned Mrs A. 'A nicer word is glamorous. I can see she is his type, the sort he *would* go after.' Cornered as he climbed into his white Merc, Romeo Ron blasted: 'I can never understand why a football manager's personal life should affect his job or his club.' For once, Martin Edwards agreed, rather understandably.

'Mr Atkinson is still the manager at Old Trafford,' he intoned. 'I'm not interested in what happens outside this club.' There was curiously little sympathy for Atkinson's wife Margaret, perhaps because almost everyone at United had known about the affair for months. After all, Harrison had turned up on club trips abroad, and had even gone over to Spain in 1982 for the World Cup at which her lover was commentating. Discreet was certainly not Big Ron's middle name. His wife finally found out the truth in a series of anonymous phone-calls in mid-1983.

MR BOJANGLES: BIG RON WITH THE SORT OF WOMAN HE WOULD GO AFTER.

The identity of the caller was never revealed. Just who could it have been?

But what really spiced up this relatively routine mid-life crisis, albeit by one of the best-known men in football, was an extraordinary offer by Margaret Atkinson to Maggie Harrison to share Big Ron with her. The rejected wife's plan was this: you have him during the day, but send him home to me every night. Poor Margaret was desperate to keep the 45-year-old husband she had been with since they were both teenagers. But Atkinson declined this novel and flattering, if highly unlikely, solution to his emotional turmoil. He had heard of stocks and shares, timeshares and the singer Cher – but never a husband-share. Days short of his twenty-fourth wedding anniversary, he walked out. Maggie Harrison was certainly impressed with her capture. 'Ron is just my type of guy. He's big and powerfully built,' she gushed. 'All my favourite film stars are the Charles Bronson and James Coburn types. And my favourite singers have deep voices, like Neil Diamond.' All very tasteful. But just when did Charles Bronson ever use the phrase 'early doors'?

The woman he left behind got some sort of revenge by spilling the beans on the type of man her husband really was – and how the powers-that-be at Old Trafford had turned a blind eye to his playing around. 'Despite his "Mr Flash" image, all gold jewellery, Gucci shoes and sharp suits, he's always been my Prince Charming since we first met twenty-nine years ago,' explained Margaret sadly. Her initial reaction to her husband's affair had been thoughts of suicide. At first they had kept up appearances. 'That meant doing the driving for Ron, chauffeuring him to and from games. I carried on my social life at United, mingling with directors and their wives, fully aware they knew about the affair.' When they asked how she was, Margaret simply replied, 'I'm fine,' and kept on smiling. She wasn't, of course. The humiliation of it all hurt. But what could she do? Looking back, she wishes that Martin Edwards, to avoid yet another scandal at United, had told Atkinson at the outset to choose between his mistress and his job. 'If he had,' said Margaret, 'I *know* Ron would have chosen his job. Football is Number One in his league table of affections. It has always been that way: soccer first, Ron second, me third. Maggie should remember that.' Mrs A also revealed how Big Ron had cheated on her once before, years before he got that nickname. He was playing for lowly Oxford United at the time and seeing his fancy woman in the afternoons while Margaret was working as a hairdresser. But when a private detective hired by the other woman's husband confronted the illicit lovers, Romeo Ron became runaway Ron and the liaison ended. Now her husband was leaving her again – except this time he was going for good.

Nobody seriously suggested Atkinson should resign as United manager over the affair, and capturing the FA Cup again in 1985 showed the wisdom of his staying on. The fact that he did so was proof positive of Old Trafford's belated conversion to an amoral attitude towards their staff's many personal indiscretions. Thus, when the saintly Sir Bobby Charlton – OBE, club director and winner of every honour in the game during a nineteen-year career with United and England – was banned in 1990 from receiving FA Cup Final tickets for three years, none of his fellow members of the

Old Trafford board condemned him. The Football Association acted against one of its most illustrious servants – 106 appearances for England as well as 751 for United – after a ticket allocation to Charlton for the 1988 Liverpool v. Wimbledon final ended up in the hands of a tout. 'It's all very embarrassing. It's my fault and therefore I accept the punishment,' admitted Charlton with typical good grace. No one mentioned the words 'sleaze', 'disgrace' or 'resign' – and the world somehow kept on turning.

Consciously or not, the recruitment of Alex Ferguson in late 1986 was a throwback to the old days, when discipline on and off the pitch brought trophies. Despite the fact that he was the club's first non-Roman Catholic manager in living memory, Fergie was an almost teetotal, strict Scots disciplinarian in the mould of Matt Busby, someone who was seen as having the right stuff finally to bring the Championship back to Old Trafford. There was also the rather wild reputation the club had earned thanks to the antics of some of its biggest names. That had to be sorted out too. As one United-watcher remarked later, Fergie 'has had his work cut out controlling the excesses of some high-living stars'. That was putting it mildly.

Yet United's Govan-born gaffer has been as erratic as Ryan Giggs' crosses in applying his supposedly cast-iron views on how professional footballers should conduct themselves. Ferguson bought two players who had both fathered a love-child while at previous clubs: Paul Parker at QPR and Dion Dublin at Cambridge United. Those unfortunate episodes clearly did not stop the manager thinking they were the right sort of players for Old Trafford. It is doubtful whether Matt Busby would have taken a similarly enlightened view. Yet Ferguson fined another of his signings, Neil Webb, a whopping £5,000 in 1992 after what was called a 'drinking incident'. In fact, the midfielder's only crime was to have one drink with a meal the day before a match – against club rules, yes, but hardly a hanging offence, especially compared to the alcohol-fuelled antics of some of United's other big names. And when Clayton Blackmore was accused of rape in late 1987, Fergie took no action despite the damaging publicity that accompanied the claim.

The scandal occurred while United were in Bermuda in December 1987 on a two-match friendly tour. The Welsh midfielder and most of the rest of the players had spent the evening drinking at the Oasis disco in the sunshine island's capital of Hamilton. According to the 'victim' of the alleged rape, a 22-year-old American beautician called Patricia Savoy, Blackmore followed her into the ladies' loo just before the club closed at 3 a.m. and sexually assaulted her on the floor. The 23-year-old player, who had married just a few months before, strenuously denied the woman's claims. But the Bermuda police arrested him and he spent thirty-two hours in custody before being released on bail. Up to seven years in jail awaited Blackmore if he was found guilty.

At first the five-foot, seven-stone brunette claimed: 'My life has been shattered. I am living a nightmare. No one will ever know what I have suffered, and am still suffering.' Back home in Manchester, Blackmore's wife Jackie anxiously waited for proof of her husband's innocence or guilt, always believing that he had done nothing wrong. Then, curiously, Savoy suddenly asked the Bermudan authorities not to proceed with any prosecution and the case was dropped. She explained her surprise about-turn as a gesture to spare Blackmore's wife: 'I was told that he had recently been married. I felt sorry for his wife who knew nothing about these events. I put myself in her position.' Not only that, but: 'I did not feel I could cope emotionally with all the inquiries. I wanted to get on with my life and put this nightmare behind me.' Significantly, however, Savoy also pointed out: 'By asking the police and the attorney general not to prosecute does not mean that I withdraw the statement I have made to the police.' Regardless of that, Jackie Blackmore was 'happy and relieved. I never had any suspicions.' The Blackmore 'scandal' was a very mysterious affair which, if nothing else, gave a whole new meaning to the phrase 'Savoy shuffle'.

In Bermuda, though, some MPs were angry about the mysterious conclusion to an incident which had shocked the usually calm island community. Austin Thomas of the National Liberal Party explained: 'There has always been unrest about the handling of the affair. The feeling is that because this gentleman was a famous footballer and a court case would bring considerable embarrassment to his club and family, proceedings were dropped.' But in Blackmore's parents' house in West Glamorgan, there was rejoicing that their boy had been freed and the stain on his character removed. His father Colin dismissed Savoy's story as 'an astonishing claim' and said his son could not have been involved in any attack. Footballers, he explained, were vulnerable to tales concocted by people who wanted to create scandals. Whatever the truth of the 'rape', no court ever tested the evidence of the alleged assault and Blackmore returned to Britain to be reunited with his bride of six months, secure in the knowledge that he had been found guilty of no impropriety whatsoever.

The Blackmore 'rape' furore was the first big off-field scandal which Alex Ferguson had to deal with as United manager. Three of the club's best players – Bryan Robson, Paul McGrath and Norman Whiteside – posed the next headache. Nicknamed 'the Wild Bunch', they were notorious for their heavy boozing. Whiteside, for example, had gone on a 24-hour bender during a club trip to Malta, and often turned up to training with his breath reeking of drink. McGrath was, if anything, worse. He would regularly go AWOL, and once went missing for a whole week. As Fergie himself admits: 'When I arrived at Old Trafford, my first concern was to get rid of the idea that Manchester United was a drinking club – not a football club.' In his memoirs, *Six Years At United*, the manager detailed the problems he faced. McGrath, for instance, was sozzled so often that United even called in a priest to give him counselling and support. It was the first time McGrath had sought spiritual aid from anything other than a bottle. Sadly, though, even that didn't work. Fergie was exasperated. 'I knew if we were to meet supporters' visions of United as a club of class and style, somewhere in the profile there would have to be discipline. Without it, all the talents could go fluttering off in a million directions. I knew I would have to separate Norman and Paul.' One week in particular, which the pair spent making their way round the pubs and clubs of Manchester, helped him decide firm action was required. 'Their journey was charted by supporters phoning in to let me know where they were and what state they were in on the merry-go-round,' he recalled. 'It was like a treasure trail.'

The manager's assessment of the two players was scathing. On McGrath: 'I sensed he was on a self-destruct course which was gathering momentum by the time I reached Old Trafford. I don't know if he lacked the intelligence to understand what was happening or whether he had gone too far down the road to ruin.' And on Whiteside, the man who had scored the winning goal in the 1985 FA Cup Final when United were down to ten men: 'I have the greatest admiration for him and sincerely believe most of his problems were down to disappointment and depression caused by his continual knee injuries. [But] I believe he sought refuge in a lifestyle which naturally created conflict with my concept of a United player.' Eventually Fergie broke up 'the Wild Bunch' in 1989 by selling McGrath to his predecessor, Atkinson, now at Villa, and Whiteside to Everton, the team he had scored against in 1985. Robson, England's Captain Marvel, was allowed to stay because his boozing had never affected his performance on the field.

That drastic action may have turned Ferguson into Public Enemy Number One in the eyes of United supporters. And it allowed Tommy Docherty, hardly a man to start throwing stones from a glass house on the subject of discipline, to speculate that 'The only possible reason for getting rid of them is that they like a drink and he won't tolerate it.' That policy was short-sighted, said the Doc, who inquired: 'Name me a great player who didn't like a jar or a drop of wine. George Best, Jimmy Johnstone, Peter Osgood . . . the list is endless. The fans couldn't care less as long as they do the business on the park.' But Fergie was determined to do things his way, whatever the cost. The board backed his judgement. They, too, were sick to the back teeth of the bad reputation Old Trafford had acquired since Busby's heyday.

After that, discipline seemed to have been restored among the United playing staff. Misbehaviour in the years following the ruthless 'Wild Bunch' purge was usually of the low-budget, harmless variety. There was the time the red-haired, fiery-tempered midfielder Nicky Butt, one of the so-called 'Fergie's Fledglings' who had made an effortless transition from the youth team to the first team, was charged with assault after allegedly headbutting his girlfriend's ex-boyfriend in the loos of Charlie Chan's, a Manchester Chinese eaterie popular with the city's big names. Peter Oldbury, the victim of Butt's alleged attack, took to wearing a patch over his left eye after the encounter. He complained bitterly that: 'I'm not going to let Nicky Butt get away with this. He has broken my nose and blackened both my eyes.' But the subsequent court case led to Butt being acquitted. And during the Reds' ill-fated assault on the Championship in the spring of 1992, for example, Lee Sharpe and Ryan Giggs – then both relatively unknown rising stars, if such a thing seems possible now – were fined an estimated £8,000 and £6,000 respectively after disobeying Ferguson's explicit orders to stay indoors in order to enjoy a night on the town. It was Easter

Monday 1992 that the rot set into United's title bid with a 2–1 defeat by Forest. The manager, aware that an historic honour was possibly slipping away from his team's grasp, told his players to go home and rest up before they travelled to London to play already relegated West Ham in a crucial game. But Sharpe and Giggs chose instead to head to Blackpool for a party. At first, they seemed to have got away with it. Both went to London for what turned out to be a catastrophic 1–0 defeat by a Hammers side Fergie later accused of putting in an 'obscene' effort. But they were rumbled when Fergie heard that they'd been seen out enjoying themselves when they should have been indoors. He went ballistic and immediately drove round to Sharpe's home. There he found Sharpe, Giggs and three United apprentices preparing for yet another night out – even though the Reds were due to play Liverpool just seventy-two hours later. The first-teamers wisely owned up to their Blackpool jaunt – yet another occasion in which the seaside town's many attractions had intervened during the climax to the title race. Just like Chelsea in 1965, though, destiny rather than indiscretion in the shadow of the famous illuminations decided the outcome of the Championship that year.

But the arrival at Old Trafford of *enfant terrible* Eric Cantona forced Alex Ferguson once again to relax his regime, and ignore his more punitive instincts. Once upon a time at United, where priests have long been a common sight in the best seats, the Reverend Ian Paisley would have been made more welcome than a kung-fu fighting Frenchman. But not any more. Ferguson, though, can hardly have one rule for the red card-prone *monsieur*, whom he treats with kid gloves, and another for the rest of United's stars. Another explosion from reckless Eric seems almost inevitable, and Irish wildman Roy Keane – already a veteran of several skirmishes with the police and one court appearance – looks as if he too may sooner or later test the patience of the manager whose players call him Taggart, after the dour, humourless fictional Glaswegian TV detective (but only behind his back). While the late, lamented Matt Busby's aura usually guaranteed order on its own, Alex Ferguson may well find himself ringing Maryhill CID in his native Glasgow, and not a Catholic priest, when the next crisis breaks among his aptly nicknamed Red Devils.

20 Choses Que Vous Ne Saviez Pas D'ERIC CANTONA

1. It's no coincidence that the four letters of Cantona's Christian name are spelled out in the middle of the word 'maverick'. Reckless Eric is the supreme individualist, both as a footballer and as *un homme*. As Bryan Robson once joked: 'When the season ends, he jumps on his Harley Davidson, roars off to the Camargue and paints . . . just like the rest of us!'

2. Cantona's antics over the years have been so regular, so scandalous and so headline-grabbing that few people in France are surprised by anything he does any more. '*Il est fou*' – French for 'he's mad' – is a typical shrugged reaction among his compatriots to his latest indiscretion.

3. Asked to name the people they really admire, most British players are predictable. Their checklist of heroes usually includes George Best, Sevvy Ballesteros, Oasis, Michelle Pfeiffer, Del Boy Trotter from *Only Fools and Horses* and, for the daring few, Nelson Mandela. Cantona's pantheon of idols, however, involves left-field characters from the worlds of art and literature such as Picasso and Kandinsky, Rimbaud and Camus, and Jim Morrison of the Doors. Interestingly, his favourite footballer is Maradona, another player with a persecution complex.

4. In his early days in France, Cantona's repeated run-ins with players, managers, referees and the beaks of the French FA led to him being nicknamed Le Brat. Despite regular punishment for his sins, the young upstart was unrepentant. 'Nothing will ever make me wiser. And there's nothing I need to be wiser about,' he declared. 'There are bad sides to my character, but without them I wouldn't be what I am. You either accept me as I am or you don't.'

5. Or, in the words of the famously articulate Howard Wilkinson: 'Eric likes to do what he likes, when he likes, because he likes it.' Er, yes, Howard, we know what you mean.

6. Cantona's career began at Auxerre in 1981, when he was signed aged fifteen by his friend and mentor Guy Roux. He showed early promise as a football bad boy but then he married Isabelle. That, he admits, was 'the end of my bohemian life'.

7. His catalogue of on-field crimes and misdemeanours began with him punching Bruno Martini, the French national 'keeper. It wouldn't have been half as bad except that Martini was his team-mate at the time!

8. Within weeks of joining Olympique Marseille, his boyhood heroes, Cantona was banned from playing for France for a year. His crime? Calling manager Henri Michel 'incompetent' and, worse, '*un sac de merde*' – 'a shitbag'. That left Eric firmly in the *merde* himself.

9. Angry at being substituted by OM after scoring three goals in a charity match, he threw his shirt at the referee and stomped off bare-chested. The club suspended Cantona, suggested he seek psychiatric help and loaned him to lowly Montpellier. After a defeat at Lille, Eric ended up fighting with team-mate Claude Lemoult. Result: yet another ban.

10. When Cantona confessed to having 'warm feelings' for the sexy French actress Isabelle Adjani, the French press sniffed *un sex scandal*. The married player insisted he simply admired Adjani's 'ability to play difficult and complex roles in films and for being her own person'.

11. Transferred to Nîmes, he cemented his reputation as the wild man of French football when he reacted to being booked by throwing the ball at the referee's head. The French League's disciplinary panel invited Monsieur Cantona to pay them his umpteenth visit. The tribunal chairman told Eric he couldn't be judged like any other player because 'behind you there's a trail of the smell of sulphur'. Suspended for a month, Cantona reacted by screaming 'idiot!' at every member of the panel. When they banned him for another month, Cantona announced his 'retirement'. He was just twenty-five.

12. French football's *enfant terrible* resurfaced in England. But he walked out on Sheffield Wednesday, outraged that Trevor Francis had asked him to stay on a bit longer so he could have a closer look at him. 'As an established international, this wasn't something I expected to undertake', huffed Cantona.

13. Howard Wilkinson paid just £1 million to take Cantona to Elland Road. 'He likes hunting and painting. He's turned on playing for France, by English football and the fanaticism of the crowds here,' explained Wilko. 'We'll climb a mountain together.' They did. Leeds stole past arch-rivals Manchester Untied to sneak the League title in 1992.

14. Ooh-ah Cantona became a folk-hero in Yorkshire in the process – then stunned British football by signing for Alex Ferguson's team several months into the new season. The player claimed Wilko couldn't live with his massive popularity among the Leeds faithful. His boss insisted that Cantona 'had a history of pissing off from other clubs when things didn't suit him. I could see Leeds being the latest in line.' Cantona dismissed as 'malicious nonsense' rumours that he'd been forced to leave Elland Road because he'd been having an affair with a team-mate's wife.

15. Ferguson was delighted with his capture. 'I've been told I'm taking a risk,' he said. 'But you gamble on every player. You might as well gamble on one who lifts people out of their seats.' Quite so. With Cantona on board, United finally ended their 26-year title hoodoo in 1993, then won the Double in both 1994 and 1996. The mad Frenchman was the inspiration for it all.

16. United supporters fell in love with Cantona; many wore red shirts bearing the number 10 and one word – '*dieu*' – to show their affection. But besides playing some beautiful football, Eric also showed the dark side of his nature. The disciplinary problems began to mount. He spat at Leeds fans, got involved in a ruck with Turkish riot police after United lost to Galatasaray in the European Cup, stamped on various opponents and managed to get himself arrested at the Brazil v. Sweden World Cup semi-final in Pasadena in 1994.

17. An explosion seemed inevitable. On the night of 25 January 1995, it happened. Verbally abused by a Crystal Palace fan after he'd been sent off yet again, Cantona vaulted over Selhurst Park's pitchside hoardings and kung-fu kicked the offending fan – a foul-mouthed petty criminal called Matthew Simmons. At the time, it seemed to be the greatest crisis English football had ever faced. Soon, though, sympathy began flowing in Cantona's direction.

18. Initially sentenced to two weeks in jail for common assault, that was reduced to 120 hours community service on appeal. At the press conference to celebrate his lucky escape from the clink, Cantona said just eighteen enigmatic words – 'When the seagulls follow the trawler, it is because they think sardines will be thrown into the sea' – then scarpered. It was apparently meant to be funny.

19. He returned in October 1995 from a record nine-month playing ban better than ever. But despite hitting new heights of brilliance with United, he did not make it into French coach Aime Jacquet's 22-man squad for the Euro '96 finals in England.

Publicly he didn't care; privately he was gutted.

20. Cantona's ultimate epitaph lies in something he said after one of his many mad moments. 'Just as I can bring happiness to people through my footballing instincts, so there are also going to be dark shadows and black stains. You've just got to live with that.' We do, Eric, we do.

le fin

ERIC CANTONA TAKES OFFENCE AFTER PALACE FAN MATTHEW SIMMONS QUESTIONS RIMBAUD'S POETIC TECHNIQUE.

9

Gunning for Trouble

'Arsenal remind me of the Army a little bit – a group of highly-trained professionals who can so easily step over the line into illegality. They are simply too close to the edge.'

Duncan McKenzie

When **Woolwich Arsenal** were just another small-time football club, struggling on without much success in an anonymous corner of south-east London, their home was at Manor Field in Plumstead. The players changed at either the Railway Tavern or the Green Man pubs near by, and dozens of spectators got a free view of the action by standing on a large overground sewage pipe which ran alongside the ground.

In 1913 the Gunners shunted north of the river Thames, buying land in Islington owned by St John's College of Divinity. The deal was agreed with the Ecclesiastical Commissioners, and the deeds were signed by no less an eminence than the Archbishop of Canterbury himself.

Arsenal's blessing from heaven always looms large in any official Highbury history, since stability, dignity and tradition are the principles which have guided the Gunners ever since. Like the Church of England, Arsenal FC has always seen itself as part of the Establishment. When the club's West Stand was built in 1932, it was opened not by some local civic dignitary but by the future King Edward VIII. And when a tribute was sought for 1930s manager Herbert Chapman, it was no jobbing sculptor commissioned to carve a bust but the world-renowned Jacob Epstein. His work sits reverently in a niche in the elegant 'marble halls' of the East Stand. Upstairs in the boardroom is Chapman's carved chapel seat, presented to the club by his Yorkshire congregation in 1931.

No, Highbury Stadium was never intended as a mere church, a run-of-the-mill venue for fortnightly gatherings of the faithful. This was soccer's first cathedral, a monument to a club with a saintly reputation. A national institution, almost.

Or so we were led to believe. When the pillars supporting this edifice of apparent virtue and honour began cracking in the late 1980s, and finally crashed down on the elegantly coiffed head of manager George Graham in 1994, the real sensation was that the most morally upright club in football had turned out to be as bent as the rest.

Ever since Arsenal uprooted from Woolwich before the First World War, the club had been intent on preserving a carefully cultivated myth. But when player

GEORGE GRAHAM SHOWS WHAT IT TAKES TO BE A MODEL MANAGER.

after player began turning up in court on drink-driving charges, and Graham was sacked for pocketing a cut from transfer deals, the story of the Gunners' early days took on a supremely ironic complexion. For what could be more fitting for a club which would nurture Tony Adams, Paul Merson and George Graham than the fact that the red and white shirts were first pulled on by men who prepared for matches in a pub – and that filth flowed within feet of where they played?

Anyone believing that the misdeeds of Adams and his generation have betrayed a glorious legacy would be wrong. The lofty corridors and marble halls of Highbury have echoed to whispers of Machiavellian intrigue since the early part of the century. Forget bungs and match-rigging: in 1919 the ferociously dictatorial Sir Henry Norris, then the club's chairman, engineered a scam which has never been bettered in more than seventy years of soccer scandal.

Arsenal had finished only fifth in Division Two at the close of the 1914–15 season, but when the Football League reconvened at the end of the First World War, Norris somehow convinced its president and his close friend, 'Honest' John McKenna, that the Gunners deserved to be in the First Division because of their 'loyal service' to the competition. McKenna duly made a speech at

The Highbury Bad Boys XI

1. David Seaman: In 1994, dumped wife Sandra and two sons for Arsenal promotions girl Debbie Rogers. His greatest mistake was being photographed leaving Debbie's flat . . . to go fishing.

2. Peter Storey: One of football's all-time lads done bad. In 1979, two years after leaving Arsenal, fined £700 and given a six-month suspended jail sentence for running a brothel, the Calypso Massage Parlour in east London's exotic Leyton High Road. In 1980, jailed for three years for financing a plot to counterfeit gold coins. Two years later, given two six-month jail terms for car theft. In 1990, jailed for four weeks for importing twenty obscene tapes inside the spare tyre of his jeep. The following year, given a 28-day suspended sentence for swearing at a traffic warden.

3. Nigel Winterburn: In 1990, fined £2,000 and sent home from a club tour of Singapore along with Paul Merson, Perry Groves and Kevin Richardson after a late-night drinking session.

4. Andy Linighan: In 1993, forced to apologize to Jewish taxi-driver Harold Levy after making anti-Semitic remarks and refusing to pay a £63 metered fare from the PFA dinner at the Grosvenor House hotel in London's Park Lane to his Harpenden home. Admitted being 'over the drink-driving limit' at the time.

5. Tony Adams: Spent fifty-six days in jail in 1990 after being convicted of drink-driving. In March 1993, needed twenty-nine stitches in a head wound after falling down concrete steps during a night out. Seven months later, helped Ray Parlour spray Essex pizza-eaters with a fire extinguisher. Allegedly spent part of 1994 FA Cup Final day frolicking on stage with a stripper. Confessed in September 1996 to being an alcoholic.

6. Ray Parlour: Adams' sidekick with the fire extinguisher. Made his own headlines in November 1994 by suffering a depressed fracture of the cheekbone after being 'glassed' during a brawl at Butlin's in Bognor Regis, and was fined £330 after assaulting a Hong Kong taxi-driver during a twelve-pint drinking binge on the club's tour of the Far East the following May.

7. Anders Limpar: In August 1992, fined £50 after being stopped by an Arsenal-supporting PC for driving his BMW through red traffic lights while hurrying to a fashion show at London's Olympia.

8. Paul Merson: In 1989, fined six weeks' wages and barred from Highbury after being banned from driving for eighteen months; suspended and fined two weeks' pay after a rumpus at a sponsor's dinner. The following year, sent home from a club tour of Singapore for late-night drinking. In August 1994, questioned by police after running away from an incident in which he wrote off his £25,000 Land Rover Discovery, and not reporting the accident until the next day. That November, confessed to an ability to sink fourteen pints of lager top in a night, and to out-of-control addictions to gambling and cocaine.

9. Ian Wright: Spent five days in Chelmsford Jail as a teenager after refusing to pay fines for driving two cars without tax, insurance or MOT. Fined £5,000 for calling a linesman a 'wanker' during that year's FA Cup Final, having been fined and banned for three games for delivering an off-the-ball right hook to Tottenham's David Howells the previous December. In February 1995, made a £750 out-of-court settlement with Queens Park Rangers security officer Mary Russell after spitting in her face, and paid £600 costs to her solicitors.

10. **Kevin Campbell:** In December 1992, fined £1,800 for drink-driving – one of the heaviest monetary punishments ever meted out for the offence. The magistrates clearly reckoned he could afford it.

11. **David Hillier:** In January 1996, fined £750 and ordered to pay £970 compensation after stealing two holdalls at Gatwick Airport. Hillier and Bolton Wanderers player Wayne Burnett lifted the bags, which belonged to a Danish businessman and contained clothes and computer equipment, on their return from a golfing holiday in Marseille the previous May. At least Hillier, unlike his former manager, did not claim that he thought the bags were a gift and he always intended to pay back the money, with interest, at a later date.

Substitutes

12. **Paul Vaessen:** In June 1994, the ex-Gunners starlet confessed to burglary and theft to fuel a £175-a-day heroin habit. Stabbed six times in a street fight over a drug deal that went wrong.

13. **Kenny Sansom:** Confessed to spending the 1987–88 season in 'a nightmare of shattered dreams and empty bottles'.

14. **Charlie Nicholas:** Competing for the last place on the substitutes' bench with Tony Woodcock and Alan Sunderland, all three being convicted of drink-driving.

Manager

George Graham: The most successful Arsenal supremo since Herbert Chapman in the 1930s, sacked in February 1995 after accepting backhanders worth £425,000 for arranging the transfers of John Jensen and Pal Lydersen.

FORTY YEARS AGO, FOOTBALLERS USED TO WEAR FLAT CAPS AND HANKIES ROUND THEIR NECK. IAN WRIGHT STILL DOES.

the League AGM proposing that a third club be promoted, a vote was taken, and Arsenal were suddenly back in the top flight. No one to this day knows why the other chairmen were swayed by McKenna's oratory – although rumours of large wads of money passing from Norris' wallet persisted for years afterwards.

But Norris eventually got his come-uppance. A decade later, two incidents saw him banned from football for good. In 1928 came allegations that Arsenal had deliberately lost at home to Portsmouth and Manchester United, in a stop-at-nothing bid to ensure that their deadly rivals Tottenham were relegated. Then the next year an FA Commission of Enquiry (heard of them before?) set up to investigate under-the-counter payments found that not only had Norris' personal chauffeur been paid by the club, but that £125 shown in the accounts as settling a bill for the team bus had in fact been used to induce the legendary Charles Buchan along to Highbury. Norris sued the FA for libel in implying he'd acted dishonestly – and lost. When asked why he'd done it, he replied: 'Because otherwise we would not have got the players.'

Did George Graham say the same about the equally legendary John Jensen and Pal Lydersen?

Sir Henry Norris clearly deserves his place in the annals of footballing infamy, but the most lawless period in the Gunners' century-long history is far more up-to-date. It was presided over by the man who himself featured in Arsenal's Double-winning team of 1971, and who went on to become the club's most successful manager since Herbert Chapman half a century earlier.

'When I was playing at Arsenal, Bertie

Mee was a stickler for discipline and organization,' recalled George Graham. 'Looking back, he was 100 per cent right.' Not for nothing did Graham earn his nicknames of 'The Ayatollah' and 'Colonel Gadaffi' from the players: 'I'm a very demanding person and I believe in professional standards,' he once declared with unwitting irony. This is the very conundrum which demolishes the notion that Arsenal FC could ever consider itself a bastion of footballing propriety. No other club in England has produced such an extensive and illustrious roll of shame – nor a Bad Boys XI which, providing its members were not otherwise engaged in court or in jail, would have every chance of emulating the Gunners' justly famous achievements on the pitch. From Peter Storey with his brothel and dirty videos to Paul Merson's tootin' and boozin' revelations, via a litany of driving bans and drink-fuelled escapades on tour, the Arsenal boys have done the lot. But the misdemeanours of one Highbury hero deserve particular attention, since they were committed by a player who has earned the highest accolade both his club and country can offer – the skipper's armband. Tony Adams is often called 'the ultimate Gunner' – a man whose unswerving commitment to the cause made him the perfect Sergeant-Major to General George. Throughout his career, Adams' philosophy has been that you must always play football with conviction – which is more than a touch apt for someone whose route to the England captaincy took a little detour via Chelmsford Prison.

The A13, the cruiseway to the Essex coast immortalized in song by Billy Bragg, passes through some of England's ugliest scenery. Clapped-out factories, the Ford car plant, dingy council estates and ranks of pylons dominate this unappealing swathe of London overspill. Half-way down the road to Southend-on-Sea stands Rainham, with its surprisingly stately red-brick hall built in 1729. However, the town has taken on a greater cultural significance in recent years. This is where Alex and Caroline Adams live, and where their son Tony was brought up.

Rainham is slap-bang in the middle of West Ham heartland – after all, the Boleyn Ground, customary haunt of Essex lads, is but a short spin in a Ford Escort XR3 away. And Tony, born three months after English soccer's one and only great moment at Wembley in 1966, grew up supporting the Hammers like most of his mates. The claret-and-blues were interested in signing the skinny defender who first kicked a ball around with Dagenham United, but this was Arsenal territory, too. It wasn't long before Adams was up at Highbury for coaching, and he was taken on as a trainee in 1982. Just a year later, he made his debut against Sunderland – but anyone looking for composure beyond Adams' seventeen tender years would have been disappointed. The match was barely two minutes old when he received the ball from a throw-in. In an uncanny echo of the kind of error which would later see a tabloid newspaper graft donkey's ears on to his head, Tony lost possession and let Colin West in to score for the Wearsiders.

It was not until George Graham took command at Highbury that Adams became a fixture in the first team. Graham had first watched him play when he was in the England junior squad being put through its paces at Lilleshall. 'He just had something about him,' drooled his future boss. This was no Peter Marinello, Charlie George, Paul Merson or Anders Limpar, flair players whose maverick genius has always been mistrusted at the club. Instead, Graham saw Adams as a disciple of the 'Arsenal way' – of collective responsibility at the expense of individuality – and installed his protégé at the heart of the Highbury back four. Before the season was out, he had helped the Gunners to win the Littlewoods Cup, had copped the bulk of the vote as 'PFA Young Player of the Year', and had even been summoned into the England side for a 4–2 victory against Spain in Madrid. In March 1988, when he was still only twenty-one, Graham chose him as the youngest captain in Arsenal's history. 'I make him from the same mould as Frank McLintock,' boomed his manager in Churchillian mode.

The reference to the captain of Arsenal's Double-winning side, and a tackler to rate alongside Tommy Smith and Ron 'Chopper' Harris from that fearsome 'bite-yer-legs' era, was a massive compliment. Yet McLintock did not have the aggravating habit of playing with one arm permanently stuck in the air, like a school swot itching to tell Miss the answer. Nor of clapping like a demented seal in mock praise whenever a linesman spotted one of Arsenal's tedious offside ploys. Indeed, legend has it that when Tony Adams arrived at church for his wedding, he organized the bridesmaids into a flat back four across the nave, pushed them up to the altar when the bride arrived, and wildly applauded the vicar when he raised his hand to make the sign of the cross.

The idea that here was an England captain in the making took a dent in February 1989, when millions of TV viewers heard Adams abuse referee David Elleray. ITV's *Out of Order* programme wired up the man in black for an Arsenal v. Millwall clash, with the full knowledge of both clubs, to show the pressure that refs are put under by the players. The Gunners had a goal disallowed, and Tony was not too happy about it. As he ran past Elleray, he screamed 'cheat'. There was a word preceding it, too – but that was bleeped out.

However, Adams' place among football's figures of ridicule was more than secure by this time. After a series of gaffes in Arsenal colours, with fluffed back-passes a particular speciality, he was part of the England team humiliated by Holland in the 1988 European Championships. True, there was unquestionable class about Marco Van Basten's hat-trick which left the England defence looking like a bunch of circus animals in desperate need of a ringmaster – but that wasn't going to stop the tabloids. In April 1989, after a 1–1 draw at Old Trafford in which Tony scored both goals, the *Daily Mirror* produced its celebrated montage of his head sprouting a pair of outsize donkey's ears. Stadiums soon echoed to the cruel but hilarious chant of 'ee-aw! ee-aw!' whenever the name of 'Adams T.' appeared on the team-sheet.

For a man who once claimed to hate all vegetables, let alone the carrots which Tottenham fans in particular started to fling at him, this was a crisis point in a career which had seen Adams rise through the ranks with the self-assurance of a born fighter. Yet the mental toughness which has always been part of his character prevented him slipping back among the legions of foot-soldiers doing duty at club level. However, there was an unexpected kick-back to Tony's renewed efforts – and it arrived, fittingly, with the force of a mule. While his performances on the pitch became ever more disciplined and determined, his life away from Highbury veered alarmingly in the opposite direction.

In May 1990 Adams celebrated the end of the League season at a Sunday lunchtime barbecue in Rayleigh, Essex. It was a warm day, and the demob-happy mood clearly had an effect on the Arsenal star as he stepped into his £18,000 Ford Sierra XR4 to drive home. Maybe it was the sudden thought of a missed tackle the previous afternoon which forced his foot to jam down on the accelerator, but before he'd even had time to yell 'offside!' at a lurking telegraph-post, it had been reduced to a pile of splinters on the ground. A wall of the brick rather than human kind fared no better, since Adams demolished it after he had careered over crossroads at more than 70 m.p.h. And all this took place within 150 yards of the party he'd just left. The utter stupidity of his escapade was confirmed when he was breathalysed and found to be three times over the drink-drive limit.

When the case came to court seven months later, a formidable array of character witnesses had been assembled. George Graham praised Adams' professionalism and leadership, and defended his shamed skipper as 'one of the game's great characters'. Gilbert Gray QC felt that the offence was 'out of character, and Adams could not understand the very high level shown in the analysis'. Maybe that was because Tony was so legless he'd forgotten how much he'd actually had to drink, but Judge Frank Lockhart was having none of it. This was no mere yellow card offence, it merited dismissal

'BUT I WAS JUST TRYING TO GET THE WALL BACK ANOTHER TEN YARDS, OFFICER . . .' TONY ADAMS
VEERS OUT OF CONTROL.

to the slammer: nine months for reckless driving, five of them suspended; three months to run concurrently for driving with excess alcohol; a two-year ban from driving; and £500 prosecution costs. 'I hear Tony Adams is appealing,' quipped Bob 'The Cat' Bevan at the Football Writers' Association awards dinner. 'Apparently he wasn't pissed. He was just trying to get the wall back another ten yards.'

Adams came through his 56-day spell in Chelmsford jail with the help of 'Minder Mick' Webb, a burly credit card fraudster who earned the nickname 'Scotchie' for his skill at getting hold of booze. 'I managed to smuggle in some vodka,' he revealed later. 'I called Tony in and said, "Give us your mug," and filled it with vodka and Coke. He must have thought it was coffee and was about to top it up with hot water when I said, "What are you doing? Get it down ya." That's when he really opened up and

COURT IN THE ACT: TONY ADAMS WONDERS IF HE'S PAST HIS CELL-BY DATE.

started talking about his family and how much he missed his dad and girlfriend. It was ironic. He was saying how booze had put him in jail . . . we were in stitches.'

But it wasn't all cosy chats with his guardian angel for Prisoner LE1561. Webb had to save Adams from a two-man coshing in a toilet, and foiled a plot by two Liverpudlians to smash his kneecaps and put him out of the game for good. 'It was pure jealousy. But, of course, beating up a celebrity like Tony Adams would have made their names in the nick.'

Even though his spell in jail was not an entirely sobering experience, George Graham was confident that his star defender had learned his lesson. 'You find out a lot about people at times like that,' he announced. 'The true test of character is how they come through those times, and Tony has . . . grown up.' The Arsenal supremo even paid Adams' wages while he was definitely not at liberty to spend them – a move hardly designed to deter any other player from driving while three times over the limit. It was amazingly hypocritical behaviour for a club so keen to proclaim its occupancy of the moral high ground.

In spite of being greeted at grounds up and down the land with reminders of his recent offence – 'Jingle bells, jingle bells, jingle all the way, oh what fun it is to see Adams put away!' and 'Tony, Tony Adams, Tony Adams in the nick!' to the tune of 'Ging-gang-goolie' were both long-runners – the Arsenal skipper seemed reluctant to mend his ways. Just four months after being released from Chelmsford and making his comeback for Arsenal reserves before an astonishing crowd of more than 8,000, Adams was fined by the FA for flashing 'V' signs at Queens Park Rangers fans. 'People make mistakes in life,' he admitted after his spell inside. 'In any case, what happens to me off the field has no bearing on what I do on it.' Good job.

In February 1993, on their way back from a day at the races, Adams and a few pals went for a drink to celebrate his son Oliver's first birthday. But at 3.30 a.m. the accident-prone Gunner arrived at St Bartholomew's Hospital in central London with blood gushing from a head wound. England team-mate and celebrated gore-lover Terry Butcher would have simply taped his skull together with a bandage and forgotten about it, but Tone told staff in casualty that he had fallen down and cracked his head on some concrete steps. In fact, his speech was so slurred and he seemed to be in such a confused state that a bed in the neuro-surgery ward was set aside. Then the doctors realized the cause. 'Drunken England Star Has 29 Stitches' screamed the front page of the *Sun* the next morning, just to clarify the point.

Adams discharged himself three hours later, and was driven to his home in Hornchurch, Essex, where he spent the day resting in a darkened room. 'Basically he is now sleeping it off,' confirmed ever-dutiful wife Jane. 'He's been in bed all day nursing a very sore head. I'm running around making him lots of cups of tea.'

Dad Alex was unfazed by the ballyhoo. 'Of course he has got drunk a few times. Haven't most people?' Meanwhile, General George once again refused to tear a strip off his scarred skipper: 'He had an accident – end of story,' was tight-lipped Graham's only comment after he had spoken to Adams on the phone.

If ever proof were needed that Tony might be a tad clumsy, it came just two

months later when Arsenal beat Sheffield Wednesday in the Coca-Cola Cup Final. As winning skippers are wont to do in such circumstances, he decided to hoist goal-scoring hero Steve Morrow on to his shoulders. It's hard to imagine the same outcome had Morrow been a pint of lager, but Adams dropped him. The young midfielder was rushed into hospital with a broken arm, and missed out on the evening's celebrations. Even worse, he was absent for the rest of a campaign in which the Gunners went on to win the FA Cup.

Still, young Steve must have been gratified to learn that his captain spent the close-season working on his hand/eye co-ordination, for in October 1993 he proved that his aim was now unerringly true. Just two days after he had been in the England team which lost 2–0 to Holland in a World Cup qualifier, a defeat which ended all hope of Graham Taylor's team reaching the finals in the USA and pushed the manager to the brink of resignation, Adams and team-mate Ray Parlour were accused of soaking diners with a fire extinguisher at a Pizza Hut in Hornchurch. Eye-witnesses claim that the lumbering England number five tampered with the extinguisher using a knife, then Parlour removed the safety pin and proceeded to spray two tables before running away.

'Parlour was pointing the jet all over our table and the one next to us,' stated a drenched and indignant customer, Jason Duke. 'Water was hitting the walls and light-fittings, too. All the time Tony Adams was holding the door open, laughing away. It was pathetic. They were like schoolkids.' Fellow diner Julie Williams backed him up – and had more to worry about than a soggy thin-crust and

PARLOUR GAMES: RAY DOES A RUNNER AFTER HIS HONG KONG TAXI DODGE.

saturated side salad: 'I had a jumper on and ski pants, and by the time he'd finished I looked like a drowned rat. I couldn't believe the way they behaved. They were no better than the football hooligans we've seen on telly and in the papers. They should be setting an example.' The police received five complaints of assault.

While the nation's soccer-lovers focused on the 1994 FA Cup Final between Manchester United and Chelsea, the *News of the World* found Tony Adams concentrating on something far less one-sided: the multiple charms of thirty-year-old stripper Alison Frost. The paper

claimed that after a drinking spree with a busload of mates at the Rocking Horse pub in Clacton, Essex, Adams and his pals turned up at the Crown pub in Billericay. Alison was part of a strip-show in a back room, and appeared on stage in knee-length black PVC boots and hot-pants. Soon she was down to tiny panties with stockings and suspenders. She then took Tony by the hand, and he pressed up against her and kissed her breasts before whipping off his blue short-sleeved shirt and black-and-white boxer shorts to shouts of 'handball!' from onlookers. The 'naked soccer ace', as the paper quaintly put it, then 'watched intently as Alison used a seven-inch sex-aid on herself, and did a series of acrobatic somersaults to show off her physique'. The story ran beneath the headline: 'The Life of a Soccer Yobbo . . . only this one is playing for England today'.

If Herbert Chapman could have been magically brought back to life and transported to Highbury on 13 August 1994, he would have smiled munificently on the scene before him. Here was a testimonial for one of the club's stalwart servants, a man who for more than a decade had, as the programme put it, been 'ready to sweat blood for the Arsenal'. Yet the legendary Chapman would also have been justified in thinking that the recipient of this acclaim was a paragon of virtue, cast in his own image. After all, the souvenir brochure carried articles with such headlines as: 'Tony always leads from the front', 'The man they all look up to', 'As brave as a lion' and 'Tony the people's hero'. There was a 'roll of honour', too – although a 'roll of dishonour' might have been more appropriate, since Adams' off-pitch escapades have made him arguably more famous than his exploits on the park. There was just one passing reference to the darker side of the Arsenal skipper's character: former Gunners' goalkeeper Bob Wilson insisted that, although he was jailed for being 'in the wrong', he also suffered for being 'in the wrong place at the wrong time. He was punished to deter others.'

However, the old Highbury hero was not going to put a damper on the occasion. 'Like me,' he gushed, 'the fans also admire Tony for the way he's overcome his problems. He was set up by a ridiculous newspaper article' – which one, Bob? – 'and had to endure some of the worst taunts I've ever heard. He could have come out bitter and twisted. Instead, he turned the taunts upside down and proved his critics wrong.' It was as if 13 August 1994 marked the start of Year Zero. Like Pol Pot, Arsenal wanted the world to believe that Tony Adams' past had never happened.

It was a similar story two months later, when Adams was chosen by England coach Terry Venables to captain his country for a friendly international against Romania. 'Stirway to heaven!' trumpeted the *Daily Star*, as the man who swopped handcuffs for armband asked: 'I hope youngsters will look at me and see I'm proof that there is a second chance.'

For as long as George Graham was at Highbury, there was never any question that he would always receive that second chance. 'Tony Adams epitomizes Arsenal,' declared the soiled supremo, and while the Gunners are governed by discretion rather than dash – no matter who occupies the manager's hotseat – then he always will. Even his revelation in September 1996 that he was an alcoholic, and that England's Euro '96 semi-final defeat by West Germany, plus his wife's cocaine addiction, sent him on a spectacular binge after four months without a drink, brought the usual tight-knit response from Highbury. Why take risks with unmuzzled guns when you can play it safe with Sergeant-Major Adams, dedicated to Queen and country?

Even if part of that service was at Her Majesty's pleasure?

1. George Graham was Arsenal's most successful manager since the heyday of Herbert Chapman some half a century earlier. After taking over in May 1986, he won six trophies, including two League Championships, the European Cup-Winners' Cup, and a unique FA Cup and League Cup double.

2. In February 1995 Graham was booted out by the Gunners for accepting £425,000 in what he called 'unsolicited gifts' from Norwegian agent Rune Hauge after signing John Jensen and Pal Lydersen. Everyone else in football called them 'bungs'.

3. Graham was born in the village of Bargeddie, near Glasgow, in 1944, the youngest of six children. His dad, a steelworker, died when he was two weeks old.

4. As a laconic centre-forward-turned-midfielder with Aston Villa, Chelsea, Arsenal, Manchester United, Portsmouth and Crystal Palace, Graham earned twelve caps for Scotland and featured in the Arsenal Double-winning side of 1971. He was not a success at Aston Villa, making just eight first-team appearances, but Tommy Docherty had seen him play for Scotland's youth team and signed him for Chelsea during the summer of 1964. The Doc insisted he had been doomed to failure at Villa and so christened him 'Doomed George'. It was a name he hated, although it became rather more apt once he met Rune Hauge.

5. Graham has been vain for as long as any of his friends can remember. His interest in clothes developed when he set up a tailoring business in Soho's Old Compton Street with Chelsea team-mates Terry Venables and Ron Harris, operating under the horrendous name of Grateron (Graham, Terry and Ron). Norman Wisdom was a regular customer, which was no recommendation, given his stage appearances in crumpled suits two sizes too small. The business bombed. However, Graham's debonair demeanour saw him signed up by Aquascutum in 1989, and the £99 George Graham stadium coat topped their winter collection.

6. Graham married Marie, a Turkish-born former actress and dancer, on the morning of the Arsenal v. Tottenham match in 1967. Terry Venables, then playing for Spurs, was best man. After the service, the guests went to the reception while the two principal males went to the football. Arsenal won easily with Graham, showing no signs of saving himself for his wedding night, playing a blinder.

7. Graham's concern for his appearance extended to the pitch. Kicked in the head during a game for Chelsea, his main worry was the position of the gash. 'It's above the hairline,' said Venables. 'Thank Christ for that,' came the relieved reply, 'I'm going dancing tonight.' As a manager he was less sympathetic. When Andy Linighan scored Arsenal's winning goal in the 1993 FA Cup Final despite a broken nose, Graham retorted: 'I never thought of taking him off. They're nothing. I tried to get one throughout my career because it adds character to your face.'

8. An elegant and unruffled footballer throughout his career, Graham's nicknames were 'Stroller', 'The Ringmaster' and 'The Peacock'. When he moved into management, the terms became less complimentary: 'Ayatollah', 'Colonel Gadaffi' and 'The Loner' were among the names given to their ruthless manager by the Arsenal players.

9. When his playing days finally ended in 1977, Graham thought about following in the footsteps of dozens of other ex-footballers and opening a pub. He decided against it when Venables offered him the post of youth team coach at Queens Park Rangers.

10. Wife Marie left Graham in December 1988 claiming, 'You spend more time on football than on me.' She moved in with her boss, dry cleaning magnate Roger Bliss, after the pair had been spotted at the Body Magic health club in the north London suburb of Cockfosters. A friend, Brian Baum, added: 'George lives for Arsenal. No one else is involved as far as we know.' Graham was granted a quickie divorce in July 1989 because of his wife's adultery. The couple were due to meet in the High Court but he settled before the case came up, offering a reported £300,000 pay-off.

11. Just two weeks later, photographer Hy (Hyacinth) Money confessed to finding Graham 'stunningly charming'. The divorced mother-of-four had first met him while she was the Crystal Palace snapper and he a player, and later bumped into him when he was in Scotland with the Arsenal team. 'We had a great time,' she declared enigmatically.

12. Graham enjoys champagne and fine wines and collects rare Scottish malt whisky. 'Quality rather than quantity' is a fine philosophy: perhaps he should have taught the lesson to his Arsenal players.

13. Shortly after his marital break-up, Graham began seeing twice-wed French-American divorcee Arianne Accristo. However, their four-year relationship ended in acrimony in 1993, when Accristo claimed he had offered to pay her £30,000 to get out of his life. She insisted that Graham was 'fantastic' in bed, but added, mysteriously, that he was a hoarder: 'He has so much money he doesn't know what to do with it all apart from saving it for retirement.'

14. In the midst of a fixture pile-up in 1991, Graham declared: 'It's hard to be passionate twice a week.' We assume he was talking about football.

15. Gardening is another of Graham's fascinating hobbies: 'I like planting and pottering around. I like the sense of creating something, much like creating a football team. My garden gives me peace of mind.' Shame so many of his players preferred booze to begonias.

16. In April 1994, Norwegian fashion store owner Ellen Dengin admitted that she had been Graham's 'away fixture' for the previous eight months. Her Oslo flat was above a bar rejoicing in the curious name of 'Highbury', where the two had met after the Gunners played a friendly match in the city in 1992.

17. Just eight months later Graham went public on his latest relationship, this time with blonde mother-of-four Sue Schmidt, nine years younger than him. They met when her friend Barbara, wife of Arsenal vice-chairman David Dein, took her to a match at Highbury. While her computer tycoon husband Dan was away on business, Sue and George met up for romantic *tête-a-têtes*, she driving her black Porsche 928 with the registration number 594 HOT.

18. Graham's sacking forced some hasty rewriting of history at the Arsenal Museum. The club's disgraced ex-manager was the voice on a twenty-minute film of the Gunners' great moments. Within days of his departure a new commentary was in place, narrated by the king of blandness, Bob Wilson.

19. In September 1996, three months after his FA ban ended, Graham replaced Howard Wilkinson as manager of Leeds United. 'I come from a background that believes in the work ethic,' he declared, having already calculated that his exile had cost him £2 million in lost income.

20. Graham once admitted what drove him on so remorselessly: 'Those little brown envelopes that come through the letter box every month.' The dirty money which helped to pay those bills is what he'll always be remembered for.

10

Merseyside Madness: Liver Girls, Likely Lads

'I haven't got a clue about anything apart from football and scoring goals.'

Liverpool striker Robbie Fowler

Robbie Fowler drinks Budweiser or Becks, fancies any glamorous woman on telly 'as long as they've got a fanny and breathe', and his favourite chat-up line goes like this: 'Do you like jewellery? Well suck my cock, it's a gem.' Team-mate Steve McManaman, however, is a considerably more sophisticated guy. Favourite tipple: Budweiser or Guinness. Top celebrity babe: Bella Emberg from *The Russ Abbott Show*. And opening gambit to hormone-jingling single females: the much more alluring come-on 'Do you like fruit?'

Quite what the designer-dressing, club-loving, long-haired winger from Liverpool likes to do next with the apples and oranges, once the target of his super-smooth approach answers 'yes' – as they usually do – can only be guessed at. Whatever it is, it's bound to be a lot classier than the aptly named Fowler's crude intentions. McManaman boasts the sort of easy patter and angelic face that are as likely to win over middle-aged mothers as their nineteen-year-old daughters. Fowler, though, has the sort of features only a mum could love. Worse, he supported Everton as a boy, appreciates

Kylie Minogue's music and thinks break-fast TV queen Anne Diamond is a sex symbol. Good taste, like subtlety, is not Robbie's strongest suit.

Perhaps the young striker's ultra-direct attitude towards the female sex merely reflects the no-nonsense tactics which have made him Liverpool's most prolific goal-getter since Ian Rush in his 1980s heyday. A stunning total of thirty-one goals in the 1994–95 season, his first full campaign as an automatic choice on the Anfield team-sheet, earned Fowler a deadly reputation. Over thirty strikes the next season, including two in an FA Cup semi-final win over Aston Villa, and an England call-up, proved Anfield had witnessed not a flash in the pan, but the birth of a goal-scoring legend to set alongside the names of Dalglish, Toshack and Keegan. But sadly for the moptop marksman, his scoring exploits appear to be limited to the pitch. Fowler is known to his team-mates as 'God' and even has a top with Jesus Christ printed on it – 'Because everything he touches turns to gold,' according to his Liverpool colleague Steve Harkness – but he appears nevertheless to be a man so desperate for female attention that he yearns for women to send him their knickers. Although Fowler hits the back of the net far more often than Ryan Giggs, and gets fan-mail just like the Manchester United heart-throb does, he still envies the Welsh wonderboy this one thing: 'I'd love to have some undies sent to me,' admits the apparently sex-starved Scouser with horrifying candour, 'so I could sniff 'em.'

We know all these intimate personal secrets of two of the English game's brightest young talents because, in possibly the daftest move of their careers so far, the pair of Liverpool-born likely lads gave a joint interview in early 1995 to *Loaded*, the magazine 'for men who should know better'. As it turned out, it was Fowler and McManaman who should have known better than to talk to a publication renowned for its obsession with babes, drinking and toilet humour.

There, spread over four pages of the New Lad bible, was a confessional which would have taxed the powers of forgiveness of even the Pope himself – who, as an ex-footballer, might look benignly upon such indiscretions as occupational hazards. 'Beer, sex and BMWs – Robbie Fowler and Steve McManaman talk about the hard life at Anfield,' teased the introduction sarcastically. It was downhill all the way after that, with the interview confirming every fan's suspicions about the glamorous lifestyle enjoyed by top players. Fast cars; yuppie £80,000 pads; bars; night-clubs; and, of course, girls. One classic moment came when the Liverpool likely lads were asked their views on sex before matches, something the great George Best had no problems fitting in, but something which modern players are meant to avoid. 'I know someone who had a wank two hours before a game and went out and scored three,'

replied Fowler tantalizingly. 'I know him. He captains his country,' continued McManaman intriguingly. 'But I think the no-sex thing is a load of shite really.'

Precisely which pre-match masturbator they were talking about was unfortunately not revealed. That, though, was the boys' only saving grace. When the chairman, directors and manager of Liverpool saw the *Loaded* article, they went ballistic. The powers-that-be were angry and embarrassed, even more humiliated than Graeme Souness after yet another third round FA Cup defeat to otherwise-useless First Division opposition. Yes, such things *are* possible. The club's two home-grown stars, Fowler and Shaggy – McManaman's nickname is because of his likeness to the ultra-lean character in *Scooby Doo* and not a reference to his legendary pulling-power – had unwittingly tarnished the image of a footballing institution which has always maintained an air of quiet, superior authority and employed clean-living men such as Shankly, Paisley and Dalglish to run a team rightly known as 'the mean machine' for the ruthless efficiency with which it functioned. In such an environment, free-spirited individuals can be a liability.

Fowler the Toxteth Terrier, though, has become a vital part of the Anfield team despite his indiscretions. There was the mystery of the damaged hotel room during an England Under-21 trip to Portugal. Although the room was booked to Trevor Sinclair and Kevin Gallen of Queens Park Rangers, it was Fowler who had to explain things to then England boss Terry Venables. Then there was the hilarious, farcical bust-up with team-mate Neil 'Razor' Ruddock. One of the great mismatches in modern footballing fisticuffs began on a plane back from

Russia after Liverpool had notched up a useful UEFA Cup win over Spartak Vladikavkaz. Ruddock, for a joke, had cut up a pair of the young striker's trainers; Fowler responded in kind, demolishing a pair of fancy shoes which had cost the hardman defender a cool £200. On board, stubble king Ruddock and bleached-blond Fowler traded insults, with both refusing to admit they'd made a mistake, while several Anfield stars relieved their boredom by chucking food at each other. At Liverpool's Speke Airport, Razor's frustration boiled over and he suddenly lived up to his heavy-weight nickname by landing one on the goal-getter's face. Blood began to pour and Fowler was taken to hospital. Anfield boss Roy Evans decided not to discipline either of them. 'The incident was no more than a high-spirited accident,' he dead-panned. 'There was a bit of banter and high-jinks between the two lads but absolutely nothing malicious.' Ruddock, he explained, 'caught Robbie with a flick of his hand, causing a nosebleed. Robbie went to hospital purely as a precaution.' Stan Collymore saw nothing of the unscheduled boxing bout except for a trail of blood the colour of Liverpool's famous red shirts going right through the green Customs exit. Those two moments of madness forced Merseyside's latterday Jimmy Greaves to admit: 'I am still learning to grow up. I realize I have to mature off the field and cannot afford to do stupid things.' Echoing the immortal words of so many football miscreants before him, Fowler insisted: 'I am not a bad lad, and the last thing I want to do is jeopardize my England prospects.'

It's hard to imagine Robbie entering politics when he finally hangs up his boots but, if he does, he's unlikely to find a sponsor in Labour MP Peter Kilfoyle. In May 1996, Kilfoyle's twenty-year-old daughter Amy confessed to scoring with the Liverpool ace on the kitchen floor of his £250,000 house after meeting at a club. 'It was an unbelievable night,' she gushed. 'Robbie's got a great body. It wasn't the best sex I've ever had, but it was Robbie Fowler – and I wasn't going to pass!' However, Amy was concerned about dad's reaction: 'He'll kill me when he finds out – he's an Everton fan!'

Reading the *Loaded* interview, the most crushing blow for manager Roy Evans, though, must have been Fowler's answer to the question, 'Who are your favourite footballers?' Jamie Redknapp and Julian Dicks got a name-check, but so did Don Hutchison. *'Dirty' Don Hutchison!* Poor Evans probably almost choked at seeing Fowler hail in print as a role model a player he had booted out of Anfield just months before for committing one sin too many.

Gateshead-born Hutchison is a fasci-nating specimen. He could have been a footballing Marlon Brando, a real con-tender. Just twenty-four appearances and two goals for struggling Hartlepool United of the Third Division somehow led to the six-foot-two midfielder becoming the umpteenth Geordie prodigy to be fêted as 'the new Gazza'. After he sent a video of himself to all the top clubs, Liverpool signed him up for £175,000. So he had luck. Unfortunately, though, Hutch does not apparently possess a huge brain. A chronic inability to keep his manhood safely inside his trousers in public ruined what could have been for the former fork-lift truck driver a glorious career in Anfield's colours, and in the process gave a whole new meaning to the phrase 'flash player'.

Hutch's first indecent exposure occurred in Labinsky's wine bar in Liverpool one summer's day in 1993. He, team-mates Ian Rush, Jamie Redknapp and Paul Stewart, plus coach Phil Boersma, were out toasting Rushie's elevation to the club captaincy when they bumped into a party of young women who were celebrating gaining university degrees. Drinks were disappearing fast all round.

Graduate Catherine Brooks, twenty-three, was so pleased to find herself in such famous company that she pulled out her camcorder to record the event for posterity. Moments later, though, she felt a tap on her shoulder. 'I looked up and there was Hutchison. He stood back and said, "Zoom in on this," pointing to the front of his fly,' recalled Brooks, a willowy brunette. 'To my astonishment he then got his penis out and started waggling it about with his hand. I turned away in disgust, forgetting to turn the camcorder off.' She put the camera down. 'I was shaking and told him it wasn't

SOME FLY GUY: DON HUTCHISON SUFFERS SOME INDECENT EXPOSURE OF HIS OWN.

worth it.' Dirty Don, though, was undeterred. 'I told you to zoom in,' he barked, clearly unaware his tackle had already been captured on tape and would soon come back to haunt him, courtesy of a photo-spread in the *News of the World*.

That, however, was not the end of the indignity inflicted on the brainbox babes by the gormless Liverpool lads. Soon after, another of the young women, Lorien Hill, her pal Claire Holmes and some other friends were sitting at a table beside four of the Anfield revellers when one of the players called over to her, asking if she would like a glass of white wine. The unidentified player handed her a glass. 'It felt all warm and horrible. One of the guys in our party said to me, "It's got to be piss. One of them has pissed in the glass."' Hill said she wisely held the glass away from her, not daring to touch a drop of what probably was almost 100 per cent alcohol anyway.

But then, disaster. 'Claire turned round and grabbed the glass, thinking I was handing it to her. Before I could stop her she took a sip and immediately spat it out.' Rush, Redknapp & Co. reacted as if they had all, like Hutchison, recently each had a lobotomy. 'The Liverpool lot just went into hysterics,' recalled Hill angrily. 'They would have been more at home in a playground.' Like they say, simple things amuse simple people. Claire Holmes was just as annoyed as her pal. 'It was a very childish thing to do. You might expect it from a sixteen-year-old yob who gets drunk on half a pint but not from someone who kids look up to.'

The girls enjoyed the last laugh, though. When the nation's favourite Sunday paper exposed Hutchison's antics – piss and tell from the masters of kiss and tell – Holmes made a comment as bitter as the 'wine' she had briefly tasted. 'None of us even recognized Hutchison at first,' she remarked. 'We thought he was a local hooligan trying to get in on the action. I used to work as a waitress at West Ham Football Club while I was studying at college. I often bumped into the players and they were always well-behaved. I used to go and watch them play.' Her happiest Hammers memory? 'When they thrashed Liverpool 4–1 at Upton Park four years ago.'

'Dirty' Don won himself few admirers over the incident. His father branded the flashing incident 'a bloody disgrace. I don't know whether he had a few drinks too many, but it's shocking behaviour. It's not the sort of thing I would expect. I'll be having words with him!' Ex-Anfield hardman Tommy Smith was just as scathing about what Hutch had been up to. 'It's surprising what drink will do to an empty head,' he commented caustically. Luckily for Don, the police took no action, although it is a crime for a man to expose himself, carrying a maximum sentence of three months in jail. Liverpool, however, meted out their own punishment: a £2,000 fine and serious warning to the midfield madman about his future conduct.

That warning seemed to go in one ear and out the other: less than a year later the empty-headed one was back in trouble. In June 1994 he was bound over to keep the peace for six months by Newcastle magistrates after being arrested for drunk and disorderly behaviour. That earned him a final warning from the Anfield hierarchy. Stupidly, even his brush with the law did not calm him down.

Just a few weeks later Hutchison was caught literally with his trousers down –

yes, *again* – during a holiday in the Cypriot resort of Ayia Napa with team-mates Jamie Redknapp and Michael Thomas. It was the sort of healthy summer sunshine break which fitness-obsessed players prefer as a way of recharging their batteries after a long, hard season: all day boozing binges, 150-feet bungee jumps, clubbing until 7 a.m. and snogging sessions with willing females.

Hutch's latest urge to display his plonker to the masses occurred in a bustling, drink-sodden Cypriot night-club. 'One night there were families coming up saying, "Can we have a picture?"' recalled Chris Iaonnou, a friend of Jamie Redknapp, who ran the Mini Golf bar in Ayia Napa. 'In front of some holiday-makers, Don Hutchison took his trousers down, pulled his dick out and put a Budweiser label on it. Don's attitude was "Have a picture of this!" He was out of it and thought it was really funny, but everyone was shocked.' Once again it was the *News of the World* which published the incriminating photographs of Hutch in a state of deliberate undress. He had good reason to regret the incident, not least because, if he was trying to show the world how well-endowed he was, he failed miserably. The Budweiser label, by no means large, more than covered his

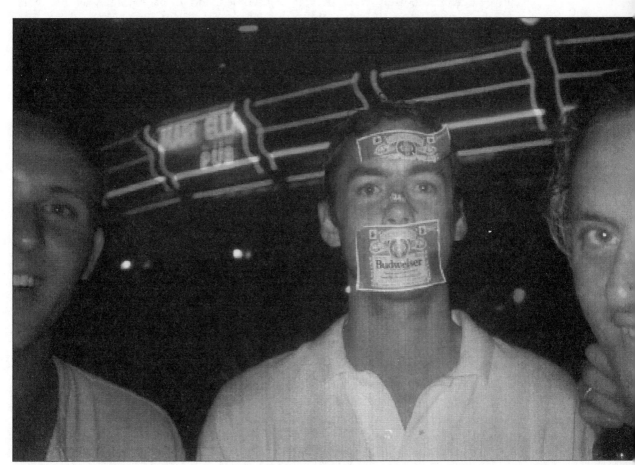

NIPPED IN THE BUD: DIRTY DON HUTCHISON IS FINALLY SILENCED.

penalty area. While Hutch may have been trying to prove that he had a massive plonker, he ended up simply confirming that he *was* a massive plonker.

Roy Evans took the news of his stars' holiday frolics in his usual happy-go-lucky way. 'Bungee jumping was crazy, but that's just kids on holiday. Copping off with birds is allowed, of course,' declared the Scouse supremo. And what about Hutch, serial flasher extraordinaire? 'If Hutchison is flashing his **** again, that's out of order.' Dirty Don was fined £5,000, slapped on the transfer-list and dropped from Liverpool's pre-season tour of Germany and Norway. Chief executive Peter Robinson said it was the harshest punishment handed down in his twenty-nine years at Anfield, but necessary because 'we are very concerned about the image of the club'. Roy Evans, frustrated at the indiscipline of such a major prospect, agreed the wayward waggler's reprimand was 'very strong action. But we won't accept this type of behaviour from any player,' he explained. 'It is disappointing because football-wise Don has a lot of talent.' Before long it was an impetuous talent under the control of Harry Redknapp at West Ham, whose £1.5 million represented possibly the biggest transfer gamble of the 1990s. The brainless one left Anfield saying, 'Liverpool have been very good to me. They did not cause me any problems. They were very tolerant, considering. I caused my own problems. I did silly things and I have to get on with it.' Hutchison's new team-mates in London's East End had just one piece of advice – keep it zipped, Don. And they didn't mean his mouth.

Dirty Don's Cypriot cock-up led to Liverpool taking their toughest-ever action

against a player for committing the sort of shameful sins which young men of that particular employment are peculiarly prone to commit. But he was by no means the first Anfield player to prove himself more of a piss artist than a football artiste. Jan Molby's jail-inducing car trouble is well documented elsewhere in this collection of capers. And any team which employs Bruce Grobbelaar can hardly expect to live a quiet life.

Grob has enjoyed an eventful career, to say the least, both on and off the pitch: a drink-driving conviction, alleged 'bung'-taking to throw matches and the reported enjoyment of the intimate company of women, none of whom was his wife. There was also the time he nearly chinned his team-mate, Jim Beglin, during an FA Cup Final and a very similar incident when, during a tense Merseyside derby, he punched yet another Liverpool player – Steve McManaman – whom he blamed for gifting Everton the first goal of a 2–0 win. Goodison Park was still celebrating Mark Ward's opener when the crazy 'keeper raced after the young winger and began remonstrating with him, in the sort of strong language fans usually reserve for clangers dropped by the most useless players, for causing the goal by failing to clear the ball. They briefly traded insults before Bruce, his face contorted with rage, and acting more like Bruce Willis than Bruce Forsyth, landed a right-hander on the left side of the England Under-21 star's head. You might say that poor McManaman was Grob-smacked.

The reaction of Graeme Souness, supposedly one of football's hardman bosses, was surprisingly relaxed. 'When things are going wrong players tend to blame each other rather than themselves. I've told them to go home and take a look at themselves.' Since then, however, the Anfield club has decreed discipline both on and off the pitch to be vital. After Souey, Grob and flasher Hutch, they have had enough headlines for the wrong reasons. From now on, as Don Hutchison knows only too well, tabloid tales will result in a short spell in the reserves followed by a rapid transfer to a team boasting little of Liverpool's allure. Souness went to Turkey, the mercurial Molby ended up managing Swansea and Hutch is engaged in a constant battle with relegation at Sheffield United and the darker side of his wayward nature. Fowler, 'Shaggy' McManaman and Redknapp have been warned.

Anfield's biggest bad boy of recent times has been centre-half Neil Ruddock. Until recently his greatest 'crimes' had been eating his toenails, going unshaven for days and grabbing a ref's groin while lying injured. But then came the airport scuffle with Robbie Fowler. A week later it was revealed that he had left his wife for another woman – a six-foot tall, blonde lingerie model, no less. Ruddock insisted he hadn't set out to have an affair with 23-year-old Fiona Robinson but pleaded: 'We just couldn't help ourselves.'

If he was trying to stop wife Sarah from finding out, he made a poor job of it. For months he and the leggy honours graduate were spotted together in pubs, night-clubs and even the Anfield players' lounge. And the hotel trade in the north-west experienced a sudden boom. Inevitably, gossip had started. One evening the lovebirds were enjoying themselves in the Kingsway night-club in Southport along with Blackburn duo Alan Shearer and Mike Newell and their wives when in walked Mrs Ruddock. Angry at having finally twigged what was going on,

she confronted her errant husband. First she inquired who Fiona was. Naughty Neil admitted she was his girlfriend and that he loved her. At that point the object of his desire wisely made a sharp exit. Sarah then asked her husband if he was prepared to promise never to see his other woman again; but Ruddock said he wasn't. Instead he told his wife he was sorry to have let her down but that he loved Fiona, couldn't give her up and was going to move in with her.

Devastated Sarah headed with the hardman's two children back to her mother's Essex home. Fiona, meanwhile, was jubilant that she had got her man. 'It's not a whirlwind romance that will blow itself out,' she proclaimed. Her married lover was obviously keen, too. 'The first thing I noticed about her, of course, was that she's a real stunner. But she's also intelligent' – presumably a rare characteristic among players' bits on the side. 'When you're a well-known footballer, girls always come on strong,' Ruddock explained. 'Usually we just give them a peck on the cheek and send them on their way.'

With this brainy blonde, though, it was different. When they first met, she asked him what he did for a living. Ruddock replied that he was an athlete. It was only when people began asking for his autograph that she realized he was famous. She quickly found out what a superb athlete he was – off the park, that is. 'Neil is a wonderful lover with a great physique,' gushed frisky Fiona. 'He's very attentive and has great stamina. We're very physical people and are so much in love that we can't keep our hands off each other.'

That was in September 1995. Just two months later, Ruddock showed his glamorous girlfriend the red card and returned home to his wife and kids – something both Terry Venables and Roy Evans had privately urged him to do. The affair Fiona denied was a whirlwind romance had blown itself out. Heartbroken, she tried one last desperate move to lure the Anfield stopper back into her life. But it didn't work. Ruddock had pledged to ditch his hellraiser reputation and wasn't going to get caught up in any more monkey business.

Within weeks, however, his new-found and highly unlikely Mr Clean image seemed to have vanished when the boys in blue were called to a traffic accident. Ruddock's £56,000 silver Porsche Carrera had gone out of control, uprooted a tree, bounced back on to the road, overturned and landed in a cycle lane. The stubbly centre-back was duly arrested – outside his favourite pub, The Grapes in Formby, a well-known footballers' haunt – and when he failed a breath-test, things looked bad for him. But he didn't stay in the cells for long. Ruddock insisted he had not been driving the car when it crashed. Initially, the cops were unable to prove who had taken the flash motor from outside The Grapes and written it off; tests showed the seats were set for someone shorter than either him or his by-then ex-girlfriend Fiona, who was also questioned. 'It's a bit of a mystery,' admitted a police spokesman. Months later, though, the police charged Razor with obstruction and he was fined £300 with £200 costs.

Today, the Merseyside club best-known for its bad boy antics is Everton. They were responsible for one of the most farcical moments in recent footballing history back in September 1990 when, after losing the first three games of the new season, beleaguered boss Colin Harvey decided urgent action was needed. The manager, who had spent £10 million on new faces without winning any silverware, hit on what seemed to be the perfect way to rebuild dressing-room spirit and put the fire of desire back into a team which, after tasting glory at home and abroad in the 1980s, had entered the new decade struggling to reproduce anything like the old panache. His brilliant idea? A first team squad night out in a Chinese restaurant, with taxis laid on so the players could drink as much as they liked. It would be a morale-booster, Harvey reckoned, an ideal opportunity for his stars to chew the fat – of the club's crisis, that is, not of the sweet 'n' sour.

The Everton lads took their boss at his word, and noisily thrashed out their differences as they gleefully tucked into spring rolls, chow mein and endless pints of lager at a Chinese eaterie in Southport, then repaired to a local hotel to keep on drinking – all at the club's expense. As a fellow diner recalled: 'There was a lot of loud conversation coming from their corner all night.' The Goodison good-for-nothings certainly had plenty to talk about, like being bottom of the league and wondering where their first points of the season might come from. All went well until Harvey headed home, leaving his players to continue their pow-wow over a few late drinks. Not long after, though, an intense debate on one of football's finer philosophical points – so is Martin Keown crap or not? – got out of hand, and the man proposing that popular notion, Everton's Republic of Ireland midfield maestro Kevin Sheedy, ended up in hand-to-hand combat with the object of his ridicule. Keown, understandably, took grave exception when his team-mate called him 'a lousy wanker of a player', punches were thrown and soon the Toffees' morale-booster was in tatters.

Next morning, the deadly duo were hauled before Harvey, who was appalled at their shocking antics. He fined them £2,000 each. 'It was a heat of the moment thing. They were having a discussion about football which got out of hand,' deadpanned the boss with considerable understatement. 'We went to Southport initially to have a chat and relax – and a few good points came out. I do not think you will ever get a group of men working together, whether on a factory floor or at a football club, without there being friction from time to time.' One of the evening's more visible scars was Sheedy's face. Despite wearing dark glasses, a black eye was still visible. He too adopted Harvey's 'Crisis? What crisis?' line, explaining: 'It was a petty disagreement between Martin and myself. We have apologized to each other and to the boss and we are sorry for any embarrassment we have caused the club. There has been no fallout in the Everton camp.' Only an announcement from Sheedy that he was retiring to become secretary of the Martin Keown Fan-Club would have stretched credulity further.

If the previous night's fisticuffs did not constitute a fallout to Sheedy, it is hard to imagine what would. Eyewitness Steve Jennings testified to what a vicious encounter it had been. 'One was saying, "You can't play, anywhere." The other one got up and started pounding him with his fists. Other players dragged him off, but he broke free and kicked him four times. You could hear the thuds,' recalled the 32-year-old clerk. 'The victim put his hands over his face to protect himself and was slumped in his chair. It was a very violent attack and he meant what he was doing.'

Mark Ward was another Everton player whose character apparently owed more to *Brookside*'s Barry Grant than the cuddly Cilla Bl-a-a-ack of *Blind Date* fame. The fact that he had been out of action for several months with a broken leg did not stop the diminutive winger getting involved in a fracas the night before New Year's Eve in 1992. The former West Ham star was drinking at the Fisherman's Rest in the posh Merseyside suburb of Birkdale with team-mates Ian Snodin and Peter Beardsley, a teetotaller, and ex-Goodison favourites Graeme Sharp and Neil Pointon, when the beer suddenly began to cloud his judgement. His big mistake was to block women on their way to the toilets, then pinch their bums. Understandably, some regulars got annoyed. When one complained, Ward tried to pick a fight with him. A bad move. Landlord Colin Calvert threw the troublesome Toffee out, warning him not to come back. But the bother continued outside in the pub car park and before long the boys in blue were on the scene. 'I never want to see him again,' said Calvert. 'Ward's behaviour was disgraceful. He is barred from this pub. The other players are welcome, they are gentlemen and it's a pleasure to serve them.' But not Ward. Ouch.

That incident happened at the same time as Everton fans were trying to solve the mystery of precisely how, just days before, another of their heroes, the fiery Scottish striker Maurice Johnston, had been ruled out of action for several weeks after he sustained a broken cheekbone. Friends of the controversy-prone redhead claimed he had been injured in a fall at his home. So it was a domestic accident. Or was it? Mo-Jo's wife Karen fuelled speculation about a more sinister explanation when she insisted cryptically that: 'He is a footballer and he has a football injury.' What could it all mean?

The Merseyside public has certainly known some rogues in its time, not all of them lovable: John Lennon, Derek 'Degsy' Hatton, the Toxteth rioters and, most recently, almost all the male characters in *Brookside*. 'The Scousers', Harry Enfield's hilarious skit on Liverpool life, portrayed the entire male population of the city as shellsuit-wearing, curly-permed, musta-chioed scallies with a love of drinking, swearing and fighting (except, of course, for the one who jumps in saying, 'Calm down, will ya? Calm down!'). Whether this is crass stereotyping or accurate parody, the Scouse masses are clearly familiar with the sort of man who likes to walk on the wild side. So the presence among them of Mo Johnston, the latest in a long line of Scottish footballing *enfants terribles*, should have made the more way-ward side of the Celtic character familiar. Nothing, however, could have prepared them for the arrival at Goodison from Glasgow Rangers late in 1994 of Duncan Ferguson, quite the baddest bad boy Scottish soccer had thrown up for quite some time.

Even by the high standards of misbe-haviour from some of football's real head-cases, big Dunc is exceptional. Once a yob, it seems, always a yob. His criminal career began at the tender age of nineteen when he was fined £125 for butting a policeman during a brawl at a taxi-rank in his home town of Stirling in central Scotland. The experience should have encouraged the emerging Dundee United striker to steer clear of taxi queues, which are renowned for attracting late-night mouthy drunks. But he was soon in trouble again. Before long he picked up a second conviction, this time for assaulting a nineteen-year-old Heart of Midlothian-supporting postman who was on crutches at the time – and at the very same taxi-rank as the previous flare-up! Result: £200 fine. There was also a question mark over Fergie's burgeoning Scottish international career after a Swiss hotel ended up mysteriously getting damaged when Dunc and the rest of the lads enjoyed its hospitality. Ferguson denied suggestions that he had set fire to Rangers and Scotland team-mate Ally McCoist's bedroom, while Coisty was still inside!

The rising star of the Scottish game had always been a cocky, aggressive, swagger-ing kind of fella, never one to walk away from a challenge – which, being six-feet-four, sometimes came his way. Smashing the British football transfer record by signing for Glasgow Rangers in July 1993 for a cool £4 million – £700,000 more than Blackburn had paid Southampton for Alan Shearer – made matters worse. He began to indulge his favourite on-field ploy: taunting opposition defenders about how much money he was earning compared to them. With no one else on £5,000 a week, no wonder some people got annoyed. Fate intervened two months later when this footballing loadsamoney was convicted of assault yet again, this time after attacking a fisherman in the bar of the Royal Hotel in Anstruther, a sleepy town in Fife where only the most deter-mined can find bother. Bizarrely, at the time big Dunc was wearing one glove, a woman's earring and a flower behind his ear. Dressed like that, it's easy to see how he ended up in trouble. Sheriff Charles Smith placed Ferguson on a year's proba-tion – a sentence criticized as unduly lenient – and advised him to 'grow up' and cut down on his drinking. He also warned him about his future conduct and revealed that he had seriously considered finding a space for him in Scotland's over-crowded jails. Smith declared that this was the last time any judge would show such understanding to the big man with the short fuse; next time – if there was a next time, of course – would have to mean a spell at Her Majesty's pleasure.

All this added to the fast-growing Ferguson legend in Scotland. He was quickly nicknamed 'Duncan Disorderly' and found his every move reported by the Scottish press in the way that the indiscretions of a certain Spurs number eight became front- as well as back-page news at the height of Gazza-mania after the 1990 World Cup. Eyebrows were raised, for example, when big Dunc fell off a pub's bucking bronco machine just after being sent home from a Scotland Under-21 squad because of injury! Despite all the attention, though, Rangers' record signing couldn't break into the first team. Injury didn't help, and Ibrox manager Walter Smith was keen not to break up the ageing but lethal partnership of Mark Hateley and Ally McCoist just yet. When Ferguson appeared for Rangers reserves against Glasgow rivals Celtic in late 1993, a phenomenal 20,000 fans turned up to see him play. Always a man for the big game, Dunc duly scored.

It was four long months before he finally netted his first goal for Rangers' senior team, however, in a 4–0 demolition of lowly Raith Rovers. But even that vaguely historic event was overshadowed by something altogether more significant: Ferguson's headbutting of Rovers' full-back Jock McStay, a vicious off-the-ball assault that left the other player writhing on the pitch clutching a cut lip. This time, instead of there being only a few witnesses in a taxi-rank or hotel bar, there were

44,000 seated ring-side at Ibrox – plus millions more watching on TV, which replayed the incident. The referee missed it, though, and DD wasn't even booked. But after reading headlines condemning Dunc as a '£4 million thug' and 'head-banger', and aware of a growing public feeling that a highly paid footballer already on probation had got away with yet another psychopathic outburst, the authorities felt obliged to act. The police interviewed Ferguson and before long he was facing his *fourth* assault charge. And he was still just twenty-two!

A few days later, the Scottish manager Craig Brown explained he was not picking Dunc to play in a European qualifier because he was 'short on fitness – and maturity'. The player's latest brush with the law led one Scottish sportswriter to wonder if some players were simply not suited to the huge exposure that football stardom brings. 'To go from housing scheme or suburban obscurity to sporting fame and fortune is a transformation that wreaks havoc,' wrote Graham Spiers in *Scotland on Sunday*. 'Suddenly, they have more money than they can spend. Suddenly, they are fêted and acclaimed. Suddenly, they seem to have unlimited access to anyone and anything.' Then the killer line: 'Suddenly, the door in the pokey is clanging shut behind them.'

Those comments were to prove prophetic. In the months before the case came to court, the world found out more about exactly what sort of loon Duncan Ferguson really is. One warm day in July 1994, he suddenly went berserk and began trashing his car – a sponsored £15,000 Audi – outside a pub in Stirling. Maybe it was stress-related. That September, his pal Eddie Conville, a lower-division player, was fined £200 and ordered to pay another £200 in compensation to a woman he had assaulted. The legal definition of the offence hardly does justice to its full horror. Conville had actually urinated on the woman as he and big Dunc watched a Benn v. Eubank boxing match on TV. 'I felt something hot on my face and ear and that's when I jumped up and Eddie was standing over me, urinating over the top of me,' recalled victim Margo Laird. She admitted 'being cheeky' to Conville – by lifting up her top but not showing him her breasts – during the bout. Further proof that Fergie likes to keep only the choicest company came two months later when Thomas Begley, his former bodyguard, was jailed for three months for non-payment of a fine after he was convicted of car fraud. With friends like that, big Dunc didn't need enemies.

Moving to Everton on a three-month loan in October that year was meant to be a new start for Dunc, both on and off the park. Under-the-cosh Goodison boss Mike Walker was desperate to turn round a team which had not won since the last day of the previous season. Just how desperate was shown by the compensation he agreed to pay for Ferguson's services: £30,000-a-week 'rent' to Rangers on top of the player's usual £5,000 wage. As hired guns go, £35,000 a week should buy a lot of firepower. Initially, it didn't. Walker, inevitably, was sacked and ex-Evertonian Joe Royle took over. Ironically it was only then that Dunc began scoring, grabbing one of the Toffees' two goals in the Merseyside derby in November 1994, Royle's first game in charge, to help make the boss's home-coming as memorable as they get.

Ferguson duly became an instant cult hero at Goodison Park. He donned the number nine shirt worn so famously in the past by the likes of Bob Latchford, Andy Gray, Gary Lineker and Royle himself. Here was six feet four inches of the rawest red meat Everton regulars had come across for quite some time, and they liked what they saw: Dunc was tough, skilful, competitive and marvellous with his head – in football, at least. As one newspaper commented: 'Not since Charlie Nicholas brought his designer skills to Highbury eleven years ago has the arrival of a Scottish forward in English football created such a sense of anticipation.'

Initially the move seemed to suit Ferguson. Soon after arriving he told friends that his wild days were over, that he had given up drinking and abandoned the services of martial arts expert Stephen Dennehy, a long-time friend, as his £100-a-night minder. Dennehy confirmed that Duncan Disorderly was now a reformed character, 'confident he'll be able to keep out of trouble. He's asked me not to go down there (from Scotland) because he's off drinking and not planning to go out.' That was on 9 October.

Sadly, just six weeks later, on 20 November, all those fine intentions lay in ruins. Ferguson was stopped by Merseyside police outside the Moat Hotel in Liverpool, his base since moving down from Glasgow, in the early hours of a Sunday morning, the day before the derby game. The cops' interest was aroused when they saw him driving at speed through an entrance into a bus station marked 'no entry'. The player, it transpired, had been to a party, had a few bevvies and . . . So much for staying in, not drinking and steering clear of trouble. Not for the first time, trouble had found Duncan Ferguson. He was fined £500 – loose change to someone on his wages – when he admitted drink-driving.

The conviction meant big Fergie had opened his scoring in England in both the ways which had distinguished his life so far: on the pitch – and, of course, in the law courts.

Perhaps the most remarkable aspect of big Dunc's career up until that point was that he had somehow avoided a spell in the pokey. He had demonstrated his thuggish tendencies enough times to deserve some porridge. The feeling grew that if he had not been a famous footballer, he would already have heard the cell-door close behind him.

His luck finally ran out, however, when he appeared at Glasgow's Sheriff Court charged with assaulting Raith Rovers' Jock McStay. The clash, he insisted, was accidental, the result of him being 'clumsy' with his head after 'eyeballing' his opponent. 'Eyeballing' happened all the time in football, he told the court. 'Two players do it just to show a bit of aggression. I stepped forward, misjudged my distance and my head came into contact with Mr McStay.' Fergie had, though, no recollection of actually striking McStay full in the face. 'I made slight contact with his forehead and he fell to the ground.' Crucially, he also admitted being annoyed and aggressive, characteristics Dunc-watchers knew about only too well already.

Others saw the same events rather differently, as suspiciously like an oversized bully snapping, lashing out and being very economical with the truth in a bid to beat the ensuing rap. The Scotsman's plea of innocence fell on deaf ears. Sheriff Alexander Eccles reached the conclusion that everyone else had arrived at long ago, that the headbutt was indeed deliberate. Two weeks later he handed out the first jail sentence ever imposed on a British footballer for on-field violence: three months in Glasgow's notorious Barlinnie prison. The punishment, said Eccles, was 'in the public interest and to bring home to you that such behaviour cannot be tolerated. You are in a prominent position and you are looked up to by younger people.'

Initially Fergie managed to avoid captivity. An appeal by his lawyers guaranteed him four more months of freedom – enough time for him to pick up an FA Cup winner's medal at Wembley when the Blues beat Manchester United 1–0. After a decidedly sticky start to the season, the Toffees had certainly got out of jail – thanks ironically to goals from a man who was heading for that very place. Fergie could not avoid his fate. The appeal failed and he became the so-called 'Birdman of Barlinnie'. Forty-five days later he was free. Everton sent a chauffeur-driven Daimler limousine to collect him and soon he was on his way back to Liverpool to do what he knew best: playing the Terminator to opposition defences. Prisoner EFC09 had done the crime and now done the time. A hero's reception greeted him at Goodison the next day when he was paraded before the fans.

Ferguson's tightly packed criminal CV did not deter Everton splashing out for Dunc when the time came. At £4 million, it was a hell of a risk. Perhaps Joe Royle secretly shared the opinion of Duncan Disorderly articulated by that other legendary wildman of Scottish soccer, dribbler – and drinker – extraordinaire, Jim Baxter: 'I read that big Fergie likes a few pints, loves to stay out late and chase the birds, and gives a bit of lip at training. In my book he has all the perfect ingredients of a great footballer.' Until we find out, it's probably best to avoid late-night taxi-ranks in Liverpool city centre.

11

Aston Villains

'My reputation had painted Birmingham red before I even turned off the M6 in search of Villa Park.'

Paul McGrath

Andy Gray was the first genuine superstar of West Midlands soccer. When Aston Villa's notoriously dour manager Ron Saunders paid £110,000 to Dundee United in 1975 for the leading striker in the Scottish First Division, he bought a player whose roller-coaster lifestyle splashed a streak of pop art colour across Birmingham's bleak industrial canvas.

Andy Gray, now familiar to all Sky TV viewers as the channel's excitable and plain-speaking resident match pundit, was the darling of the claret-and-blue faithful in England's second city. His place in their hearts was assured when he netted on his home debut against the hated Manchester United. Every time he scored, he sprinted towards the masses in the Holte End, arms aloft, flinging himself on their affection.

Here was a nineteen-year-old who met his new employers wearing platform shoes which made him look four inches taller than he actually was. A forward who, four years later, earned a wedge of a different sort when Wolves paid a world record £1.46 million for his services. Here was the man dubbed 'He Who Dares' by

admiring pressmen for his courage in the box. Who became the first footballer to collect Player of the Year and Young Player of the Year awards in the same season. Who won twenty caps for Scotland. And who copped an FA fine of £27.50 per finger when he flashed a double 'V' sign at baying Manchester Reds.

But it was Andy Gray's first foray from the protective bosom of Villa Park which made the biggest impact on his adopted home. Like others before and after, the dashing young striker lived up to the universal truth defined by that well-known student of the game, Jane Austen: that a single man in possession of a good fortune must be in want of a crazy scheme to blow it on.

Holy City Zoo in San Francisco is a legendary clubland haunt for California's rich and famous. But Holy City Zoo under the viaduct at scummy Snow Hill station, just off Brum's unlovely city centre? As an address it didn't have much going for it. But in the late 1970s, it had Andy Gray going for it. And, more to the point, it had Andy Gray's money going for it.

Gray was twenty-two and earning riches

of £400 a week when, in March 1979, he, his older brother Duncan and a pal from back home in Glasgow, Rab Jackson, threw open the doors on a new addition to Birmingham's burgeoning night-club scene. It was, in the parlance of the time, tasteful but stylish. There were softly-lit lounges, a disco, cabaret room and a five-star restaurant. It cost £60,000 to convert the old railway station into this sophisticated rendezvous for West Midlands socialites, and, on its launch night, Ron Saunders to his credit let Gray off early from a match to see where his money had gone. He had scored one of three first-half goals against Bolton but took a knock on his right knee. Saunders told him not to bother going out after the break but to get changed and hit the town.

Down in Livery Street, Birmingham's well-heeled clubland set were having a ball. But then, they could hardly fail to enjoy themselves if local comic Dave Ismay was behind the bar. Ismay never remembered the price of any drinks, so everything was £1. You wanted a bottle of Bollinger, a pint of lager or a bitter lemon? With Dave Ismay, it all cost the same at Holy City Zoo. Billy Connolly, another Glasgow lad, visited when he was in the area. So did chicken-in-a-basket crooners the Three Degrees, and TV faces like Jim Davidson and Russ Abbot. It was any footballer's idea of sheer class. All these 'celebrities' were attracted by a club which sold the cheapest bubbly but the most expensive soft drinks in Birmingham – and where, so rumours went, you could even stroll behind the bar and serve yourself, if you were famous enough.

A couple of years on from her bath-sharing exploits with the players at Crystal Palace, sex queen Fiona Richmond sashayed through the front door. She left behind a flock of men with flames in their Y-fronts, and a signed photo: 'To Andy, love and lust, Fiona'.

Not that randy Andy ever went short in the ardour department. Long before the Sky Strikers appeared on the scene, he demonstrated a penchant for leggy lovelies. He secretly married model Vanessa Crossland-Taylor in 1979, confessing himself 'fabulously in love', but the relationship lasted barely twelve months and the couple later divorced. The next object of his affections was Janet Trigg, a nursery nurse voted 'Face of the '80s', and they had two daughters. Gray was on the move again after just two years, his self-confessed itchy feet taking him into the arms of another model, six-foot blonde Jackie Cherry. 'I've known some beautiful women,' he admitted, 'but whenever I get this feeling of anyone putting shackles on me, I have this urge to break free. I'm a bad man to live with.' When reports in March 1995 claimed that he had dumped Jackie and their three-year-old daughter Sophie for an unnamed divorced mum, the Sun found an inevitably anonymous but talkative 'friend' who concurred with Gray's own description of himself: 'Andy has always been a bit of a lad and a womanizer,' confirmed the secretive side-kick.

Gray's twenty-fourth birthday celebration was the Zoo's bash to end all bashes. In the entrance hall, a solid silver fountain flowed with champagne. The idea was that guests would help themselves to a glass when they arrived but, in keeping with the hedonistic mood, someone forgot to switch it off and it frothed away all night.

There was never any suggestion that

BLONDES ON FILM: JACKIE CHERRY AND DAUGHTER SOPHIE, UNSHACKLED BY ANDY GRAY.

Gray's penchant for a party affected his performances on the pitch. He only went to the Zoo twice a week, and didn't get involved in the running of the club. However, it was this arm's-length approach to the business which turned Gray from claret-drinking to blue. Duncan and Rab had warned him that he should keep an eye on the other two partners in the Zoo, but he ignored them. And so, after eighteen months of working together, Gray's brother and mate announced that they were quitting. This was the move which prompted him to call in accountants to carry out an independent audit, and they confirmed his now growing fears: Holy City Zoo was deep in debt, and losing more money by the day. The two errant partners vanished, the club closed, and Gray, now a severely chastened soccer celebrity, was saddled with a bill for £40,000.

'At twenty-two I was still naïve and easy meat for the big game hunters who came offering a golden business opportunity,' he admitted afterwards, reflecting ruefully on how he had lived up to that old adage, there's a sucker born every minute. 'I paid up and put it down to experience.'

When Gray was then photographed walking barefoot round Birmingham city centre, some suggested that the debt had left him literally on his uppers. In fact, he'd slipped his shoes off after stopping at a café for a coffee, and run across the road without them to accost a traffic warden who was about to ticket his car. The rumour machine went into overdrive, however, when Gray asked for a transfer. Villa followers are to this day convinced that he needed ready money to save himself from the impending financial disaster that was Holy City Zoo. On the contrary, protested Gray, it was a breakdown in communication with Ron Saunders which forced him into a move.

Saunders could have out-grumped Victor Meldrew. Jim Smith recalled that when he was in charge at Birmingham City and the bosses around the West Midlands got together for a drink and a chat, Saunders never came. And so it was no surprise when the stone-faced, dictatorial Villa supremo and his brash, individualistic striker came to blows, verbally speaking at least. Gray's first transfer request was slapped down – and he was fined £100 for speaking in public about it. Eventually he was saddled with a £1 million valuation, a fee which seemed designed to scare off potential purchasers. But Gray's gift for putting the ball in the back of the net was rightly prized, and the sum was almost fifty per cent larger by the time Wolves beat off Liverpool, Manchester City and Nottingham Forest for his signature.

It was an unseemly three-month squabble between Gray and Saunders, a rumpus ill-befitting a club which always maintained an air of aristocratic aloofness in matters monetary. Villa, after all, had religious origins to live up to, being formed by members of Aston Cross Wesleyan Chapel. They were one of the founders of the Football League, and had a glorious reputation in the FA Cup – even though the original trophy was nicked from a shop in Aston after they put it on display in 1895. Villa had long vied with the Reds of Merseyside and Manchester to be considered the most fashionable club outside London. Villa had a noble history to call on. In fact, Aston Villa FC was, in the eyes of its devotees, an upstanding and morally incorruptible bastion of the football establishment.

So why did they ever buy Paul McGrath?

As the 1980s staggered to a close, Paul McGrath was a dodgier purchase than a second-hand Picasso at a car-boot sale. The defender whom Manchester United's then manager Ron Atkinson had plucked from League of Ireland football with St Patrick's Athletic was, in the eyes of Big Ron's successor, Alex Ferguson, nothing more than damaged goods – both physically and mentally. A knee injury sustained against Sheffield United in the last reserve team game of the 1981–82 season had brought McGrath the first of eight operations, constant pain and a brooding introspection about his fitness. The player christened 'The Black Pearl of Inchicore' – a reference to his colour, as the orphaned son of a Nigerian father and Irish mother, and to the part of Dublin where St Pat's were based – began to seek solace in booze and kindred company.

Ferguson, a staunch Protestant from working-class Glaswegian stock, and McGrath, brought up in a Protestant orphanage but a wayward Celtic Irish soul brother by instinct, were utterly contrasting personalities. McGrath liked a drink and the crack with his pals, and made no secret of it. So did many other United players at the time – Kevin Moran, Norman Whiteside and Bryan Robson were his regular beer buddies around the watering holes of sedate Cheshire towns like Hale and Altrincham. Strait-laced Ferguson, in contrast, saw drinking in public as a breach of professional protocol. McGrath was often fined and warned to keep his boozing in check. Nor did it help his image in the eyes of the Old Trafford hierarchy when, in 1987, he lost control of his club Ford Granada after a session with Whiteside at the Four Seasons hotel in Hale. The number of gardens McGrath's motor skidded through – three – was, by a neat coincidence, identical to the number of times by which he was over the limit. He landed a two-year driving ban for his exploits.

Irretrievable breakdown came on 7 January 1989. United were due to play Queens Park Rangers in the third round of the FA Cup, and McGrath, who had only come back into the team during the Christmas period, wasn't fit. His knees were not yet ready for heavy ground and tough tackles so soon after surgery. According to McGrath, Ferguson knew

this, because they had discussed the matter and the manager had not named him in the squad when he announced it to the players the day before. That meant McGrath was off duty, with no pre-match rules and rituals to abide by. He was a free man, along with drinking partner and long-term injury victim Norman Whiteside.

Their night out began with the now-customary few bevvies, before the two Red Devils appeared together on the Granada TV programme *Kick Off* – the same show on which Willie Morgan famously called former United boss Tommy Docherty the worst manager he'd ever known, and sparked off one of the most sensational libel trials of the 1970s. The interview went well. So well, in fact, since McGrath is no natural before a camera, that some viewers thought he and Whiteside were pissed. Again.

When McGrath reported at Old Trafford the following day, Alex Ferguson's thunderous face said it all. Lee Sharpe had gone down with flu, and the only possible cover was the man standing in front of him – injured, and in no condition to play football. It's not hard to imagine the dressing-room dressing-down which followed: Ferguson stomping around telling McGrath his experience on the pitch could be vital and that he was bloody well playing, McGrath retorting that he was in no fit state even to lace his boots, let alone cope with a high-pressure cup tie. The manager relented only after physio Jim McGregor intervened on the player's behalf – but demanded a show-down with his errant stopper on Monday morning.

Not only did Ferguson want McGrath out of the club, he wanted him out of football. For good. The offer, according to

McGrath, was £100,000 plus a testimonial – in Ireland, mind, not at Old Trafford – if he decided to heed his complaining knees and quit the game. Meanwhile, he was sent to Coventry, Old Trafford-style: training with the YTS kids and playing for the 'A' team. 'My first concern was to get rid of the idea that Manchester United was a drinking club – not a football club,' rapped Fergie in explanation.

And then Aston Villa manager Graham Taylor came in for him, and it took just one phone call for Manchester United to offload thirty-year-old P. McGrath, trouble maker, for £450,000. 'I felt at that stage he needed a bit of loving,' explained Taylor. On the pitch, it was a new start for the player in whom Republic of Ireland manager Jack Charlton saw only good, and made a linchpin of his team through three World Cup and European Championship campaigns. Off it, however, the move to the Midlands meant cuddles from a different manager but the same grief from the bottle.

October 1990, and the man for whom the Irish fans had invented their own much-copied rap at the players' home-coming from the World Cup finals two years earlier, was in disgrace. Instead of being at Lansdowne Road, where the Republic were playing Turkey in a European Championship qualifier, McGrath was hiding in the Dublin International Airport hotel, slowly coming to terms with the hangover of a lifetime. Away visiting his sick mother – that was how Charlton had explained his failure to meet up with the team. Getting plastered on a three-day grand tour of Dublin bars was the real story. Irish physio Mick Byrne eventually rounded him up from the house of a friend in Mulhuddart – there were kids outside chanting 'Ooh, aah, Paul McGrath' as if it were a scene from a Roddy Doyle novel – and hurried him into bed at the hotel. 'I woke up late, looked in the mirror and I wanted to die with embarrassment,' he confessed later. 'This was not Paul McGrath the footballer. This was Paul McGrath the mess.'

Villa booked him into the Woodbourne detox clinic in the leafy Birmingham suburb of Edgbaston. He was given tablets that made him sick if alcohol touched his lips, and examined inside and out. The verdict was that McGrath was a binger rather than an alcoholic – someone who can give up when they want, but keep going for days if they get a thirst. He left, apparently cleaned out, after four weeks of a six-week programme, and returned for another dose a year later.

But the man Aston Villa's next boss Ron Atkinson was to call 'the best defender in the world, bar none' was still shackled by the demons in a pint glass and in his rheumatic knees. His ten-year marriage to Claire was in shreds and, after fathering a love-child with brunette Paula Hilton, he had now taken up with 27-year-old Liverpudlian Caroline Lamb. McGrath was making George Best look like a model of reliability, while Lord Lucan would have been envious of his disappearing skills. In May 1993, he failed to appear for Ireland's trip to Tirana to play Albania in a World Cup qualifier, choosing instead the old haunts of Cork, the sun of Israel and the company of Caroline in preference to the halibut farms and tractor factories of the glorious socialist state of Enver Hoxha. Two months later, he skipped a Villa trip to Japan when Claire was in hospital and his three kids needed looking after, and was fined two weeks' wages by Atkinson. In

Ooh-er Paul McGrath. The Black Pearl of Inchicore gets to grips with the home leg.

January 1994, his timetable again went awry when he missed the coach to Exeter for an FA Cup tie, complaining of painful knees, and decided to indulge in some extra rehabilitation work in the Barley Mow pub near the Villa training ground. That was another two weeks' pay – about £10,000 – down the pan.

This time, though, an exasperated Big Ron spent the money on McGrath's long-suffering team-mates. He took them for a five-day break in Tenerife before the fourth round game at Grimsby.

'Ooh, aah, Paul McGrath' was a chant born of affection and admiration. And its recipient knew it. 'I have tested Jack Charlton and Ron Atkinson to the absolute limits,' he confessed with commendable understatement. 'I have done enough to have been sacked by Villa and discarded by Ireland.' But neither ever happened. Players of McGrath's calibre don't come floating across the Irish Sea very often, and followers of both country and club were willing to forgive him anything provided he turned up and did the business on the pitch.

When Villa were at home to West Ham in early 1994, McGrath took a ball full in the face and ended up flat on his back. As he rose groggily to his feet, the West Ham fans responded with a chorus of 'Have a drink, have a drink, have a drink!'. McGrath obliged with 'a Merson', placing his hands round an imaginary giant Guinness glass and glugging the contents. 'Wino! Wino! Wino!' shrieked the terraces, and a smile and a thumbs-up flashed back in their direction from the pitch. Paul McGrath was a far better footballer than any of them, but to fans everywhere he would always be one of the lads.

If Andy Gray was a gentle poke in the back of Aston Villa's establishment image, and Paul McGrath a dig in its ribs with an empty bottle, then Dalian Atkinson's bid to undermine the foundations of the club would be carried out with a battering ram of unpaid bills and a very fast car.

The 6-foot, 13-stone striker had cost Villa a club record £1.6 million when Big Ron brought Big Dalian back to Britain from Real Sociedad in 1991. According to the hype, here was the player who would guarantee that the claret-and-blues went one better than the league runners-up spot achieved in Graham Taylor's final season, 1989–90. The pace, bustling demeanour and extravagant natural skills were there for all to see, along with a deliciously mercurial temperament. Yet stories from Atkinson's reckless reign in Spain soon winged across the Continent. There was the £58,000 Porsche he pranged; his words of farewell from the Real Sociedad secretary: 'There goes the most indisciplined player I've ever known'; and his nickname: 'Jelly ankles'. Villa fans soon added two more tags of their own: 'Sicknote' and 'Santa', because he only seemed to appear once a year.

'If I was still at Ipswich, I wouldn't be where I am today,' said Atkinson, with remarkable profundity, of his early career at Portman Road. His manager at Villa, however, wasn't sure whether his under-achieving striker would be better off back there: 'I always write "Atkinson D." on the team-sheet,' muttered Atkinson R. 'Sometimes I wonder if I'm making a mistake.' The supporters began to wonder, too, after three seasons on a reported salary of £3,000 a week yielded just eighty-seven appearances and twenty-three goals while the object of their impatience whizzed about in a £48,000 limited edition Lotus Carlton.

DALIAN ATKINSON BOUNCES ONE PAST THE POSTIE.

However, Birmingham City chief executive Karren Brady had the best explanation for Big Ron's loyalty to his namesake striker. Visiting Villa Park for a game, she noticed 'Atkinson D.' listed on the team-sheet and innocently asked if it was his son playing up front.

Maybe he had been taking lessons from Paul McGrath, who once described him as a 'not very well-mannered young man', but Atkinson's disregard for footballing propriety surfaced throughout 1994. In August, he bounced two £100 cheques on village postmistress Shirley Owen at Newborough in Staffordshire. When she tackled him about it, he settled up – with three more rubber cheques. 'I presumed a well-paid footballer like him must have plenty of cash,' said Owen with understandable dismay. Atkinson blamed it on a mix-up with his bank accounts, but did at least proffer some thoughtful and conciliatory words to his victim: 'So what if a few cheques bounced? It's hardly unusual, is it?'

It was Atkinson's seeming inability to spend his three grand a week wisely which landed him in the bankruptcy courts three months later. Perhaps there had been a lot of Clubcall interviews to give, but Intercell found the Villa man strangely reluctant to pay a mobile phone bill of £1,984.79. Nor was this his first brush with bankruptcy proceedings: a year earlier, a firm of Sheffield solicitors had spent six months chasing a £3,000 bill for conveyancing on Atkinson's house before the force of the law finally compelled him to cough up.

Like most Villa followers, Dave Woodhall, the editor of fanzine *Heroes and Villains*, had a lot of time for Dalian Atkinson the player: 'Any striker, be it Cole, Klinsmann or Shearer, would be grateful to have a bit of him attached to their repertoire.' But rival publication *The Villa Bugle* spoke for the disenchanted thousands when an article headlined 'Behave yourself' thundered: 'Is this really the type of footballer Villa fans want at their club?'

In December 1993, Dalian finally completed a spectacular double hat-trick. But it wasn't on the pitch. After being banned from driving for six and two months respectively in 1991 and 1992, he notched a third conviction for smashing head-on into another car when overtaking a lorry at 50 m.p.h. in his Golf GTi. The second treble came when the list of charges was read out in court at Lichfield: careless driving, no insurance and two bald tyres. He was landed with a bill of £1,120 in fines and costs, and his speedy motor was garaged for two years.

A year later, when Atkinson was ordered by a Walsall County Court judge to pay damages to two of the people hurt in the collision, word went round Villa Park that a clause would be inserted in his next contract restricting him to vehicles under 50 cc. After all, when travelling at any speed, he tended to lose control of whatever he was in possession of – be it a car or the round spherical object he was so handsomely paid to boot about.

This final episode in Dalian's diary of dirty deeds did, however, provoke a response which only a true footballing bad boy could come up with. Contrition oozing from his every pore, the former Villa striker explained to his victims: 'I've just had a run of bad luck.' Paul McGrath will have nodded in approval, and raised his glass to that one.

WOULD YOU BUY A USED CAR FROM THIS MAN? DALIAN ATKINSON GETS INTO A GOLF CRISIS.

12

Lust Horizons
(Sex, Lies and Videotape)

'I spent most of the night hanging off the bed in one room or another. I couldn't believe my luck.'

Soccer groupie Sarah Moore

It takes a lot to shock the world of football. It's common to find razzle mags lying around some clubs' training grounds and there's always plenty of sexual banter among the lads. Straight sex is usually considered part of everyday soccer life, while playing away is more or less expected by both players and commentators.

Only something far more unusual, or just plain sleazy, really excites the cynical hacks and stuns the authorities; kerb-crawling managers and players, alleged orgies and gay centre-forwards have all had the press salivating and the great administrators of our game choking on their gin and tonics.

It's not often a manager gets caught with his trousers down. Particularly with a vice girl. But in June 1987 a stunned soccer world gazed in disbelief at the front page of the *Sun*. Tottenham boss David Pleat was accused of being a kerb-crawler. Pleat had previously been cautioned by police while he was manager at Luton: he had been found picking up prostitutes in the notorious Bury Park red-light area, near Luton's Kenil-

worth Road ground. Prostitute Wendy Branagan told how Pleat had asked her into his car. He declined Wendy's offer of scoring at her flat, as he was worried that he might be recognized, claimed Wendy. Instead, Pleat drove her to a car park right next to Luton's ground and within sight of the manager's office. Perhaps, like his team, he felt more at home playing on plastic (car seats, that is).

During their fifteen-minute session Pleat did not want to talk about himself, but, showing admirable dedication to his chosen sport, did talk about football, revealed Wendy. Pleat then politely drove her back to her street corner, but his clever tactical plan was thwarted by the arrival of the police who pounced when they saw the hooker leave his car, cautioning the Luton supremo. Three days later Pleat was in the penalty area once more, again cautioned by Vice Squad officers in the same locality.

After the June 1987 revelations, Wendy Branagan claimed that Pleat had paid her and another prostitute £80 to perform lesbian acts in the back of his car – well, it must have been more entertaining than watching Luton. Following Branagan's revelations, another prostitute, Heather Barrett, claimed that the £90,000-a-year Spurs boss was as shrewd in his dealings on the street as he was in the transfer market: 'He asked me once if I was prepared to do business and I told him the price was £15. But he wanted to do it for a fiver! I told him to **** off.'

The Tottenham board stood by Pleat, but he was at the centre of a further sex scandal in October of that year. Unbelievably, he'd been done for kerb-crawling again. Earlier that month the randy Spurs boss had been cautioned in George Street, in London's West End. He was stopped by a Scotland Yard under-cover squad as he cruised in his blue Mercedes, cautioned and allowed to go.

This time Pleat had little choice but to resign as Spurs manager. His wife Maureen loyally stood by him, vowing: 'We're determined to go on, because if we didn't we'd just lie down and behave like wimps. We're worth a lot more in this family.' Pleat and his wife handled the situation with great dignity, and he later achieved remarkable success again at Luton – but he will forever be haunted by the T-shirts Arsenal supporters subsequently had made up, featuring the *Sun*'s memorable front-page headline 'Spurs Boss Is Caught Kerb Crawling'. Dealers rapidly ran out of supplies.

There must be something in the Luton air that generates an unusual interest in personal services. It's rumoured that more prostitutes can be seen on the street-corners of Bury Park than spectators at the Hatters' home games. John Dreyer came to regret demonstrating his ball skills in 1989, when he was fined £200 for picking up a prostitute just yards from Luton's ground. Police watched the defender kerb-crawling before he stopped on a corner and talked to a blonde woman. They tailed Dreyer's car until he parked behind a shopping-centre and when his car lights were turned off the police pounced. His lawyer said that Dreyer was 'deeply sorry'.

Footballers can't be too careful in their choice of girlfriends. Nottingham Forest striker Kevin Campbell was sitting at home watching a Belgian blue movie featuring a busty blonde beauty bedding both men and women, when out popped something familiar. It was his girlfriend Lisa, whom he'd met at a topless beauty contest. The ex-Arsenal forward was prepared to tolerate Lisa being a topless model, but the hard-core porn movie was too much. Setting a moral example rarely seen in a former Gunner, Kevin ditched her. Only, if Campbell really is so virtuous, one does wonder why he was watching the blue movie in the first place.

Leeds United's Gary Speed wasn't too careful in his choice of bedroom partners either – two blondes stole his valuables and ran off with his clothes. After a January 1996 FA Cup tie at Bolton was postponed, Gary booked himself in for an extra two days at the luxury Copthorne Hotel at Salford Quays, Manchester.

On the Sunday night, Gary, due to marry his girlfriend that summer, went drinking at Mulligans wine bar and disco in Hale. He returned to the hotel with two blondes, whom he took up to his bedroom. After what we can only presume was a vigorous discussion of Howard Wilkinson's tactical plans, Gary fell asleep. When he awoke, the hapless star discovered that his £2,000 watch, all his credit cards, £150 cash, his mobile phone and his clothes had been stolen. In what must have resembled a scene from a Brian Rix farce, the trouserless midfielder informed hotel staff of the robbery and the police were called.

Can you remember the girls' names, sir? Erm, no, officer. Floundering Gary could only tell the police that the robbers were both white, slim, blonde and about 5 ft 5 ins tall. Which puts just about every footballer's wife or girlfriend in the frame. And no, he didn't remember what they were wearing.

Still, the Thelma and Louise of Manchester did have some sympathy for Gary. A taxi drew up at the hotel and the driver handed over Gary's clothes. The girls had taken pity on him by returning his kit – but kept everything else.

And what's this at Watford, a homely club that brings forth pictures of Elton John, John Barnes and Graham Taylor? *Blue Moves*, the title of one of Elton's albums, sums up the shenanigans. 'The Orgy at Vicarage Road' – as the *People* put it – might sound like Agatha Christie meets Jackie Collins, but it happened next to Watford's ground. Caligula (that's the Roman Emperor not an AC Milan star) would have blushed at the goings-on at property developer Robert Culverhouse's Watford flat in March 1991. Culverhouse organized wild parties that went on until dawn and offered mirror-lined bedrooms, blue movies, partner-swapping and group sex, and he often invited footballers.

On this occasion, two footballers were secretly videoed in a sex orgy – both were big names and one a former England international. They were filmed by hidden cameras having sex with a 22-year-old waitress dressed in suspenders and stockings and a French maid's outfit. Culverhouse then attempted to sell the videos to a Sunday newspaper for

£200,000 and promised to set up three more First Division stars, but was then himself trapped when the paper reported him to the police. He claimed that he had lost a lot of money in the property recession and had to get it back somehow.

Luckily for them, the bedroom secrets of the two footballers were saved as the police burnt the videos of the orgies. Just imagine if they'd got out, what Alan Hansen and Trevor Brooking would have made of the replays . . . 'He's got round the back there and you have to say that is criminal defending from the young lassie.' Over to you, Trevor. 'Well, the lad made a bit of a mess of that, there was a slight bobble, the keeper came too soon and I don't think he'll be very pleased with that effort.'

Take a group of footballers gathered for the Professional Footballers Association awards, add a self-confessed 'soccer groupie', and you have another orgy. In March 1993 Sarah Moore claimed that she had sex with seven footballers at the Embassy Hotel in London, and that Manchester City goalkeeper Andy Dibble came off his line to make love with her an astonishing seven times in three hours, as well as sharing a shower after two hours' snatched sleep. Who knows what Dibble and his footballing chums had to drink that night, but judging by his performance between the sheets perhaps we should assume that Dibble was quaffing Carling Black Label.

Sarah arrived at the hotel with her book of photos and a camera and was asked upstairs for a drink by a footballer. After sex with one player she agreed to some action with another. As they lay together, there was a knock at the door and Dibble and another man took over the sexathon. She then went from room to room with ten blokes, scoring repeatedly with seven of them as they took saucy snaps of the action for her scrapbook. At one point she claimed to be in a single bed with five men, all covered in Nivea cream. 'It was my wildest fantasy come true,' sighed Sarah.

Moore, apparently not wise to the ways of males and soccer stars, was miffed at her breakfast treatment, though, when all the players ignored her except gentleman Dibble. 'They were all fine when they were getting it off me . . . For three solid hours I was on my back and couldn't get up. But they just turned their backs on me the next morning.'

When they read about their heroes' sex lives, it's hardly surprising that some fans try to cash in on their attraction to women. In 1993 randy salesman Mike Gregory, a lookalike of Oldham defender Steve Redmond, was caught offside impersonating the player. Gregory had been advertising as a professional footballer seeking 'adult fun' in a lonely hearts column.

When women replied he claimed to be Steve Redmond and boasted of his friendships with Bryan Robson, Paul Merson, John Barnes and Les Ferdinand. He even claimed that he advertised as he was too famous to go to night-clubs. The real married Steve Redmond was mightily relieved when his doppelgänger had been exposed. 'People always believe the worst of footballers and if this guy had done something stupid the finger would have been pointed at me.'

Amid all this heterosexual activity in football there's one thing that really shocks the soccer community – homosexuality. This is surprising, as most insiders could easily name a team of gay footballers and an accompanying agent to manage their deals. Justin Fashanu deserves praise for at least having the courage to come out – although his spectacular love life does indicate he might be a half-volley short of a golden goal.

How Fashanu, best known for his spells at Norwich and Nottingham Forest, managed to combine born-again Christianity, gay romps in the Speaker's chair of the House of Commons, an affair with *Coronation Street*'s Bet Lynch, a run-in with Brian Clough and being questioned by police after the death of Tory MP Stephen Milligan, defies rational analysis.

Clough, his manager at Forest, wasn't too impressed by his non-goal-scoring striker's (three in thirty-one games) sexual mores. Clough recites a famous tale of how he confronted the then still in the closet player, after he'd received phone calls saying Fashanu had been seen in gay night-clubs in Nottingham.

'Where do you go if you want to buy a loaf of bread?' asked Cloughie.

'A baker's, I suppose,' said Fashanu.

'Where do you go for a leg of lamb?'

'A butcher's.'

'So why do you keep going to that bloody poofs' club in town?' inquired Clough.

Fashanu shrugged and got the point. After that, according to his boss, 'It was not long before I could stand no more of him.'

Fashanu finally came out as gay in 1990, claiming that he had had sex with other footballers, pop stars and a married Tory MP. His younger brother, Wimbledon's macho striker John, was horrified. 'John thought the news would reflect badly on him. He offered me more than the *Sun* to keep quiet,' claimed Justin. John Fashanu was quoted as

JUSTIN FASHANU CLAIMED TO HAVE SCORED WITH A RIGHT HONOURABLE MEMBER.

saying of Justin: 'I wouldn't like to play in the same team or even get changed in the same vicinity as him.' The two brothers eventually made their peace, but maintained a distant relationship.

But it was still early doors for Justin. Two years later, in a love match made in tabloid heaven, the thirty-year-old marksman, assistant manager at Torquay United, was now 'bisexual' and going out with busty blonde Bet Lynch, aka 49-year-old actress Julie Goodyear. Justin's Bet on the side found him 'adorable', while Fashanu admitted that he had told Julie about his past flings with men: 'She is very philosophical. She understands it is individuals that matter rather than a way of life.'

Fashanu attributed his past homosexuality to the time he became a born-again Christian. He was living with a woman but the Christians disapproved of sex outside marriage. 'I stopped having sex with my girlfriend and that's when I started to have homosexual feelings' – surely a twentieth-century example of a Christian being thrown to the loins.

'I'd have thought he'd have been more likely to ask out Jack Duckworth,' was Brian Clough's comment, as Fashanu declared, 'I never thought I could be happy with a woman.' But only a year later Fashanu, amid tears from both parties, dumped Goodyear for being too old: 'I love Julie more than I've ever loved anyone and all the ingredients were right – except her age.'

Fashanu, while still claiming to be predominantly gay, said that in five years' time he would want to start a family. Sounding more rampantly heterosexual by the minute, he announced: 'My dream is to have a big house and fill it with lots of kids. I can't see that sort of future with Julie.' What a stunning awareness of human biology.

The affair was notable for one remarkable effect on Fashanu, though, marking the rover's return to women: 'When you have curled the ball into the back of the net once, you know you can do it again.' If only he'd met Bet while he was at Forest, it might have prevented such pub toilet graffiti as 'Jesus laid on the cross, but Fashanu couldn't put it in'.

By 1994 Fashanu and the tabloids enjoyed an almost symbiotic relationship. When Tory MP Stephen Milligan was found dead wearing stockings and suspenders with an orange in his mouth, after indulging in the bizarre practice of auto-asphyxiation, Fashanu then tried to demand £300,000 from a Sunday newspaper for a story claiming he had enjoyed three-in-a-bed sex romps with senior members of the government. Realizing this would involve a top-level investigation, Fashanu later withdrew his allegations. After his claims that he knew Milligan, and that the dead MP had introduced him to a top Tory sex ring, Fashanu was interviewed by police in connection with Milligan's death, but was not considered to know anything of interest to the case.

The controversy was too much for Fashanu's then club Hearts, who sacked the striker. He was last seen in January 1995, bereft of designer clothes, and living in a former Coal Board house in the Lanarkshire village of Greenrig with a female friend. Fashanu was unable to play football, as his registration documents were being held by a club in Canada when he ran out on them after accepting their signing-on fee. Whether he was now consorting with Brian Clough's butcher, baker or candlestick-maker was a matter of speculation.

Kerb-crawling, orgies, infidelity, they all occur in football. But is there no place left for more traditional values? Yes, there is. You might not believe it, but a number of Christian footballers are trying to elevate the spiritual nature of their fellow soccer sinners.

Let us seek solace from the example of Chelsea's Gavin Peacock. When young Gavin was playing for Gillingham it was a case of born-again versus porn-again. While his team-mates salivated over pornographic videos on the coach to away games, the bashful Peacock hid in the luggage hold rather than view the steamy scenes on screen. Who says there is no morality left in football?

13

Love Hurts

'If one of my girls walked in and said "Daddy, I'm going out with a footballer", I'd say, "No, you *were* going out with a footballer!"'

Andy Gray

Like Andy Gray, most sensible parents would prefer their daughters to go out with a bowls-playing accountant rather than a footballer – unless he was Gary Lineker, of course. As a former player, Andy knows exactly what the species is like. True, the footballer does have a certain glamour: regardless of whether God gave him Giggs-like handsomeness or Dowie-like dourness, he is hero-worshipped by millions and also has a massive wad.

On the other hand, after a couple of hours playing one-touch in training, the more roguish player spends his time boozing all afternoon, drink-driving, getting arrested in night-clubs, and chasing 'models', page 3 girls, football groupies, Chris de Burgh's lady in red, and anything in a micro-skirt including a Scotsman – well, all right, maybe not Alex Ferguson or Kenny Dalglish.

Consequently, for the soccer ace, the course of true love runs about as smoothly as his sponsored car after he's drunk eight pints of lager. Relate should set up a special branch for footballing couples. In comparison to the average player's relationship fiascos, Morrissey has a successful and contented love life.

Take the case of Frank McAvennie and Jenny Blyth. It is surely the dream of every former Glaswegian road-mender to date a page 3 girl, and while at West Ham and Celtic Frank did just that. Frank and Jenny were the definitive 1980s *nouveau riche* footballing couple.

They had everything. Frank had the archetypal footballer's haircut, dyed blond with long bits at the back – enough to embarrass even a member of the cast of *Neighbours*. Jenny was also heavily into peroxide and regularly appeared clad only in a thong on page 3 of the *Sun*, with her Hammers scarf out for the lads, and subtle captions exclaiming that 'Frank and his lads could do with a couple of extra points!'

They first met at Stringfellow's night-club in London. Old romantic Frank presented her with a £5,000 engagement ring during a dinner at the swanky Langan's brasserie, a well-known West End showbusiness haunt. And they had a dream home, a mock-Tudor mansion in – where else – Essex, next door to Jenny's page 3 bosom pal, Maria Whitaker.

The mock-Tudor house has, of course, for many years been the footballer's idea of class, and Frankie Mac was no exception to its lure. 'Frank's so sweet, all he wanted to know was when we could move in,' gushed love-struck Jenny, after she suggested buying the £450,000 five-bedroom, *Birds of a Feather*-style Hornchurch love nest in 1989.

Did it last? Of course not. Frankie now says: 'My advice to blokes is to stay well away from page 3 girls' – surely the footballing equivalent of the Pope deciding to advertise Durex.

One problem was that Jenny's modelling work tailed off as soon as she started going out with Frank. 'People have seen us as a cliché – footballer and page 3 girl – and assumed we spend our whole lives out on the town and at parties,' complained Jenny. She was quite right, this was a most unreasonable conclusion to jump to, particularly from the numerous people who had actually seen them at night-clubs across Essex and London.

'But every time we go out, our picture appears in a newspaper,' she continued. How stupid of those snappers not to realize that professional photographic model Jenny was desperately camera-shy.

By 1994, in the wake of Paul Merson's cocaine revelations, Frank, now aged thirty-five, short of dosh and back at his first club St Mirren, revealed the full torrid details of their affair. For four years he had snorted cocaine around London's clubs, admitted the blond 'golden boy' of thousands of fans. For a year their relationship was fine ('She was a sex symbol and we never had a problem about sex'), but after that, drink changed Jenny, said Frank: 'Our home was like Beirut, we did nothing but argue. She couldn't stand playing second fiddle to me.'

In addition, McAvennie clearly had all the financial mastery of Dickens' Mr Micawber. He claims to have blown £700,000 on Jenny. McAvennie says that at Celtic he was spending £2,000 a weekend flying from Glasgow to London to see her; that they were drinking two or three £100 bottles of champagne per night before going out; that they went on £10,000 jet-set holidays; and that he had a 'beautiful house' in Essex that Jenny, in a fit of jealousy, refused to live in, as he had lived there with a previous girlfriend. Instead, she insisted on buying the £450,000 Hornchurch dream home: 'I

FRANK, JENNY AND BUBBLY: A MARRIAGE OF MINDS MADE IN ESSEX.

hoped to make a killing out of the property market, but it crashed. I lost a fortune.'

After 'two years of hell' McAvennie finally left Blyth, and today he charitably declares: 'I can't describe how I feel about Jenny now, I just want to exorcize the whole memory of drugs and Jenny.'

The attraction of the page 3 girl lingers on among younger players, though; certainly no credible £5 million striker would be seen without a pin-up stunna on his arm. Blackburn's Chris Sutton married model Samantha Williamson in January 1995. When she met Sutton, Williamson gave him a caution; her first move was to stop his gambling and 'trawler' parties. No, the Rovers hotshot didn't have a nautical bent – his football pals enjoyed 'trawling' around the pubs in Thorpe St Andrews and inviting lone women back to his – inevitably mock-Tudor – house near Norwich for a party.

Perhaps Sutton had done too much trawling in the past. In December 1993, his engagement was ruined by the revelation that former air hostess Lynn Briggs, aged thirty-eight, struggling on income support while Sutton earned £250,000 a year, was the mother of Sutton's child, whom he had never even seen.

The romance had taken off when the couple had a fling in the United States on a post-season Norwich tour, when Sutton was only nineteen. Lynn said the couple fell 'madly in love' and after an intimate week in a five-star hotel she was given VIP treatment at Norwich games. Only when she became pregnant, he 'got cold feet' and dumped her. Sutton was not at the birth of their son Jordan: 'It should have been the happiest day of our lives, but I never heard from Chris, got a card or even a phone call,' said Lynn.

Sutton countered that he had been used as a toyboy: 'I was young and naïve. I didn't realize at the time but it was her last chance to have a kid . . . I asked her to have it aborted and it's her decision that she didn't.' At a court case in 1993 the ex-trawlerman was ordered to pay £100 a week towards Jordan's upkeep.

There is a long history of footballers and page 3 girls teaming up. Maria Whitaker went out with Watford's Andy Kennedy for a number of years. But the stunnas can also present other problems. When Teddy Sheringham was photographed being hugged by Samantha Fox while they both modelled Tottenham's new kit in the summer of 1995, it was obvious that he was pleased to see her. However, the supply of page 3 girls is, of course, finite, so how about the ex-wife of a Rolling Stone? As Pat Van den Hauwe's career was going downhill at Spurs he decided to go out in show-biz 'style' by leaving his wife and moving straight in with Bill Wyman's ex-teenage missus, Mandy Smith.

Apart from Mandy arriving twenty-five minutes late, Pat and Mandy's 1993 marriage went as smoothly as one of Van den Hauwe's tackles. Ex-wife Susan immediately revealed that the £30,000 engagement ring Pat gave Mandy was at the centre of a court battle – Pat had tried to remortgage his and Susan's mock-Tudor home in Chislehurst, Kent, to pay for it. Susan tried to stop him in the High Court but was too late, although the judge did agree to a temporary injunction, preventing Pat from disposing of any more assets. Susan also stated that Van den Hauwe's solicitor had sent a letter to her solicitors threatening to take her to court if their six-year-old daughter Gemma wasn't allowed to attend Pat and Mandy's wedding.

PAT AND MANDY: 'I CAN'T WAIT TILL WE GET HOME AND SWAP OUTFITS . . .'

Then, in October 1993, with Pat now at Millwall, ex-wife Susan was infuriated by Mandy advertising Molson Ice beer. 'Beer poisoned our marriage,' she warned Mandy, 'and if Mandy's not careful it will destroy hers.' She claimed that alcohol turned shy Van den Hauwe 'from a loving husband and dad into a monstrous Mr Hyde' and described his giant booze benders and drunken rages. Oh, and another legal battle over maintenance was looming. Only days earlier Mandy Smith had admitted that hardman Pat had turned to drink after being banned from bonking. Mandy blamed the sex problems on the effects of her past slimming illness and her relationship with Bill Wyman.

In the middle of their turbulent marriage Mandy and Pat received yet more publicity when a thief with a crowbar raided their home, knocked down Pat and stole £100,000 of jewels – all uninsured – including, inevitably, the £30,000 engagement ring.

By June 1994 the couple had even made it on to the cover of *Hello!* for their first wedding anniversary – and the 'curse of *Hello!*' immediately took effect. Despite the glossy pictures of an idealized lifestyle, featuring the couple gazing lovingly into each other's eyes amid a perfectly furnished home, and Pat's admission that 'the highpoint in my life was marrying Mandy', they split up a month later. Mandy threw Pat out of their Muswell Hill house amid rows over his jealousy – in future it was going to be Mandy post-man Pat.

Poor old Pat then had to stay with his parents. Only in a final dénouement to the whole sorry saga, the mock-Tudor mansion where Pat's ex-wife Susan and their daughter Gemma lived was set to be repossessed, as the mortgage was £12,000

in arrears. Susan had agreed to take a rented property when Van den Hauwe stepped in, offering to pay the arrears off in instalments and move in himself. Susan was instructed to hand the keys over at a 3 p.m. kick-off and complained: 'He saved it from repossession for himself, not us . . . It felt very strange handing over the keys to him.'

Still, things could have been worse for Pat – left with two broken marriages, his first wife still talking to the tabloids, a nicked uninsured £30,000 engagement ring, a heavily mortgaged mock-Tudor mansion he couldn't sell, and given a free transfer from Millwall – but not much worse.

It was Pat himself who provided the final ignominy, revealing that, following long sex droughts, Mandy would then insist that the hardman of soccer dressed in a nurse's uniform. On another occasion she painted his wedding tackle with lipstick and they then put ears on his manhood to make it look like a mouse. At this point Mandy's mum walked in and Pat hid behind the door. Mandy said there was a mouse in the room, Mrs Smith asked 'where?' and Pat revealed the trouser rodent: 'She was a bit shocked but Mandy and I thought it was hysterical.'

The couple even cross-dressed and once went out to a restaurant in Muswell Hill, Pat wearing one of Mandy's dresses and Mandy in Pat's suit. Pictures of Pat in a dress and nurse's uniform were printed alongside his confessions – we can only speculate as to the cross-dressing-room stick reserved for a Millwall star in a frock. No wonder he decided to try his luck abroad.

Even more bizarrely, while Mandy's mum was marrying Bill Wyman's son,

Mandy's sister Nicola began a relationship with Teddy Sheringham.

'From the outside, some things about the Smith family look odd,' confessed Teddy. What, one teenage sister marrying a Rolling Stone thirty-four years her senior, then marrying a famous footballer, her mother marrying Bill Wyman's son, the other daughter dating an England striker, doesn't this sort of thing happen in every household? 'But when you know them they're just like any other family,' explained Sheringham. Yes, typical girls-next-door, really.

And just to keep up the Tottenham/showbusiness connection, early in 1995 hunky goalkeeper Ian Walker was being linked with ex-East Ender and one-time coke addict Danniella Westbrook, who at the time was engaged to East 17's Brian Harvey. After Walker showed Danniella his safe pair of hands in a bedroom at the Swallow Hotel in Waltham Abbey, Essex, an irate Harvey had turned up at reception, demanding to see 'his bird', finally leaving after being told that Danniella wasn't booked in. Walker's agent Geoff Weston admitted that Walker and Danniella were in the same room. 'It was pure coincidence she was in the hotel, and she knocked on his door out of the blue.' What a lucky meeting, a perfect opportunity for Danniella to observe Ian's clean sheets.

Newcastle's Les Ferdinand prefers a bit more style in his relationships. Despite living with his long-term girlfriend Angelea and their son, Les managed to score a hat-trick in the love stakes. For seven sizzling months he dated stunning Dutch-born model Eva Dijkstra, a cover girl with *Vogue*, *Options* and *New Woman*, after they met at The Spot nightclub in Covent Garden, London. Eva

TEDDY SHERINGHAM AND GIRL-NEXT-DOOR NICOLA SMITH.

revealed that the first time they made love, when Les was still at QPR, they slipped sticky raspberry jelly into each other's mouth and then dribbled champagne over themselves. When fruity Ferdie was naked Eva poured more champagne over his body and then licked it off; now Les is at St James' Park we can safely assume that his foreplay features Newcastle Brown Ale instead of Bollinger.

Kevin Keegan has always fancied players with a good engine capable of lasting the pace right into injury time, and so does Eva. Les performed like the six million dollar man he was set to become: 'It was amazing. Les made love to me for well over ninety minutes. He swept me off my feet and blew my mind,' sighed Ferdinand's jelly babe. Although she did add that Les, like any self-respecting man, checked the football results on Teletext before making love.

Les told Eva that he was always arguing with girlfriend Angelea and that they only stayed together for the sake of their son. Eva said that he even talked of marriage. She said that the striker's fantasy was for her to dress in blue stockings and suspenders. However, naughty but nice Les was caught out when Eva saw a magazine article in which Les was pictured as a happy family man with Angelea. In the feature, he boasted: 'Angelea has a great body and knows how to be extremely desirable in bed. I like her to wear slinky sexy underwear – matching, clean and neat.'

Ferdinand told Eva the article was written a year ago, before he'd met her. Eva took him back, but eventually Les told her he'd met someone else. Eva asked him if it was TV presenter Dani Behr, who'd previously dated Ryan Giggs, remembering that on the second time they met in February 1995, Les had Dani on his arm. Jilted Eva then revealed that tactful Les had the Behr-faced cheek to ask her if she still wanted to 'do the bed business'. She didn't, funnily enough.

Later, and despite further romantic linking with Behr, Ferdinand would only admit: 'I'm a good friend of Dani Behr, but it doesn't mean I'm having a relationship with her.' And who wouldn't want to be a good friend of Dani Behr?

Ferdinand's old team-mates at QPR also had problems keeping their women happy. In January 1996 winger Andy Impey was involved in a bizarre fracas, when he was punched on the jaw during a row between the two lovers he had made pregnant.

Long-term girlfriend Michelle, who had just had Impey's son, was furious when Andy confessed that he had made another woman, Natasha Kerr, pregnant. Michelle demanded a face-to-face meeting with Natasha. Andy and Michelle arrived at Natasha's house and the mother of all arguments ensued.

The two women began to punch and kick each other and Impey tried to intervene. 'Andy looked like he'd seen a ghost and I punched him on the jaw. It was like "Yes!" I knew he wasn't going to hit me back,' was how Natasha described the brawl. As Michelle left Natasha tactfully shouted, 'I had him in this hallway.' What followed would have graced any Brian Rix farce. 'She came running back going mental,' recalled Natasha. 'She came for me and we ended up on the ground spinning around. Andy was trying to pull me off. He was on top of me and I was on top of her.' Inevitably the police were called and Impey was interviewed about what the law euphemistically described as 'a domestic incident'.

At least Impey's hunky team-mate Trevor Sinclair escaped physical violence. Early in 1996 the mother of his child, Nicola Finlay, publicly accused the dreadlocked winger, earning £5,000 a week, of being 'miserly' in only allowing her £100 a week. They had once lived together in Blackpool and Nicola had thought they'd get married, 'but after the baby was born he was more interested in going out clubbing it with the lads than being at home.'

Other footballers have to settle for the girl-next-door – and life for the average football wife is often even more difficult than it is for page 3 girls. After splitting up with husband Imre, Jane Varadi wrote to Leeds United asking for help, because no maintenance bills were being paid by her former partner.

After the couple had parted, Jane changed the locks on their home. Imre's response was to break in and smash up the contents of the house, causing an estimated £10,000 worth of damage. 'The place was trashed. Because Imre was technically the owner, the police could not charge him. For the same reason there was no insurance for me,' says Jane.

Jane's reply from Leeds United's solicitors accused her of trying to blackmail the club. In 1993, with Imre owing £10,000 in maintenance arrears, Leeds were ordered by a judge to pay Jane maintenance direct from Varadi's wages.

Jane Varadi blames much of what happened between Imre and herself, his affairs, gambling and smashing-up of their house, on football, saying her biggest dread was the summer holiday and the week before Christmas. 'The wives are virtually never invited on those trips for one very good reason. It's playtime for the boys, married or not.'

Managers are notoriously bad relationship counsellors. Jane Varadi was disappointed in Howard Wilkinson after she went to see him with her marriage problems. She thought he would have a quiet word with Varadi and not reveal her visit.

'Instead Imre came home from training in a rage, saying the boss had told him I was making trouble and it could cost him his career.' Jane Varadi also claimed that Wilkinson wasn't worried what happened off the pitch; he had once told her he'd sign Jack The Ripper if he thought he could play . . .

Either managers say they are only concerned with three points on Saturday – as Brian Clough told Brian Rice's wife Helen, when she went to him about her marriage problems – or they interfere too much. When at Sheffield Wednesday Tommy Tynan recalls falling out with Jack Charlton over his choice of girlfriend; she had been married previously, had two children and, even worse, worked in a night-club.

As for childbirth, Karen Wigley, wife of Steve, the ex-Nottingham Forest and Portsmouth player, recalls that as the head of her first child emerged, a voice on the hospital Tannoy announced that Steve's manager wanted to know if he'd be back for the game. And West Ham's 'new man', Martin 'Mad Dog' Allen, actually left QPR after boss Trevor Francis tried to insist he play football rather than be at his wife's side for the birth of their child.

There is also the constant moving for wives and girlfriends involved with a footballer's career – and former Norwich City receptionist Eunice Beckett made a big mistake when she left her job and relocated to Manchester to be with former City striker Darren Beckford, then at Oldham. Only a month after she had given up everything to join him, Beckford dumped Eunice – to go back to his wife, in possibly the only recorded example of a footballer actually trying to be faithful to his marital vows. Jilted Eunice sighed: 'All he gave me was a cheque for the removal man to get out of his flat – and that bounced!'

Such problems are exacerbated by the fact that footballers are not exactly noted for their Gabriel Oak-like constancy (whoever he played for). With the temptations of regular trips around the country and abroad it's hardly surprising that many footballers are caught playing away from home in more ways than one.

Tottenham's Romanian import Ilie Dumitrescu, now at West Ham, soon adapted to the ways of English football. Within weeks of joining Spurs in August 1994 he was caught two-timing his wife Nila, holding secret trysts in his car with policeman's wife Dawn Pyles and kissing her while her husband was out on the beat. 'It was purely a goodbye kiss that perhaps went on a little longer than it should,' explained Dumi.

But it didn't stop there. During his brief stay in England before being loaned to Spanish club Seville, Dumitrescu seemed determined to make George Best look like a man about to enter cloisters. When Dumi flew over two teenage models from Spain, he opted for a low-profile five-day liaison – booking two £400-a-night suites at London's Dorchester Hotel for the models, an aide and himself, followed by champagne in the Ritz, more champagne and clubbing in Manchester (and a brief trip to the Man United versus Barcelona European Cup tie) while staying in the same hotel as Terry Venables.

He paid the £850 Manchester hotel bill with his gold credit card, and then made a brief trip home to his wife and two sons, followed by a swift return to the Dorchester for some souvenir snapshots in bed with the models. He then paid a Dorchester bill of £3,000 as the models flew back to Spain. Still, what's £7,000 in

seven days on two hot babes when you earn a whacking £10,000 a week? Pass the Bolly, Dumi.

Predictably, Arsenal's Paul Merson was not quite as salubrious in his sexploits as Dumitrescu. Merson confessed to straying from his wife after a lager and coke session at the Broadway Boulevard nightclub in Ealing. He went to a woman's house for three hours of sex but couldn't remember her name, only that she was a 'Cindy Crawford lookalike' – but then after fourteen pints of lager top even Nora Batty would probably look like Cindy Crawford.

After Merson's confessions of coke, booze and gambling addictions and infidelity, Gunners fan Shelley Miller described how married Merson made love to her in the most exotic of venues – a dimly lit alleyway, after they met at the Ra Ra club in Islington.

Shelley once worked at Highbury escorting VIP visitors to executive boxes, and she and Merson had first met at Tony Adams' testimonial dinner. And Merson certainly received VIP treatment from the knickerless Miller during their twenty-minute alley romp. 'He was a gentleman,' swooned Shelley. 'He made me feel so good, as though I was the best thing on earth.'

Other Merson conquests emerged in the wake of his admission that things used to go better with coke. Air hostess Suzanne Handley also claimed to have made love to Merse in the kitchen, lounge and bathroom of his family home, and that Merson sometimes interrupted their love-making to watch videos of himself scoring – on the pitch that is.

Even Gladiators get caught out. John Fashanu was in trouble in 1995, by which time he was engaged to Melissa Kassi-

Mapsi, daughter of an African diplomat and niece of the president of the Ivory Coast. Niki Thompson, the daughter of an RAF officer, and Anna Odell from Sweden had found themselves sharing Fashanu's £500,000 flat in Paddington – which proved to be a spectacular own goal on Fash's part. Niki paid the millionaire footballer £50 a week and Anna stayed rent-free – although in emotional terms, Fash was soon hit by a double dose of negative equity. The girls started talking and hell hath no fury like two women scorned. Fash himself was, for once, given the elbow.

'When we started comparing our notes, we discovered we were making love to John on the same day and sometimes at the same place, just hours apart,' raged Niki, who, after a ten-year on-off affair, had believed that John loved her. Rule one for amorous footballers: don't move your

JOHN FASHANU AT HOME: 'IT'S GOT A FITTED KITCHEN, WASHING MACHINE, NO DEPOSIT AND A VERY ATTENTIVE LANDLORD . . .'

lovers into the same flat. It all makes Frank Worthington seem like a new man.

Anna, who met Fashanu in a Swedish night-club while he was on a club tour, fumed: 'To put two lovers up in the same house when they had no idea he was sleeping with both of them, is beyond belief.'

The two women's comparisons read more like *The Lover's Guide*. Anna claimed that Fashanu had made love to her in his changing-room at Wembley, during a break in a live *Gladiators* show: 'We did it there and then, and then he went back on stage.' And Niki insisted that she and Fash had once bonked, Merson-style, in an alleyway near Millwall's ground.

In a phone call to Niki, sex warrior Fash told her: 'We had a good friendship. OK, once in a while I slept with you. Anna, when she didn't have somebody there, when I wasn't going out with Melissa.'

Both women left Fashanu's flat while he was on police bail, along with fiancée Melissa Kassa-Mapsi, Southampton's Bruce Grobbelaar and Wimbledon's Hans Segers, after being questioned over a bribes enquiry. 'He's a snake! He lured us into his trap,' raged a vengeful Niki, adding that she never wanted to see the Aston Villa number nine again.

John Fashanu! No points!

Even British Bulldog Bobby Robson was exposed in 1990 as having had a six-year extra-marital affair with 37-year-old divorcee Pauline Ridal, a translator, shortly before the World Cup finals. They'd met at a testimonial dinner for the former Sheffield United player Les Tibbott at Bramall Lane.

Red-haired Ridal said that at the dinner Robson asked her to dance. 'We liked the same music – Lionel Richie.' Pauline also claimed that, unlike most of his forwards, Bobby was able to boast of scoring a hat-trick in one evening match under the lights.

Robson booked into hotels under the name of Mr Holmes and would call Pauline 'Mrs Watson' and left his keys in a sock inside an envelope for her to collect. She confessed that they once made love in Robson's house in the bed he shares with wife Elsie, a staunch Catholic. The affair was a whole new ball game for Robson. Once while they were in bed he said to Pauline, 'To think I've reached my fifties before experiencing this!' Yes, she'd finally convinced Bobby to abandon the flat-back four for a sweeper system.

Pauline claimed that the affair ended when she became pregnant, and Robson begged her to have an abortion. (She later lost the baby.) In a tearful showdown with Ridal, Robson's admission was typically patriotic. Pauline said he told her: 'I have deceived my country. I have deceived people, I have deceived my wife and my family.'

Even worse was to come for Robbo. A week later another redhead, Janet Rush, claimed that she'd had an affair with him. 'He is a very good-looking man and I was instantly attracted to him. Wham! That was it.' At the time she was married to millionaire farmer, John Rush, and Robson was manager of Ipswich.

Rush's husband John had found her Boots diary in her desk detailing their affair and had threatened to cite Robson in divorce proceedings, she revealed. John Rush himself later fumed: 'The details destroyed me . . . It was a blow-by-blow account of her affair with Robson.' For the sake of their three children, the couple were eventually divorced on the grounds of Janet's adultery with 'person or persons unknown'.

Janet said that she realized that when Robson became England boss, 'I would discreetly fade into the past, as your position as England manager was the most important thing in your life,' yet soon afterwards he was seeing Pauline. Rather disingenuously, she went on to claim in an open letter to Robson that she'd gone public because, after reading Pauline Ridal's revelations, she felt that, 'Some of the more personal things you told me which I thought were unique and special were repeated to another woman.'

The England supremo retreated to a secret hideaway to talk things over with Elsie, who decided to stand by him. Although Robson never admitted the affairs in public, he did confess that after 'the worst forty-eight hours of my life' he might end up a better manager. Asked how he could enforce discipline he replied: 'Having had this dreadful experience I may be in a better position to enforce things better with players – especially with the high risks involved.'

Bobby is the sort of patriot who would make love even with a Terry Butcher-style head-gash oozing blood, and when the affair with Pauline Ridal became public he talked of resigning, as he had been dishonourable to his country. But even Pauline Ridal insisted he must keep his position. 'He's the best man for the job,' she pleaded – the England job that is.

However, footballers' partners can also play away. Poor Tony Cottee had just completed a £2 million move from West Ham to Everton in the summer of 1988, when a bizarre Essex love triangle was revealed. His live-in fiancée, 'top model' Lorraine Blackhall, had been scoring with builder's labourer and convicted burglar

Eddie Hagan. Hagan summed up the situation as he perceived it, with building-site succinctness: 'She has me as her bit of rough and Tone because he's loaded with money.'

'Tone', as Lorraine called him, had given Lorraine a £10,000 Ford XR3i and a £3,000 engagement ring. But that didn't stop a night of passion with Hagan in a Brentwood hotel, followed by a confrontation between Cottee and Hagan in that quintessentially Essex venue, the night-club Hollywood in Romford. 'Obviously the bloke got the hump and we had a bit of a set-to,' was how Hagan described their meeting.

Thankfully, despite two-timing Tone, Lorraine and the diminutive striker repaired their relationship. Lorraine admitted an affair with Hagan after she became engaged to Cottee, but said their friendship didn't develop until she and Cottee split up briefly: 'Eddie and I had what I considered to be a wonderful relationship. And for a few months I suppose I did love him.' But after her relationship with Hagan soured, underwear model Lorraine decided that TC was top cat: 'I realized just how much Tone meant to me.'

With all the aforementioned pressures on their relationships, it's hardly surprising that footballers and their partners are involved in that delightful euphemism, the 'domestic incident'. A select few are even injured in the process. The most notorious case was in March 1991, involving 'Tricky' Trevor Morley, the West Ham striker.

Let us picture the scene in Essex. It is the small hours of Monday morning, and a row has erupted at Morley's luxury Waltham Abbey home after Trevor and his Norwegian wife Monica have been out with Ian Bishop and his wife and a third couple. Worried neighbours first hear shouting. A few minutes later they see a body in a pool of blood in the driveway. It is Trevor Morley, a striker once nicknamed 'rag doll' for his knack of winning penalties. Only this is no dive – Morley has been stabbed several times, one of the wounds narrowly missing his heart. His wife hurriedly calls an ambulance at around 3 a.m.

As the ambulance drives off, shocked neighbours learn that Morley has been attacked with a kitchen knife, in a fracas involving Monica. In hospital Morley is operated on for stomach and arm wounds and loses several pints of blood.

The next day his manager Billy Bonds and fellow player Bishop visit the sickly striker in hospital. All the diplomatic Bonds will say is, 'It's very sad. I've lost a striker, but my main concern is for his family.'

Morley's health couldn't have been improved by the fact that his wife was being questioned by the police. Neighbours looked after their three children while Monica was quizzed at the local police station for twelve hours, and later released on bail. Despite the seriousness of his injuries, Morley was 'not keen to see his wife charged', and wanted the incident to be treated purely as a 'domestic matter', which was the approach the police adopted.

It was several weeks before Morley, West Ham's top scorer, played again, and his long absence hardly helped West Ham's failed bid for the Second Division championship.

Hardened Hammers fans had been used to bizarre injuries such as Phil Parkes' septic elbow and the legendary two-year 'Devonshire Flu' – but even they didn't expect to lose their top scorer with stab wounds.

The papers may have felt unable to give their readers, bewildered by the episode, a fuller picture of what had gone on in the Morley household that night. But that didn't stop *Fortune's Always Hiding*, the aptly titled West Ham fanzine, having a lot of fun at the couple's expense.

A few weeks after the stabbing, it compiled a spoof profile of Trevor and Monica Morley, listing Trevor's favourite films as *Jagged Edge*, *How To Murder Your Wife*, *Fatal Attraction* and *The Wrong Man*, while Monica was described as living in 'Daggernam, Essex' and her favourite album was, of course, *The Final Cut* by Pink Floyd.

In 1996 Ian Bishop discussed the stabbing for the first time in an interview. Bish said that it was up to Morley to tell the truth behind the incident when he saw fit. But he admitted he was upset by wild rumours that circulated about his involvement. 'When you go to Old Trafford and there are 20,000 people singing things, it does get to you,' said Bishop. 'I don't have a problem with gay people, but I was angry for my parents, my wife and kids. I don't want my boy getting stick for it at school.'

If you are going to have a row with your partner it's best not to be caught out in front of ten million viewers. Brentford's Barry Ashby was in a lorra lorra trouble after his girlfriend Alison watched *Blind Date*.

One of the contestants, blonde Tara McNally, told Cilla Black that footballers fancied her.

'What kind of footballers do you attract? And who are they? We want names here. Who have you been out with?' quizzed Cilla.

'That would be telling,' replied Tara coyly.

Cilla carried on her interrogation and eventually Tara blurted, 'Barry Ashby from Brentford.'

Alison was astounded. Despite Barry's red roses and claims that Tara was 'just a friend', Alison vowed to send Barry for an early bath. Particularly after Tara left a message on her answerphone saying that she was only joking. 'He let me watch it and be humiliated in front of all my friends,' raged Alison, suffering from blind hate.

Tara's verdict was: 'I just want people to forget I ever said what I did.' And you can bet Barry Ashby does too.

It's usually the wives who suffer, though, and sadly some footballers have been accused of domestic violence. The pressure of their profession might provide some explanation, but can never excuse their actions. Gazza is the most prominent example, admitting in a tearful confession that he had beaten up girlfriend Sheryl Kyle.

In May 1994, Wimbledon's Andy Clarke was very nearly jailed after he pleaded guilty to causing actual bodily harm to his ex-girlfriend Carmella Gloria, in an attack that left her with a permanent scar above one eye. He escaped jail as he had no previous record of violence, but was fined £1,000 and ordered to pay £1,000 compensation and £300 costs.

Suspecting he was having an affair, Carmella and a friend visited Clarke's house at 7 a.m. and found a strange woman in his bed. She told him they were finished and as she started packing her things Clarke rained punches on her. Carmella reported the attack to the police, who, before arresting Clarke,

rushed her to hospital where she had three stitches in an eye wound.

Inevitably, when the footballer's break-up comes, it's usually messy and public. Arsenal goalkeeper David Seaman failed to keep a clean sheet when he ran off with Debbie Rogers, a hostess at Arsenal who runs her own promotions company, in the summer of 1994. It marked the end of the keeper's ten-year marriage to Sandra, and Debbie's able Seaman gave up his £250,000 Waltham Abbey mansion for her £62,000 flat next to Wormwood Scrubs prison.

The split was bitter, even by footballing standards. When Arsenal lost an FA Cup replay at Sheffield United in January 1996, Susan Seaman phoned Sheffield radio station Hallam FM to say: 'It's Mrs Seaman here, David's ex-wife. I just want to thank him. Our two boys are over the moon that Sheffield United have won.' Ouch.

Debbie later insisted that she felt safe in Seaman's hands: 'The break-up wasn't my fault. David convinced me that even if I hadn't existed, he would have separated from his wife.' Seaman's father-in-law Harry Swift had claimed that Seaman had broken his two sons' hearts by shunning them for six weeks since the split-up.

He also claimed that Seaman's character had changed since he bought a flash sports car and began drinking with Tony Adams and Paul Merson – surely a most unreasonable assertion against these two abstemious characters. Swift had further evidence of Seaman's increasingly dissolute state: 'He became a bit trendy, wearing gold chains and drinking lager out of the bottle.' He'll be growing his hair next.

No doubt stardom does change people, from TV personalities to actors to rock and roll singers. Football exemplifies the perils of fame more than most jobs. Thanks to their high profile players receive offers of love and sex never available to their fans. If the only way Seaman had changed was drinking lager from the bottle, then perhaps he's one of our more down-to-earth heroes.

Teddy Sheringham is another player whose relationship didn't survive his transition to England superstar. In 1994 Sheringham was tackled by the Child Support Agency over maintenance for his six-year-old son Charlie. After Denise Sims and Sheringham had split up after an eight-year relationship, Denise publicly demanded that the £8,000-a-week Spurs striker increase his maintenance payments – he was only making interim payments of £51.50 a week, as he had failed to complete the CSA forms. Sheringham did eventually complete the paperwork and increase his dues.

Denise said that Sheringham had always been a family man, but after success at Millwall he got in with a crowd of footballing friends who had no responsibilities. 'He would go out on a Saturday night and not come home. Then he would go drinking Sunday lunchtime and stay out all day.' But isn't drinking all day written into every striker's contract, Denise?

Poor Denise was left at home holding the baby. 'We fell apart and we had stand-up rows in pubs, and I ended up throwing beer over him more than once.' She even claimed that Teddy's new girlfriend Nicola Smith wouldn't talk to her on the phone and sat outside in the car when he came to pick up Charlie.

In turn, that September Sheringham accused Denise of not letting him see Charlie unless he increased her payments, and declared that, although he missed his son, 'I think I pay enough for Charlie.' Just another story of family life on Planet Football . . .

Still, occasionally something does happen in a marriage split to boost your faith in footballers. In 1994 Everton's Gary Ablett left his wife, two children and his £200,000 home to move in with his lover in a £6,000 caravan with no loo. Anything that causes a player willingly to give up his mock-Tudor paradise must surely be love.

So is love for the soccer star one perpetual round of battling over maintenance payments and fighting off temptations away from home? Nothing but secret love children, love nests with page 3 models, and hacks in the bushes with long-range lenses?

Perhaps there is some hope for romance with the entry of women into positions of power in football. When 23-year-old Karren Brady became chief executive at Birmingham, sexist cynics all said it was only a matter of time before she was sleeping with the players. And indeed, she found herself admiring City striker Paul Peschisolido's first touch.

But somehow Karren carried it off, winning over the Blues fans with her marketing expertise and letting the world know that it was definitely 'luurve' with Paul, who is now her husband. Perhaps they are football's great romantic hope – the one couple who can survive the temptations of mutual stardom and still stay together.

Considering that Brady is a tough boss who sacked all but one of the staff at Birmingham when she arrived, that porn millionaire David Sullivan is her mentor and that she earns at least £50,000 a year from shares in Sport Newspapers, Brady has a surprisingly romantic streak. There's no *Sunday Sport*-style salaciousness for this stunna. 'When I saw him (Peschisolido) the world just stopped for me,' Brady cooed, although the striker was subsequently sold to Stoke as the directors thought it would be less embarrassing for everyone if he were to leave.

The only, predictable, hitch was when Peschisolido's ex-girlfriend in the US, Carmen Garforth, then declared to the press that Brady had stolen the man she planned to wed. 'They'll probably bonk each other crazy for a while, then she'll trade him for some other male bimbo,' was her wrathful verdict.

'It wasn't like I said, "there's a whole team to pick from, who shall I sleep with?"' explained Brady, pointing out they were both young and single. 'Most people do meet their partners in the workplace.' The happy couple have already had a child. 'The beautiful thing about football is that, if you have kids, Paul's home in the afternoon, so you can get someone in until one and then Paul does the rest.' Exactly: if more footballers were responsible for child-minding it would keep them out of the boozers and clubs – although they'd have to be trained not to bottle-feed the baby with lager.

For Peschisolido, it's a case of 'he shoots, he snores' on the household chores front, revealed Brady. 'It really bugs me, because he gets home at one o'clock and sits there and when I get home at nine o'clock he says, "Oh, there's some washing-up for you to do." He's a typical man!'

It might sound like a domestic incident waiting to happen, but let us end with Pesch's words to remind ourselves that not all strikers are faithless opportunists. 'I thought she was one of the most beautiful women I had ever seen . . . I don't think I ever knew what love was until I met her.'

Cue 'As Time Goes By' as Karren and Paul walk off into the sunset . . . and let's just hope he doesn't get distracted by any page 3 girl with a mock-Tudor love nest in Essex.

1. Paul Gascoigne was born in Gateshead on 27 May 1967, the second in a family of four. Hard though it is to believe, he was skinny as a child.

2. Gascoigne was given his not-very-inspiring nickname by a coach at Redheugh Boys' Club, which he joined at eight-and-a-half, eighteen months before he should have done. His dad John lied about his age.

3. In January 1989, after moving from Newcastle United to Tottenham Hotspur amid predictions of super-stardom, Gazza was accused of shattering glasses, bottles and furniture during a Christmas drinking binge at the Swallow Hotel in Waltham Abbey, Essex. 'When he caused all the damage he was legless on brandy,' claimed an unnamed assistant manager. 'He's like George Best without brains,' blasted former Magpies chairman Stan Seymour.

4. Gazza has often been compared to Best, but in November 1990 he called the Manchester United legend 'a drunken fat man' and 'scum bastard'. Best gave as good as he got: 'He wears a number ten jersey. I thought it was his position but it turns out to be his IQ.'

5. Even after the tears of the 1990 World Cup, the Gazza phenomenon had failed to register in the upper reaches of the British judicial system. In October that year, Mr Justice Harman pondered a High Court injunction to prevent an unauthorized biography using the nickname – now trademarked – as its title. 'Who is Gazza?' he asked, prompting general disbelief in the public gallery. 'Do you think Mr Gascoigne is more famous than the Duke of Wellington in 1815?' 'I have to say I think it's possible,' replied counsel Michael Silverleaf with barely restrained incredulity.

6. After the end of a long-term relationship with Gail Pringle, who moved down to London from the North-east to be with her sweetheart, Gazza met mother-of-two Sheryl Kyle in a wine bar in 1990. The following July, Gascoigne was named as 'the other man' in divorce papers filed at Cambridge County Court by her estate agent husband Colin.

7. In September 1990, Gascoigne signed a contract to endorse 'the great smell of Brut'. Instead of sticking to the script given to him for the press conference, he decided to answer off-the-cuff. 'How long have you been using Brut?' asked a journalist. 'I don't,' he replied. 'What aftershave do you use?' 'None. They bring me out in a rash.'

8. Gazza's eating habits have been a source of constant frustration for managers and fitness advisors, even though he knew what he should be stuffing away. 'Fruit is very good for you. I particularly like Terry's Chocolate Oranges,' he wrote in *Gazza: Daft as a Brush*. In December 1994, he checked into the £1,600-a-week Marc Messegue clinic in the Umbrian countryside for a five-day diet of water, vegetable juice and herbs.

9. Gazza's occasionally erratic behaviour has been attributed to many things besides a juvenile sense of humour and low boredom threshold. The writer Ian Hamilton even suggested that he suffered from a form of Tourette's Syndrome, displaying 'an excess of nervous energy, and a great production of strange motions and notions: tics, jerks, mannerisms, grimaces, noises, curses, involuntary imitations and compulsions of all sorts'.

10. Gazza was named Britain's Best Dressed Man of 1990. He turned up at the International Menswear Fair at Earl's Court to receive his award wearing a garish multi-coloured shell suit.

11. In his book *Soccer Skills with Gazza*, Gascoigne wrote about tackling: 'Keep your eye on the ball and try to force your opponent into the first move – let him commit himself before you do. Try and come out of the tackle with a bit of style and panache.'

Shortly afterwards, he failed to follow his own advice and clattered into Nottingham Forest's Gary Charles in the 1991 FA Cup Final – demolishing the cruciate ligaments in his right knee.

12. In September 1991, just four months after that fateful final, Gazza fractured the same right kneecap during a scuffle at Walker's night-club in Newcastle. He was carted off to hospital for a third operation.

13. Diplomacy has never been among Gazza's strongest features. In October 1992, an Oslo TV crew covering the World Cup qualifier at Wembley asked him for a pre-match comment. 'Fuck off Norway,' he responded. Gascoigne later claimed he did not know that the camera or microphone were live. Three months later, he was fined £9,000 for belching on an Italian TV programme. Questions about his behaviour were raised in the Italian parliament.

14. In August 1993, Gazza unveiled his latest lapse in taste – a set of hair extensions, which cost £295. Nineteen days later, after much derision, he replaced them with a £5 short-back-and-sides.

15. Gazza proposed to Sheryl in March 1994, over dinner at London's three-star restaurant Le Gavroche. The evening began with best seats in the house at the West End musical *Carousel*, followed by a drive to the Mayfair eaterie in a limousine strewn with red roses. Dessert was a heart-shaped cake with 'Will you marry me?' written in icing.

16. Gascoigne's tempestuous relationship with Sheryl reached its lowest point in May 1994, when the couple split up. Two months later, he confessed to *News of the World* reporter Rebekeh Wade that for two years he had beaten his blonde fiancée, 'grabbing her very hard by the arms, putting my head against her, stabbing at her, pulling her head back, grabbing her head . . . all for no reason'. He admitted:

'I've been a violent bastard and a coward and I want the world to know it'.

17. Gazza bought Sheryl a £28,000 fuel-injected BMW saloon as a Christmas present – but in September 1994 she was fined £400 and given six penalty points on her licence. He had forgotten to tell her that the car was only insured for three months.

18. In March 1995, Gazza agreed to pay £5,000 damages and £2,500 costs in an out-of-court settlement with railway signalman John Beach. Gascoigne had felled Beach with two punches in the face after he had accidentally stumbled into his sister Lindsay in Newcastle four years earlier. At the time, Gazza was conditionally discharged after pleading guilty to assault.

19. In his quieter moments, Gazza likes to write poems. One notable effort, penned before Lazio's derby match against AS Roma, included the lines:

> 'When we are together
> We will be the best
> We will take on Rome
> And the fucking rest.
> Then we'll take on Juve
> Sampdoria, Napoli too
> We will shit on all of them
> Especially that Roma crew.'

Eat your heart out, Ted Hughes.

20. When Gascoigne first appeared in Rome's Stadio Olimpico, Lazio fans hoisted a celebratory banner: 'Gazza's boys are here, shag women, drink beer'. But patchy performances and a succession of injuries saw the mood change. 'Paul Gascoigne, you are a big poofter,' read a later message. Undeterred, Gazza signed for Glasgow Rangers – and in the summer of 1996, he finally married Sheryl, won the Scottish Footballer of the Year Award, and helped England to the semi-finals of the European Championship. The tragi-comic tale of Paul Gascoigne, England's most naturally gifted player since the 1960s, is far from over.

14

Rich Man, Poor Man, Beggar Man, Bankrupt

'For all its popularity among footballers, players make very poor gamblers.'

Tommy Tynan

When Manchester United signed Martin Buchan from Aberdeen in 1972, it seemed that every quip about tight-fisted Scotsmen was about to be proved true. It was Buchan who gave George Best 2p to use the telephone – and asked for it back the following morning. It was Buchan, so Willie Morgan reckoned, who had refused to phone his wife from Heathrow when jetting off on an international trip until he'd passed through customs – because the calls were duty-free inside the barrier.

Martin Buchan was a player who knew his own mind, and wasn't afraid to speak it. While the United squad waited at Old Trafford for the coach to take them to their usual Friday night stopover, the Mottram Hall Hotel in Cheshire, trainer Malcolm Musgrove decided that a draw for room-sharing would help prevent any cliques forming. All went well until it was Buchan's turn to dip his hand into the hat and learn who would be snoring in the bed alongside his. He refused. Musgrove made it an order. Buchan's response was to utter sixteen words which challenged the very first rule of admission to soccer's

masonic fraternity: 'No. I do not believe in sweepstakes. I do not spend my money on horse racing.'

Straight-as-a-die Buchan had mistakenly thought they were having a sweep on the 2.10 at Kempton Park, but the damage was done. He had outed himself. Here was that little-known creature, a footballer who didn't gamble.

No one would ever accuse the classy United defender of being less than committed on the pitch. It's just that off it, his aversion to the turf was a rarity. As that lower-division roamer in search of goals, Tommy Tynan, put it, gambling goes with the lifestyle because footballers are competitive people playing a competitive game. Win on the dogs or the gee-gees, and it's a way of getting one-up on your team-mates. But it's not only players who are partial to such pecuniary pugilism – managers, even managing directors, will strike a wager on anything which moves. Or, in the case of Dave Beasant, doesn't.

Wimbledon MD Sam Hammam would turn up at the club's muddy training ground wearing his suit and leather shoes, to bet then first-team keeper Beasant that he could score more than three penalties out of ten against him. Fail, and he would stick £100 into the players' pool. Even if Beasant had kept goal with both hands tied behind his back – and critics would say that he often did – there was never much risk of him losing.

On long away trips, some players sleep, others watch videos or play computer games, a few read books or the papers. But most play cards. Plymouth's geographical isolation means countless four- and five-hour coach journeys, and during Tommy Tynan's final spell with the Pilgrims in the late 1980s there were two card schools going – the heavy school and the mediocre school, membership determined by size of wallet. It was no surprise if, over a ten-hour game, someone lost £50 – although that was small change compared to what was in the kitty at Liverpool. When Tynan went with the Reds on tour to Sweden, there were £800 pots on the table. One player lost £1,000 in a single session.

Too much spare time and too much spare money – that's the root of the intimate relationship between footballers and the gents of turf, track and casino. While his wife was out at work, Tynan would sit in the bookies' between the end of training at 1 p.m. and 3.30 p.m., the time when he had to collect his kids from school. David Platt sometimes found himself nipping down to the bank to finance a bet simply because he was bored at home during his early career with Crewe Alexandra. But although Tynan never got carried away – a tenner or £20 maximum on a horse – Platt, in contrast, used to gamble what he called 'hurting money – cash I couldn't afford to lose'. He would stand in the betting shop wagering 50p doubles to make his loot last all after-

noon. 'In those days,' he confessed, 'a fiver to win thirty quid was a big deal. The ironic thing is that when you've only got a fiver to your name you can guarantee the horse will get beaten by a short head.'

The safest wager of all, however, is that every dressing-room in England contains at least one player whose fingers have been burned by the bookmakers. God-daddy to them all is the man who, legend has it, was once so desperate for a flutter that he played Snakes and Ladders for £50 a go while waiting for the betting shop to open.

Stan Bowles placed his first punt at the age of fifteen, £2 on a 12–1 shot at the White City dog track. It won, and the £24 which ended up in his pocket turned an exploratory kiss into a lifelong love affair. However, it's one of life's eternal truths that romance is a disastrously expensive business. Bowles once won £18,000 in a single day, but how many punters close their gambling career in credit? His old Queens Park Rangers partner-in-mischief Don Shanks wished Bowles had been a big-stakes gambler, sticking a wad on a single horse, watching it lose then retiring hurt, but that wasn't his way: 'He wanted to bet all day. He just loved those places.' Loftus Road regulars of two decades ago insist that his conversations with members of the crowd were only to find out what won the last race at Windsor.

If he could have passed a betting shop like he could pass a football, so the joke went, Stan would have been a millionaire. Instead, the bookies' door was always open and Bowles blew two marriages and £750,000 inside.

But Stan the Man was not the only star from football's maverick era to fall victim to the allure of large bets and long odds.

'Jinky' Jim Smith was Newcastle's first £100,000 buy when he moved from Aberdeen to St James' Park in 1969. He was a winger who tended to decorate rather than dominate games, but after his playing days were ended by a knee injury, £15,000 from a testimonial should have helped set him up for life. Instead, Smith opted to adorn the inside of betting shops.

He frittered £27,000 in two years, his sports business collapsed, his wife left him and he fetched up in a bankruptcy court. There, he admitted gambling with creditors' money and received a four-month suspended jail sentence.

Peter Lorimer was of that same ilk, although it was force rather than finesse which typified his game. The Scottish

THE BEST HAND: GEORGE HOLDS ALL THE ACES.

international was a key member of Don Revie's Championship-winning side at Leeds United, with a 75 m.p.h. shot measured as the hardest in the country. But following a career which brought him 238 goals, and after testimonials in 1979 and 1985 had each raised around £25,000, the Official Receiver announced in 1991 that any money due to Lorimer should be paid directly to the Receiver to help recover debts of £40,000.

Problems for the former Elland Road hero began when he went to play in Canada in the early 1980s. He claimed he was owed £18,000 when he left, and borrowed from the banks while waiting for it to arrive. But the money never did come, and Lorimer started betting on the horses to try and cut his losses. He simply lost more. By the time he had paid his gambling debts, only £2,000 of the proceeds from his second testimonial remained. Lorimer reckoned he wagered away a cool million – and admitted that he loved it at the time. A decade on, though, it's a different story: 'People call me a frigging idiot and I have got to agree with them. I am.'

George Best has been called far worse, but gambling has always taken second place to boozing in the headlines which have accompanied every move of soccer's original lad done bad. In September 1974, Best and Colin Dunne, one of his co-partners in Slack Alice's night-club in Manchester, turned up at a city casino for a gentle flutter on the dice. Neither had more than £200 on them, and they lost that pretty quickly. So they started 'calling' the bets – even though they didn't have any money – and by 2.15 a.m. were £17,000 down. The house limit was £100 a throw, but Dunne asked for that to be doubled to give them a chance of squaring

up – or, of course, plunging even deeper into debt. The club agreed. Incredibly, from 2.20 a.m. until 4 a.m. the duo didn't throw a single losing roll. Instead of stumbling into the autumnal dawn seventeen grand lighter, they swanned out of the casino £9,000 in profit. Poor 'Jinky' Smith and Peter Lorimer would have killed for even a share of Best's good fortune.

In purely monetary terms, Newcastle United winger Keith Gillespie's spree at the bookies' in October 1995 takes some beating. It was reported that he blew the price of a house in a single afternoon, losing £47,000 in a desperate bid to recoup some of the £15,000 he had lost during four earlier disastrous days spent playing the dogs and horses. As the inevitable 'close friend' told the *Sun*, Gillespie 'was betting with professional gamblers' stakes but behaving like a mug punter. Once he started losing, he made the classic mistake of trying to chase his bets.' The run reached a grisly climax when the Northern Ireland international starlet staked almost a week's wages – £4,000 – on 5–2 favourite 'Innocent George' in the 4.05 race at Bangor: £3,000 that the horse would win, and another £1,000 on a first-second prediction. 'Innocent George' didn't even finish in the first three, and innocent Keith found bookie Mickey Arnott demanding that Gillespie settle his debts. Prison officer dad Harry was staggered at the sum his wayward son had allegedly run up: 'The most I've seen him bet was a fiver. I fear he may need help.' But Gillespie, who disputed the figures quoted, paid his dues within a fortnight, and vowed never to gamble again.

It's a lesson Steve Claridge would have done well to heed. The much-travelled striker confessed that he once had to squat in houses because he had frittered away his earnings at the bookies. 'It started when I was at Luton Town,' revealed the player valued at £4 million by former Birmingham City boss Barry Fry. 'I did £35,000 in two months and pretty well lived in a betting shop. But that's just the tip of the iceberg. I went to Cheltenham racecourse and over a four-day period I did five grand a day. I just couldn't stop. I went training once with £4,500 in my pocket and ran out of petrol on the way home because I had spent the lot. How much money do you think I've done? I've done it all. It's all gone on the horses – at least a quarter of a million.' Claridge has, however, managed to curb his penchant for a punt: 'Thankfully I've been on the wagon a little bit. If I start again I am going to Gamblers Anonymous.'

Many players have put off joining GA because none of their team-mates would take a bet on how long they'd stay a member. But if the organization for compulsive punters ever needed extra office space, it could do worse than contact the Football Association to ask if there were rooms for hire at Lancaster Gate. After all, FA and GA have had plenty of clients in common down the years.

Drink is the traditional enemy of the professional footballer. But according to Don Shanks, if booze is a danger then try going to the bookies' with a week's wages on a Friday afternoon. You want an account? You want credit? No problem, sir. 'At the race tracks you meet owners and trainers and it's part of the glamour. You think you're on the inside – but you're not. It's a great illusion and very tempting to think you can beat the organization.' Shanks did, when a run of good luck on the gee-gees made him a Hong Kong dollar millionaire after his career in

England was over. But he blew the lot – around £120,000 – within a year.

It was at Wimbledon dog track that Shanks bumped into Kerry Dixon, and in early 1990 he warned the striker, who was then playing for Chelsea, that he was behaving 'like a desperate punter, chasing money that he'd already lost'. Ten months later, Dixon had run up a debt of £47,000 with Victor Chandler, and the bookmaker accepted half that amount in settlement.

It was the dogs that caused trouble for former Leyton Orient defender Terry Howard, too. 'It's no secret that I had a big problem with gambling,' he admitted. 'It took hold of my life and for six or seven years it ruled everything.' Living on the fringes of Essex, Howard was in greyhound utopia: 'I could go to Hackney Wick in the afternoon, Romford on a Monday, Wednesday and Friday and Walthamstow on Tuesday, Thursday and Saturday. I often did! I was better known for my gambling than my football. People would find out what I did and exclaim: "I didn't know you were a footballer."'

Kenny Sansom didn't need anyone else to tell him he was a mug. The former Arsenal skipper, capped eighty-six times by England, said it himself. 'I used to be a bad, mad punter,' he confessed in his diary of the 1986–87 season. 'I admit that there were times when I couldn't let a day go by without a trip to the bookies.' When I was at Crystal Palace, I lost £800 in a day.' On one occasion, he even blew his wife's bingo winnings.

The Eagles' then-boss Terry Venables advised the player dubbed the 'Potty Punter' by his team-mates to contact Gamblers' Anonymous. It was an idea which might have helped Tony Cascarino, too. The Chelsea fans called him Tony Cantscorino for his singular lack of prowess in front of goal, but Tony Cantquitpokerino would have served just as well had the supporters known the truth about the target of their venom.

Cascarino and cards first communed at the family home, where his Italian grand-dad presided over money games with his seven kids. By the time he'd made it to Millwall, where he was earning £500 a week, Cas was picking up double that amount at poker. He would keep five grand in ready money stashed around the house, and was always the first to leg it from the Lions' training ground to be ready for the day's real action at 1 p.m. Games would often last for ten hours, with the Republic of Ireland international chomping on a Big Mac or Chinese takeaway instead of fare more suited to a well-honed athlete. When Cascarino went on holiday to the States with his wife Sarah and family, it was simply a chance to play the casinos – forty-eight hours in the Golden Nugget at Las Vegas, a 24-hour non-stop marathon in Atlantic City.

Sometimes he won – up to £5,000 over a couple of sessions. Sometimes he lost – a two-year-old Sierra Ghia went to one of the car dealers in his south-east London card school to help pay off a debt. But once he ended up staring down the barrels of three sawn-off shotguns.

There was ten grand on the table when five men burst into his gambling den brandishing guns and baseball bats. They ripped the phones out, took everyone's watch, and calmly scooped up £10,000 in cash. 'It was like something out of a film,' said a shaken Cascarino afterwards. 'I tried stuffing a few notes back in my pocket – a pretty daft thing to do with a sawn-off shotgun pointing at me.' There were unproven reports that the villains were a group of Millwall fans, trying to claim back some of the money they'd wasted watching their hapless centre-forward in action.

Shaken maybe, but still not stirred to do anything about it, Cascarino came back to London to play poker after his £1.5 million transfer to Aston Villa, and it wasn't until his efforts on the pitch had deteriorated even further and he returned from the 1994 World Cup as the player no one wanted, even on a free transfer from Chelsea, that he threw in his hand for the last time. 'I have let the best years of my career slip away from me by not giving 100 per cent,' he lamented. But unlike others before him, Cascarino got another chance. At the age of thirty-one, he crossed La Manche to join Marseilles and became the French club's top scorer in his first season. Those who had seen him failing to hit the proverbial barn door on the Chelsea training ground were understandably nonplussed.

Perhaps Tony Cascarino should have bought shares in Waddingtons with the money he wasted shuffling their products: taking a stake in a horse is surely a better way of indulging an interest in the turf than lining a bookie's pocket. The then Manchester City and Republic of Ireland target man Niall Quinn purchased a two-year-old colt, 'Cois na Tine', for £15,000, but doubled that figure in prize money when it won its first four races. In 1993, Quinn sold his horse to an American stable for a cool £250,000. Another owner, Mike Channon, was once on the wrong end of a volley of half-time verbals from manager Lawrie McMenemy when he trooped into the dressing-room. Channon, blasted the boss, was a disgrace to his profession. Wrong, retorted the Southampton striker: football was only his hobby. Horse-racing was his profession.

It was through Mick Channon that Peter Shilton became interested in racing. After all, the goalkeeper who made a then world record 125 appearances for his country, and was still earning £250,000 a year as a player for Derby County well after his fortieth birthday, could hardly have been short of a bob or two for a little relaxing investment away from the game. The names of the horses he owned – 'Between the Sticks' and 'Shot Stopper', for example – reflected Shilton's image as one of the greatest keepers ever to play for England. After he had been surprisingly beaten by a long-range effort against Uruguay in 1990, John Barnes said: 'Shilton criticizes himself for leaking goals that the combined talents of Clemence, Banks, Southall and Grobbelaar in the same net couldn't keep out.'

As a boy secure in the knowledge of his desired destiny but less sure of his physical potential to achieve it, Shilts suspended himself from the stair banisters of his parents' house with weights attached to his ankles. His obvious brilliance – and arms two inches longer than average for someone of his height – won him a place in the Leicester City team in 1966, at the age of sixteen, and four years later he donned an England jersey for the first time in a 3–1 win over East Germany. His reflexes and positional sense were outstanding, but what Shilton most excelled at was organizing the defenders in front of him. Keeping a clean sheet was, of

'IT'S ALL RIGHT, MR SHILTON, YOU CAN LEAVE AFTERWARDS . . .'

'ONE HOUSE IN CHILWORTH, GOING, GOING, GONE...'

course, crucial to his team – but personal reputation mattered as much, if not more. Larry Lloyd gave away a penalty when the pair were playing for Nottingham Forest in a pre-season friendly against Athletic Bilbao, and suddenly found his keeper's accusing finger thrust in his face. Half-time fisticuffs were avoided only when Forest's assistant manager Peter Taylor separated the feuding twosome after Lloyd had grabbed Shilton by the throat.

When the man who made a staggering 1,379 appearances between the sticks for country and seven clubs went into print, perfection was his Holy Grail. 'Most keepers who have natural powers of anticipation will see dangers before they happen and be able to react early,' he wrote in *Shilton on Goalkeeping*. However, it was advice which he proved disastrously unable to follow away from the security of his penalty box.

Away trips with England are just as tedious as those with clubs. The blazers might be a little smarter, but otherwise it's the same wearying round of travel, training and killing time in hotels. And that means yet more card schools. Malcolm Macdonald was an international colleague of Shilton's in the early 1970s, and always keen for a game to pass the time. But not for the stakes his keeper wanted. For Macdonald, gin rummy or cribbage for a few pence a point was enough – but for Shilts, the risk had to be higher. Team-mates would hide and organize quiet games for sensible stakes, yet Shilton, his much-vaunted reflexes to the fore, would discover where they had gone and demand to be included. And then, instead of the pot containing loose change and a few pound notes, it would suddenly fill with fivers, tenners and twenties.

'It was always go for broke with Shilts,' lamented Macdonald. 'And that was usually the way he finished – broke! There was no reasoning to the way he played cards. He never worked the percentages, he would have a go even when the odds were stacked against him.' And when he lost, as he often did, he refused to let the other players go to bed. He once owed Macdonald around £400, but was desperate to play one-card turnovers for £20 a shot. Macdonald claimed he took pity: 'I began stacking winning hands just to reduce the debt to sensible levels.'

Competitive people playing competitive games: Shilton reigned supreme in one, and thought he should be king of the other. The bookies were opponents to be beaten too. Macdonald recalled that whenever a horse came up in conversation – and in an England squad containing Channon, Kevin Keegan, Colin Todd and Emlyn Hughes, it often did – 'up would go the antennae, out would come the bundle of notes and on would go the bet'. At Southampton, after the players had eaten their pre-match lunch, Shilton would ring his bookmaker, give the name of a horse and finish with the enigmatic phrase, 'the usual'. He once struck it spectacularly lucky, winning £36,000 on a four-horse accumulator at Cheltenham.

Peter Shilton MBE, OBE, was a goalkeeper by royal appointment. And when the muscles finally started to lose their elasticity and the reflexes their panther-like edge, he sought the move into management which would offer status to match the number on his shirt: one. He didn't come cheap, though. Several clubs baulked at his wage demands, until in March 1992 Plymouth Argyle chairman Dan McCauley saw a high-profile coach as the key to launching the Pilgrims on a quest for soccer's land of plenty.

'When we appointed him, we wanted to put Argyle on a different plateau,' said the hard-nosed engineering millionaire.

Never mind that Shilton's ultimate ambitions would demand a more exalted location than Home Park – Plymouth seemed the perfect club to launch his career in management. And what was a £125,000 signing-on fee and matching salary if he pulled the team out of the Second Division?

Yet Dan was to discover that the legend he appointed was different from the man he got. Instead of a dynamic manager capitalizing on his legendary status by luring good players to the West Country, Shilts spent much of his time on the phone to his chairman asking for money. He needed it to cover what he vaguely termed 'cashflow problems'. The club advanced him a total of £100,000 in seven separate instalments.

It wasn't only McCauley whom Shilton tapped. In 1992, he borrowed £40,000 from the PFA's benevolent fund – a sum ten times larger than the Association's usual limit. And that same year, Derby County owner Lionel Pickering provided him with a £72,000 advance on a book which was never written. But it was two years later that the financial house of cards which Shilton had built around himself finally came tumbling down.

In August 1994, his home in Chilworth, near Southampton, was repossessed by the Abbey National Building Society. It was sold four months afterwards for around half its estimated value of £400,000. Nor was this the first time that Shilton had struggled to pay his mortgage: a year earlier, he had run the risk of repossession when the account was six months in arrears. Two years before that, he faced a similar threat when he owed £10,000 on a house in Leicestershire.

Then, in September, Plymouth's assistant manager John McGovern quit the

PETER SHILTON: GOALKEEPER BY ROYAL APPOINTMENT.

club, claiming he could no longer work with the man who had been a team-mate during Nottingham Forest's glory days in the 1980s. McGovern lent Shilton £7,000 of his own money in July 1993, a sum which both men agreed was to be repaid, with interest, within six months. But it wasn't. More than a year later, McGovern had still not received any of the loan back – and he walked out talking of betrayal by someone he counted as a friend. Dan McCauley was by this time getting desperate: 'I don't get any hassles from anyone else apart from Peter Shilton. I've got one big hassle and it's him. If I'd known we were going to have as many problems off the field with him, we'd have tried a different manager.'

As Christmas 1994 drew near, Shilton's early presents brought little seasonal cheer. Racehorse trainer Martin Pipe issued him with a winding-up petition for unpaid bills of around £3,000 dating back four years. The Inland Revenue pressed Plymouth for £50,000 tax still owing from Shilts' signing-on fee – and the club, right up on its overdraft limit, refused to bail out its beleaguered boss and passed the bill on to him. And on 17 December, the first team suffered its heaviest defeat for twenty-two years, going down 7–0 at Brentford. The fans, having watched a side

'SO THE CHEQUE'S IN THE POST, IS IT?' JOHN MCGOVERN WONDERS WHAT FRIENDS ARE REALLY FOR.

which reached the play-offs the season before now struggling in the bottom five, made their feelings on the affair blatantly clear. 'Bye-bye Shilton,' they sang.

'Anticipation,' wrote England's finest net-minder since Gordon Banks in *Shilton on Goalkeeping*, 'means foreseeing every possible situation that may arise.' But when Plymouth issued an ultimatum – pay the £50,000 tax or face suspension from the club – even Shilton must have known that the game was up. As the new year dawned, he arrived a quarter-of-an-hour late for a board meeting. Just six

minutes later, he emerged to announce that he had been suspended.

McCauley was more puzzled than angry, wondering how a man earning large sums of money could be in such a financial mess. 'I've never put it down to horse racing,' he said. 'Never. But when you look at the size of the amounts there must be something behind it. It's hard to imagine where his money goes.'

Stan Bowles, Jim Smith, Peter Lorimer and Kenny Sansom must have wondered the same over the years. Lads done bad? Not really. Sad, more like.

15

Always Crashing in the Same Car

'In no condition to drive I insisted on taking my car and refused the offer of a lift from Norman's [Whiteside's] wife. About half a mile from home I lost control completely, the car took off, mounted a footpath, went through a garden, then another one and came to a halt in the grounds of a third . . . When I came round someone was trying to drag me from the wreckage . . . When I moved my head blood gushed out everywhere.'

Paul McGrath

Footballers love fast cars. Visit any training ground and you'll find the players' car park stuffed full of the latest, most expensive motors. All the players at top clubs seem to drive either a BMW, Mercedes or flash Audi – and at Manchester United the players even have their initials painted on their personalized parking spaces.

The flash motor is of infinite importance to the modern footballer. In the macho world of soccer a big player has a big car, and the latest top-of-the-range model helps attract the latest model (page 3 version). At the age of nineteen Liverpool's Robbie Fowler was living at home with his mum but driving an Audi 80. At twenty-two the Reds' Steve McManaman was driving a BMW 318i. While the rest of us worry about keeping our jobs and finding a car that actually

works, the young footballer only has to consider outdoing his team-mates' vehicles.

According to Robbie Fowler, 'Stevie's big headache at the moment is not being able to upgrade his motor to a BMW M3 convertible because his age and profession would make the insurance premium a whacking £11,000!' Poor dear.

The only problem with this car culture is that the players aren't too good at looking after their prized automobiles, particularly when they've had a few drinks. Give young men sudden adulation, free sponsored cars with their names emblazoned on the side plus massive wage packets and the result is inevitable.

Famous footballers are reluctant to travel on public transport for fear of meeting intrusive or belligerent fans. So when the post-training drinking session is over, the temptation to drive home when they shouldn't is always there. The result is usually unwelcome attention from the law for the lads and endless hours of amusement for the fans.

A Bookable Offence

The casual observer might be forgiven for concluding that every professional footballer has a stipulation in his contract insisting that he be convicted at least once for speeding and/or drink-driving. No sooner do they receive their complimentary club car than the trouble begins.

A few years ago the Campaign Against Drunk-Driving listed a Boozers United XI of the footballers convicted in the previous two years, and called for tougher penalties on the stars to set an example, pointing out that 25,000 people a year are killed or injured through drink-driving.

The rogues gallery included Bryan Robson (Man United, three-year ban), John Bailey (Bristol City, seven-year ban), Alan Sunderland (ex-Arsenal, three-year ban), Tommy Caton (Charlton, three-year ban), Mick Quinn (Portsmouth, twenty-one days' jail), Gary Briggs (Oxford, three-year ban), Billy Whitehurst (Hull, eighteen-month ban), John Trewick (Birmingham, one-year ban), Brian Kilcline (Coventry, eighteen-month ban), Paul Merson (Arsenal, eighteen-month ban) and John Barnwell (Walsall manager, one-year ban).

Today, fans could complete their own Fantasy League of drink-driving sides.

Motoring (and particularly drink-driving) offences are now so common that it requires a certain flair in his convictions for a player to differentiate himself from his team-mates. Take the court case involving Gary Charles, then at Nottingham Forest.

In April 1993, Charles, an England international, was so drunk after a car crash that he could only crawl upstairs on his hands and knees. Charles' neighbours said they saw his Ford Escort XR3i 'kangarooing' along their cul-de-sac, before it smashed into another parked car. After the crash his neighbours found Charles in the car, but he got out without saying a word, and the police were called. 'It was clear he'd had a considerable amount to drink,' remarked prosecutor Gilbert Barnatt.

Charles was incapable of walking when the police arrived at his home. 'I saw him lying on a couch. He rolled off and crawled upstairs. He was in a drunken state,' said WPC Amanda Orchard. She asked the Forest flyer to come downstairs, 'but he was abusive and refused'.

How he could have benefited from the advice of his manager Brian Clough: 'Hey! Young man! Watch what you say!' But sadly there was no Cloughie present to protect Charles from engaging his mouth before his brain was in gear. When WPC Orchard told Charles that he was arrested on suspicion of drink-driving and pointed out that the engine in Charles' car was still warm, the merry man of Nottingham came out with the memorable riposte, 'My willy's warm but that doesn't mean to say I've used it!'

Needless to say, this line of reasoning did not impress the WPC. Charles then twice refused to take a breath-test and claimed to police that he had only got in the car to get some tapes (no doubt by INXS). He also claimed that a friend had been driving his car at the time. 'I refused to give a breath-test because I had not done anything wrong,' was how Charles explained his actions. For some strange reason Charles' version of events didn't convince the magistrates, and he was fined £1,600 for failing to give a breath-test without reasonable excuse. (Although surely not being able to stand up is a reasonable excuse? Strange business, the law.)

After his embarrassing court case and a newspaper article saying he no longer wanted to play for Brian Clough, Charles was dropped for the next Forest match. Cloughie was driven to despair. 'We don't need the kind of bad publicity he has attracted,' said Clough's assistant Ronnie Fenton, and, after a willy or won't he move saga, the young man was despatched to Derby.

West Ham's Ian Bishop managed to complete his drink-driving offence in real style. He was stopped by police in central London after leaving an ITV *Telethon* yard of ale contest. He was three times over the legal limit and was told he would have been jailed if it had not been his first offence. As Bishop might well have replied: 'Yes, but it was for charidee, hofficer . . . ' When asked what his favourite drink was in West Ham's programme a few months later, Bishop cheekily replied, 'Yard of ale!'

Bishop was only following in the wrong-way-down-a-one-way-street traditions of an earlier West Ham player, Keith Robson, who was adept at the old borrowing your team-mate's car scam. Trevor Brooking remembers a 1970s incident involving winger Robson at the Room At The Top club in Ilford. 'If he had a couple of bevvies he was bad news, very aggressive and he liked a gamble,' Brooking says of the man he affectionately calls 'Mad Robbo'.

At the trendy seventies disco Robson, who'd been banned from driving, asked a team-mate if he could borrow his car keys, as the disco was too noisy and he wanted to talk to the girl he'd just met. Almost inevitably, Robson could not resist taking his girlfriend for a test drive in his mate's motor. 'He'd had a few bevvies and was later stopped for driving the wrong way down a one-way street, and was pretty aggressive afterwards,' recalls Brooking. West Ham's general manager Ron Greenwood then had to go to court to plead successfully for a non-custodial sentence for the winger, so that he could help West Ham's perpetual relegation fight.

Sometimes players simply go for huge quantities of alcohol to impress their peers. Manchester United's Norman Whiteside was a mere four times over the legal limit when he was banned from driving for two years in 1990. At least he wasn't speeding, though. Whiteside was creeping home at 15–20 m.p.h. on a busy motorway after a post-training drinking session. A cunning plan worthy of Baldrick, Norman.

Just imagine the scene. If the sight of Manchester United's legendary hardman and feared drinking companion of Paul McGrath and Bryan Robson crawling at 15 m.p.h. along a motorway didn't raise the suspicions of even the dimmest policeman, then surely nothing ever would. (Rule one for aspiring police officers: footballers only ever drive slowly when drunk.)

Another way of enlivening the mundane footballing drink-driving offence is to involve your wife. In 1989 both Liverpool's John Aldridge and his missus Joan drunkenly abused police after their car crashed into a lamppost.

The couple had been drinking at a

Grand National party and were arrested shortly after Aldridge had starred in a five-goal win over Sheffield Wednesday. Joan was found guilty of drink-driving, banned for a year and fined £250. John was found not guilty of drink-driving. Charges of being drunk and disorderly against both were dropped after they agreed to be bound over for the sum of £200 for a year. (Aldridge's defence might also have pleaded that he was one of the few footballers in the country actually with his wife.)

As well as the nature of their offences, the excuses players give for their motoring madness often show more imagination and creativity than their performances on the pitch. Take this explanation from Mark Wright's solicitor in 1990, after Wright's BMW was stopped in Derby in the early hours of the morning.

As a policeman got out of his patrol car to question the former Derby, erm, stopper, he suddenly sped off in his 145 m.p.h. motor, moving so fast that his tyres were spinning. The stunned policemen realized that pursuit was useless and later picked up Wright at his house – after having to knock on his door for half an hour.

In court, Wright's solicitor explained how difficult it was for a footballer when he was considered to be public property. 'He believed he was being stopped, as he had been on a number of other occasions, by police who just wanted to speak to him about football. He thought, "No, I don't want to talk to you," and drove away.'

Despite this impressive defence – conjuring up pictures of police cars throughout the Midlands screeching along roads with their sirens wailing, in frenzied pursuit of the then Derby manager Arthur Cox's latest tactical nuances – Wright

admitted failing to stop, refusing a breath test, having no insurance and driving carelessly, and was fined £1,550.

Of course, unlike Wright, some footballers do simply run off after being tackled. When Sheffield United's Billy Whitehurst, returning from a training session in Sheffield, was stopped by Hull police in 1991 for suspected drink-driving – his Ford Fiesta was swerving with a traffic cone trapped beneath it – he asked if he could relieve himself. The police agreed – and the burly striker promptly did a Blades runner, moving faster than had ever been observed on the football pitch. Perhaps he thought the police just wanted to discuss United's relegation prospects. Billy the Kid gave himself up the next day and was later fined £250 for failing to provide a breath-test and obstructing the police, but escaped a driving ban.

A subtler tactic for dodging the blame was employed by Huddersfield's Tony Kenworthy in 1990. When he wrote off his Datsun in a head-on crash on the way home from a greyhound meeting he lied to police, claiming that his car had been stolen and crashed by the thief. The hapless Huddersfield star was jailed for nine months for perverting the course of justice and banned for two years for reckless driving.

Like his fellow international Mark Wright, Captain Marvel, aka former England skipper and current Middlesbrough manager Bryan Robson, also produced an international-class excuse when he was found guilty of drink-driving in 1988. Robson's lawyer detailed the demanding life of Bryan: 'That day Mr Robson had been involved in a number of arduous business meetings. These culminated in a meal at which he con-

Top 10 Excuses for Motoring Offences

1. Thought the police just wanted to talk about Derby's chances so didn't stop – Mark Wright, fined £1,550 for failing to stop for police and provide a breath specimen, careless driving and having no insurance.

2. Was rushing to buy a guard dog after being burgled – Graeme Souness, fined £600 for speeding.

3. Wasn't used to driving his Land Rover – Paul Merson, fined £300 for careless driving.

4. Was eager to get home to his wife – Derek Ferguson, fined £2,300 and banned for a year for driving the wrong way round a roundabout and injuring three Sunderland team-mates.

5. Only got in the car to get some cassettes – Gary Charles, fined £1,600 for failing to give a breath-test.

6. His drinks might have been laced – Tony Adams, jailed for four months for drink-driving.

7. Had been to several arduous business meetings – Bryan Robson, three-year ban for drink-driving.

8. Does a lot of work for charity – Ray Houghton, fined £2,800 after admitting drink-driving.

9. Was worried about being breathalysed – Jan Molby, jailed for three months for reckless driving and impersonating Stirling Moss.

10. Threw litter at the cat to avoid running over it – George Georgiou, fined £100 for failing to keep Britain tidy.

sumed alcohol.' Ah, the sacrifices the budding entrepreneur has to make for commerce . . .

Police had found Robson on a slip-road of the M62, standing by his car after it had run out of petrol. He failed a breath-test and admitted refusing to give a specimen for analysis – clearly no one was going to take the p*** out of Robbo. The Manchester United icon, who had been banned for a year for drink-driving in 1982, was barred for another three years.

Incredibly, a month after Robson was given the red card, the Department of Transport asked him to spearhead a new drink-drive blitz. Not surprisingly, his manager Alex Ferguson blocked the move. But that wasn't the end of Robbo's troubles. While he was banned he had to employ a chauffeur, Lawrence Sellstrom, who then revealed to the Press details of his boss's boozy days and nights out.

Robson would go out to get 'bladdered', claimed Sellstrom – and once he was so drunk he fell out of the car. Many of Robson's drinking sessions were with Paul McGrath and Norman Whiteside, said Sellstrom, although the conscientious England captain never drank after Wednesday night when he had a Saturday game.

Robson's three-year ban was lifted at the end of the second year, in 1990, after a merciful court heard that the ban had hit his business and charity work. (Just a thought, but isn't the whole point of drink-driving bans to inconvenience the miscreants involved?) His lawyer revealed that poor Robbo was forced 'to rely on family, friends and public transport to get around'. Anti-drink-driving campaigners were infuriated by the magistrate's leniency. As for the contrite England skipper, he was going to drive, but only if his wife

Denise, who now had the car keys, let him. Which presumably meant Denise was now carrying a breathalyser in her handbag.

When all other excuses fail to get a result, there's always the one employed by Ray Houghton's lawyer in January 1993: 'This is totally out of character for someone who takes great care of his physical fitness . . . and has contributed to society by working for charity.' Unimpressed by this portrayal of a latter-day Bob Geldof in footballer's kit, the magistrates banned Houghton from the roads for two years and fined him £2,800 after he admitted drink-driving while three times over the legal limit after an Aston Villa Christmas party.

Sometimes it's simply best to say nothing. Frank Worthington, a man who once nearly drove £4 million worth of talent (City's Mark Dennis and Kevin Dillon and Aston Villa's Gordon Cowans and Gary Shaw) over a cliff, during a 70 m.p.h. drive back to their hotel on an end-of-season trip to Marbella with Birmingham City, was stopped in his car by a policeman on the night Bolton had won the Second Division championship.

Worthington tested positive after blowing into the breathalyser, but then realized the copper must have been a Bolton fan. 'This must be your lucky night, Mr Worthington,' said the policeman with a wink, as the boozy star drove off without a booking.

Wheels on Fire

It's not only players who get into trouble with their cars. Many a manager has succumbed to the motorway madness, although with their enhanced sense of responsibility they tend to stick to speeding rather than drunken driving. Unfortunately for them, though, the average manager tends to assume that police officers are every bit as gullible as footballers.

Take the example of the ex-Liverpool boss Graeme Souness. In March 1992 his car reached 100 m.p.h. as he sped along the M62. The reason? His house had been burgled two days previously and he was racing to buy a guard dog. Despite his canny canine explanation, Souness was fined £600.

Strangely, managers never seem to set off for a game in good time. Even that well-known disciplinarian George Graham was done for speeding in 1989, while on his way to watch his old club Millwall play at Sheffield Wednesday. The then Arsenal boss reached speeds of 104 m.p.h. in his BMW. (Well, he must have been eager to see a game that wasn't likely to be a goalless draw, as is normally the case with Arsenal.) His solicitor claimed that Graham needed his licence to scour the country for new talent and to make transfer deals. Despite this defence, Graham was banned for fourteen days and fined £100, and Arsenal still went on to win the League in spite of the two-week hiatus in Graham's player dealing.

Ex-England manager Terry Venables has been convicted of speeding too, when he was boss at Spurs. In 1993 he was fined £700 and banned from driving for seven days by Epping magistrates, despite his defence that he was racing to an important FA Cup tie at Norwich. Venables admitted driving at 100 m.p.h. in his Mercedes on the M11.

Bobby Robson, another former England boss, has also been in car trouble.

In 1989, shortly after it was revealed that he had been lying back and not thinking of England three times a night during a six-year extra-marital affair with Pauline Ridal, Robson was caught speeding at 110 m.p.h. in a 70 m.p.h. zone. His lawyer told magistrates that he 'was keen to get home' to his wife. Keener than he had been during the previous six years, we hope.

An elaborate tactical defence rarely pays off. Far better the honest approach of West Ham's chirpy cockney boss and all-round East End geezer Harry Redknapp. When 'Arry Boy was manager at struggling Bournemouth in 1991 he was nicked for speeding while on his way to watch his son Jamie's debut for Liverpool. 'That's all right,' Harry told the motorway plod, 'I've been trying all season to get three points.' The Old Bill were so impressed that Harry's quote made it into *Police* magazine.

Even old players turned pundits (and the most inoffensive man in football) can sometimes get caught. Trevor 'Mr Controversial' Brooking had to turn lawyer for a day in October 1992, defending himself at Maidstone Court after being given a yellow card for speeding on the M20. Brooking's Perry Mason imitation failed and he was fined £75, remarking, 'I'll stick to what I know best in future – football.'

Crawling from the Wreckage

A picture of a smashed motor undoubtedly improves the bad boy footballer's CV. After Tony Adams' car crash in May 1990 his battered Sierra XR4 was gleefully photographed by the Press.

Not to be outdone, fellow Arsenal miscreant Paul Merson produced a caved-in £25,000 Land Rover Discovery in August 1994. Merson had left the scene of the crash leaving his dazed passenger to deal with the police.

Merson had already been banned for eighteen months in 1989 after twice crashing a BMW while drunk. He managed to crash into both another car and a telegraph pole as he drove from a pub car park. Merson was arrested after police found the car abandoned outside his flat; magistrates heard that he had fled after the second crash, but later returned to move the motor.

In the 1994 accident, Merson lost control of his Land Rover driving down a hill in Mill Hill, north London, on a Sunday afternoon. He clipped the kerb, rebounded into a Nissan Micra, virtually writing it off and causing Bhuendra Lakhaim and his wife Minaxi to suffer shock and whiplash injuries. He then bumped a garden wall and lurched back into the street, hitting a tree. Merson gave his name and address to Bhuendra Lakhaim but then scarpered when someone mentioned the police were on their way, leaving his dazed companion to deal with the aftermath. Merson later revealed that he had disappeared as he had a match to go to – it's strange how this argument never seems to apply to fans in accidents on their way to games. The next day Merson reported the affair to the police.

At Merson's trial in February 1995, held three months after he had confessed to cocaine, gambling and alcohol addictions, there was national outrage when he escaped a ban – because he needed his car to get to his drug clinic in Southampton and his pregnant wife could not drive. (What do they call those large red things with numbers on the front? And those

MERSON BREAKS THROUGH THE DEFENSIVE WALL . . .

long things that move on tracks? No, it's no good, it's gone now . . .)

Merse, who admitted driving without due care and attention, also got a result in only being fined £300, after telling the court he'd blown all his £5,000 a week wages on his addictions. He was given an absolute discharge for leaving the scene of the accident.

There were mitigating circumstances, though. In one of the all-time classic defences, Merson's lawyer claimed he was not used to driving the Land Rover Discovery and also begged JPs not to ban him, as he needed his car to visit school-children to warn them of the dangers of drugs.

After the verdict, victim Bhuendra Lakhaim fumed: 'It is an outrage – he left us for dead in the wreckage.' Tory MP Warren Hawksley was even dragged in, declaring, 'There seems to be one law for ordinary people and one for celebrities.' In fact, before the case a gambling man might have put money on Merson getting banned – but we won't go into that.

Car accidents can even cost a manager his job. In September 1993 poor Terry Butcher, manager of Sunderland, had just signed four players worth £3 million, and what happened? Derek Ferguson was giving a lift to team-mates Phil Gray, Ian Rodgerson and Andy Melville after a

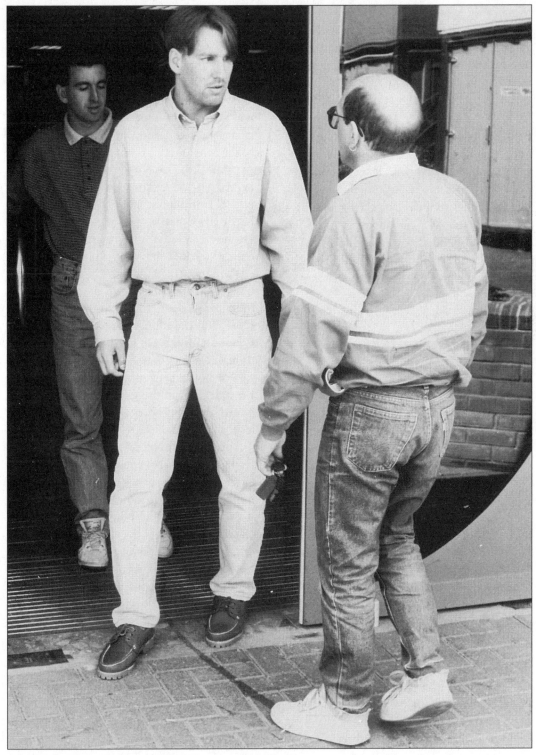

. . . AND ACCELERATES AWAY FROM THE COURTROOM.

friendly at Middlesbrough, when he was involved in a head-on crash near Roker Park with another car while driving at 60 m.p.h. the wrong way round a round-about.

Gray needed an emergency operation to remove broken glass from his eye, Rodgerson suffered a dislocated shoulder and Melville whiplash injuries. Without their crocked stars Sunderland made a poor start to the season and Butcher was sacked a few months later. In the subsequent court case, Ferguson was fined £2,300 and banned for a year. His lawyer claimed that the roundabout had been difficult to see and that he had been in a hurry to get home to his wife.

The car Ferguson hit was written off and a 72-year-old woman passenger suffered broken ribs. In court the driver, Julie Williams, testified that Ferguson had told her: 'I don't know the roads. I don't live here. I'm pissed. I'm pissed.' However, a roadside breath-test on Ferguson proved negative.

The Scottish international was also ordered to resit his driving test when the ban was over. Jobless Terry Butcher must have wished that Ferguson had retaken it a lot sooner.

Getting the Centre-Forward out of Jail

To get actually banged-up requires some special road feats, as Jan Molby and Mick Quinn can testify, your honour. When Quinn, then of Portsmouth, was jailed for twenty-one days in January 1987 for driving while disqualified (this was for a previous drink-driving offence), he had the most valid of reasons for breaking the ban. On the first occasion, when he had been stopped for speeding, his defence was that an aunt who had been staying with him had received a message saying her daughter was ill and good Samaritan Quinn had come to her aid.

On the second occasion, when Quinn was stopped by a police officer who knew he was disqualified, he said his girlfriend had been taken ill. Having no money to pay for a taxi and with the phone disconnected (now Quinny might like a bet, but a footballer with no money?) he had driven her to get assistance. Clearly Quinn is a very nice man, a very nice man indeed.

Portsmouth manager Alan Ball did his best to keep Quinn out of the slammer, telling the court that it would be a 'tragic blow' for the club if he was jailed. After Quinn had served his time he declared: 'I'm not a bad lad . . . I just wanted the feel of being behind the wheel again. The car had been in the garage for six months. I only got fifty yards before I was spotted.'

Sometimes footballers don't even have to be in cars to cause trouble. Former Liverpool star Jan 'Rambo' Molby perhaps regrets an incident involving the overturning of a Triumph TR7 sports car outside a gay club in Chester. The bulky midfielder had been out drinking with friends when his group of mates surrounded the car and overturned it, causing £1,000 worth of damage.

Molby, who admitted helping to flip the car when interviewed by police, claimed in court that he confessed because he was frightened (what, Rambo frightened of the rozzers?) and that he had really been ten yards from the incident (and we all know how long it takes big Jan to cover ten yards). It certainly wasn't a gay day for Molby when in March 1988 he was fined £100 for criminal damage to the car plus a further £150 costs, but was cleared of threatening behaviour inside the club.

The venue was unfortunate for macho Molby. 'Now they'll be calling me the poof of the penalty area,' he moaned, claiming it wasn't him, guv, honest. 'When I walked into the club I didn't know it was gay . . . It didn't take long to find out. We left pretty sharpish and there was an altercation outside. But I was miles down the road when it happened.'

This wasn't the end of Molby's motoring mayhem. In May 1988 he was banned from driving for six months for failing to stop after an accident when his BMW swerved into a parked car. Then in October of that year Molby was jailed for three months for reckless driving (and banned for another year) after a car chase. Jan might not move too quickly on the field, but he certainly made up for this in his motor.

What Molby's defence lawyer termed 'two minutes of motoring madness' took place in February 1988, and involved a two-mile police chase through Wallasey on the Wirral. In the early hours a patrol car saw Molby's black BMW, with three or four people inside, speeding towards it on the wrong side of the road. A bit suspicious that, Jan. The officer mounted the pavement to avoid a collision.

He later saw the BMW with just Molby inside. The police car followed it and two other patrol cars joined the chase. It was then that Molby appeared to be possessed by the spirit of Nigel Mansell on amphetamines. Over the next two miles Molby sped through two red lights, overtook three vehicles on the wrong side of the road and screeched round corners on the wrong side of keep-left bollards, so really he wasn't driving that much worse than most other footballers on a night out.

The lard done bad almost broke the sound barrier. Molby was going so fast, at speeds of up to 100 m.p.h. in a 30 m.p.h. limit, that the three police cars had to give up the chase for safety reasons. Molby admitted driving in a 'highly dangerous way'. His defence said that he had had two or three pints and when he saw the police he panicked as he feared being breathalysed. And drove like a man deranged instead. Very astute, Jan, but nothing could now save the Dane his bacon.

When sentencing, Judge Gerald Crowe QC told Molby: 'It is only by the grace of providence that you did not kill or maim somebody.' After he signed for Liverpool Jan had quickly developed a Liverpool accent: now it had become apparent that perhaps he had integrated a little too well into the Scally lifestyle.

When Molby made his first appearance at Old Trafford after being released from the nick he had to put up with chants of 'who's the jailbird in the red?'. The only benefit of a spell inside for the podgy playmaker was that he'd lost a stone and a half in weight as he 'didn't fancy the grub'.

Spurs' Terry Fenwick, now manager of Portsmouth, ran Molby close in sheer quantity of offences. He was jailed for four months in September 1991 for failing to give a breath-test and driving home from his own Bethnal Green pub, called, ahem, the Camel (a name which no doubt kept Arsenal fans amused) while disqualified.

The Camel, the pub that is, had been celebrating Spurs' Cup Winners' Cup victory over Austrian side Stockerau and Fenwick had shown admirable solidarity with his locals in toasting the Spurs.

The England international was never going to win any careful driving awards. He had already been disqualified for three years in September 1989 and for one year in August 1980 for drink-driving offences. There were also two speeding raps on his record.

His manager at Spurs, Terry Venables, said that Fenwick, ironically nicknamed 'Lucky' by his team-mates, had suffered a terrible run of luck, breaking his leg and being recently divorced. As Fenwick neared the end of his sentence, Venables revealed that 'the spirit he has shown has been second to none'. As, no doubt, was the spirit that he drank, Tel. At least the regulars at the Camel held a welcome-home party for Fenwick when he was released from jail – and travel home by camel was just about the only transport option left for the luckless defender.

Driven to Distraction

Most players fall short of actually getting banged up for their offences – but you name it, they can still be done for it. Another footballer floored, like Molby, by a stationary car was Norwich's Chris Sutton. On the eve of his £5 million transfer to Blackburn, the Premier League's then most expensive striker spent the night sobbing in police cells after he and his boozy mates vandalized restaurant boss Ali Askar Bari's £9,000 Mini convertible outside – where else? – a nightclub in Norwich.

Sutton and pals had earlier been on a four-hour drinking session around the city's pubs, knocking back bottles of Sol, Rolling Rock and Miller Draft. Bari saw Sutton leaning into his car parked outside Hy's night-club and called the police. 'The car lights were on and the levers that operate the indicators and wipers had been twisted around each other.'

Police found Sutton hiding in the toilets at Hy's. He fled down a fire escape and into a taxi. Two PCs hailed another taxi and after a bizarre chase (presumably a Norwich policeman achieved a lifetime's ambition of shouting 'follow that cab!') Sutton was apprehended and identified by Bari as the car vandal. Ali Askar Bari said that at the police station a tearful Sutton then offered him £1,000 to pay for any damage. Sutton was released by the police with a caution and a packet of Kleenex tissues.

Nor is the saintly Gary Lineker immune from controversy – although Gary does run people down nicely. When, in 1992, he knocked over a motor cyclist in Kensington, London, Lineker helped the injured man to his feet and offered him the use of his mobile phone to call an ambulance. (The accident victim had to refuse the offer of the phone because his cut hands and wrists were too painful to use it.)

Even the prosecutor admitted that Lineker 'had his head bowed, looking at the ground in obvious remorse'. Lineker admitted careless driving and was fined £100 and had to pay £25 costs. Even worse for the wild man of football, the Press discovered a previous motoring offence – he'd been given three penalty points after a zebra crossing offence in 1989.

Even the simplest motoring situations can get players into trouble. Shrewsbury's wideman Victor Kasule was questioned by the police in 1989 after he managed to overturn team-mate John McGinlay's car on the way to the corner shop. At the time, Kasule claimed he had just popped out to buy some fruit juice. Today he remembers: 'We wanted a few beers so I went out to get them. I didn't realize the car was so powerful and when I came back I attempted to do a handbrake turn and, bang, the car was over. It was a write-off. John wasn't too keen on the car, anyway.' Or take Ronnie Mauge, now at Plymouth. When Fulham signed midfielder Maugé from Charlton in 1988 they didn't realize that he was set to appear in court. In November 1988 he was sentenced to nine months in a young offenders' institution, after pleading guilty to two assaults. These involved smashing a bottle of Babycham over his girlfriend Sophie Stennett's head, and an incident with a bus driver.

Mauge had taunted the driver by saying, 'I f***ed your wife last night', to which the driver replied with a similar comment concerning Mauge's mother. (Mauge's mum, who was sitting in the public gallery, was requested to leave the court while this piece of evidence was being heard.) Mauge then threw a brick at the bus driver, hitting him in the groin. Let's hope Ronnie never meets an obstinate traffic warden.

In 1992 Anders Limpar suffered the humiliation of being nicked for driving his BMW through a red light by one of his own supporters. PC Christopher Joycey confessed: 'I'm an Arsenal fan, but I couldn't let him off.' Limpar claimed he was in a hurry to get to a clothes show in Olympia, but was fined £50 plus £20 costs.

There have even been cases of joyriding. Torquay's Mark Loram was jailed for one month in 1992 for allowing himself to be carried in a car taken without the owner's consent – and served a second month from a suspended sentence imposed in 1990 for indecent exposure. Clearly a man who likes a flash motor – even if it isn't his.

Rabbits can also prove a dangerous temptation for the footballer behind the wheel. Frank Worthington will always remember the time Mark Dennis came to pick him up. Dennis saw a family of flopsy bunnies in his headlights: 'Any normal person would have left it at that, but Mark isn't any normal person.' Dirty Dennis thought it would be fun to play 'chase the rabbit'. Clearly no fan of Beatrix Potter, he careered off after the creatures over a series of lawns, skidding and doing handbrake turns. 'Mark thought it was a huge joke, but I had to spend about a month dodging the neighbours,' recalls Worthington.

Perhaps the most humiliating motoring offence of all time was that committed by Fulham's George Georgiou in 1991. There was no wrapping of his car around lampposts or drink-driving for this miscreant: his threat-to-society-as-we-know-it crime was far worse than that – Georgiou was fined £100 for dropping litter from the sun-roof of his Ford Escort.

His defence was unforgettable, even by footballing standards: 'A cat ran out in front of me and my instincts made me throw litter out of the window to avoid hitting the cat.' With instincts like that it wasn't surprising that Fulham were struggling against relegation.

There was no dramatic high-speed Molbyesque chase pursued by three police cars for Georgiou. He was spotted by a member of the Keep Merton Tidy Group who took down his car's number and reported it to the council. The shame of it.

Taxi Evasion

The sensible way of avoiding drink-driving and other motoring misdemeanours is to take a taxi. Or at least it would be sensible for anyone but a soccer ace.

Blimey, guv, we had that Andy Linighan of Arsenal in the back of the cab, after a boozy 1993 Professional Footballers Association dinner at the Grosvenor House hotel in London's plush Park Lane. And strike a light! Linighan ended up being accused of racism after a row with cabbie Harold Levy over the £63 metered fare to Harpenden.

Police were called when Linighan refused to pay the fare as he argued that the cab had gone the wrong route. It was then that Levy heard Linighan make anti-Semitic remarks involving Adolf Hitler. 'He thought I was a Spurs supporter trying to get back at Arsenal.'

A contrite Linighan later apologized to the *Jewish Chronicle*, admitting that he was over the drink-driving limit at the time of the incident. 'I obviously wasn't in my right mind and said things which I do regret. I'm definitely not racist,' pleaded the drunken Gunner.

Another London player, Chelsea's Dennis Wise, a former member of Wimbledon's Crazy Gang and notorious for his discipline problems on the pitch, was jailed for three months in March 1995, after a rank taxi assault, although he was subsequently cleared on appeal.

Chelsea's not so Wise man was found guilty of assaulting a taxi-driver and causing criminal damage following an argument in October 1994. 'He is the most violent customer I have ever had,' declared 65-year-old cabbie Gerald Graham.

After a night out at England boss Terry Venables' Scribes West club in London's up-market Kensington High Street, just hours before he was set to join up with the England squad, Wise got in a cab and tried to persuade Graham to take him and his girlfriend, Geraldine Lennon, to Boston Manor, six miles away. When the driver refused, as he was entitled to do, and asked them to get another cab, a row occurred.

Wise, who had a previous conviction for criminal damage to a car door in 1988, 'flew into a real rage', said Graham. 'He kicked the cab and started punching the window. I flinched and my foot slipped off the brake. The cab, being automatic, moved forward, the door caught the girl's arm and she started screaming. Wise went berserk and started shouting, "You've hurt my girl's arm".'

Wise then leapt back into the cab and kicked the glass partition window, smashing it to pieces. Or, to quote his agent Eric Hall, Wise went 'monster monster potty'. 'Then he started trying to hit me,' recalled Graham. 'He whacked me a couple of times round the head and knocked my glasses off. He was still screaming like a lunatic and threatening me when luckily a police car came along.' The police found Wise with his hands around the cabbie's neck and promptly handcuffed him before arresting him.

Magistrate Geoffrey Breen dismissed Wise's claim that he smashed the window and grabbed Graham by the hair only because his girlfriend was being dragged along by the open door of the cab. Breen summed up: 'I am satisfied he got into the cab and smashed the dividing window, not because he wanted to stop the cab, because it was already stationary, but because he wanted to get at the cab-driver.'

And simply because a fit young athlete had attacked a man twice his age, the magistrate told Dennis the menace: 'Your reaction was that of a bully. When he

LET'S GO TO COURT. RESERVOIR DOG DENNIS WISE WITH HIS MONSTER MONSTER LEGAL AID TEAM.

made it clear he was not going to obey your demands you resorted to violence.'

Wise was dropped from the England squad following the case, even though the sentence was subject to an appeal. Outside the court special agent Eric Hall seemed more intent on intoning his tedious catch phrases to the media rather than sympathizing with his client. Hall was 'monster emotional' and declared his charge to be 'monster monster stunned'. That was nothing to the three-month monster jail sentence Wise faced.

However, at his appeal in June, Wise had a monster monster escape, as his conviction was overturned. Even so, the judge, Gerald Butler QC, said the court had reached its decision 'with no enthusiasm'. The judge strongly castigated the little man, despite the verdict: 'Even on his own account Mr Wise's conduct was quite disgraceful and does him no credit at all.'

Boom! Boom! Boom! indeed, as Eric Hall might have put it. Chelsea's captain had escaped bird bird bird . . . but the meter has been left running on Wise's promising England career.

Yes, it seems that the modern footballer can combine the automobile with just about every offence and accident known to humanity, bar, as yet, spontaneous combustion. The next time Big Ron says that a midfield dynamo has a good engine you'll know exactly what he means. It's just a shame that he isn't allowed to drive it for the next three years.

Perhaps the only solution is to ban all footballers from driving – and hailing taxis.

Maybe they should all travel by bus. Then again, maybe not, if they're like Wolverhampton Wanderers' Brian Law. After he'd drunk twenty or so pints and shorts in an all-night session, the Welsh international and three mates decided to nick a bus. They only made it half a mile. Law, who was three times over the legal limit, crashed the brand new double-decker into railings on Wolverhampton's ring road, causing £13,000 worth of damage. Perhaps he thought he was being chased by Blakey. Law ran off with the other men but was found hiding in bushes. 'It was a childish prank. I can't really understand why I did it,' pleaded the contrite defender.

Brian fought the law and the law won. He admitted aggravated vehicle-taking, driving with excess alcohol, driving without insurance, and failing to stop after an accident. He was ordered to do 180 hours' community service, banned from driving for two years and ordered to pay £13,000 compensation. Presumably he won't be receiving any On The Buses videos for Christmas.

Nor can they be trusted in coaches: West Ham players hired a coach for their 1994 Christmas beano at the Phoenix Apollo restaurant in Stratford, East London. This resulted in manager Harry Redknapp receiving a £1,162 bill for damage to both the first coach and its replacement.

In the first coach, seats were urinated on, one was slashed and needed upholstering and the vehicle was taken out of service the next day to be cleaned. The driver refused to take the players back, and a replacement coach had to be summoned. After the Hammers stars had enjoyed a boozy evening, this second vehicle ended up in an even worse state. A rear emergency window was broken, an interior light was smashed, more seats were urinated on, and another full valet service was needed.

Still, South Woodford Coaches got off quite lightly, it seems. The company's MD Dan Brown revealed: 'The year before, we supplied West Ham with a coach to the West End which ended up dirty and one of the seats was set alight.' This was surely the first case of a West Ham player setting anything alight since their 1980 FA Cup Final win.

Perhaps they should all follow the example of Everton's Neville Southall who used to come to training on his bicycle. Even footballers couldn't get into trouble on two-wheelers. Although, come to think of it, it is an offence to be drunk in charge of a pushbike . . .

16

Charlie's Angels

'People ask: "How would you like to end your days?" And I say: "Sod the records. Just give me a desert island with an *Exxon Valdez*-sized tanker full of lager with a pipe running to the shore!"'

Jimmy Greaves

When **Arsenal's** Paul Merson confessed to a £150-a-night cocaine habit, he hardly seemed to appreciate the 'style' of the designer drug. For some, the pop star's powder has a frisson of illicit decadence and glamour. Not so for Merse. There were no insights into life and the universe; his main observation on snorting 'Charlie' after drinking up to fourteen pints of lager top was: 'I thought: "This is great. I can go out drinking all night and be as right as rain the next day."' Drinking without a hangover – surely a state of nirvana for some of our professionals.

Temptation for footballers is exacerbated by the fact that they are often somewhat limited individuals. Look at all that travelling abroad. While many fans would love the chance to explore foreign cities while in European competitions or on tour, footballers usually moan about the dodgy food and the boredom of staying in their hotel. For every Gary Lineker who plays abroad, learns the language and discovers the culture, there is an Ian Rush who, while at Juventus, had to have his baked beans specially shipped over to Italy.

That might sound patronizing, but it has to be remembered that footballers lead one-dimensional lives. Often they have had limited educational opportunities, leaving school early to sign on as apprentices. From the moment they arrive at a club, everything is done for them. It is hardly an environment that encourages an enquiring mind. As the ex-Arsenal star Peter Storey said after ending up in jail:

'If I wanted to buy a new car, I told the club what make and colour I fancied and they arranged it. A house or furniture was the same. When I went on holiday they booked it all. If I got a parking ticket I just took it to the club and said "What do I do with this?" I would never hear of it again. They organized my life so much that when I left I didn't even know how to book a plane ticket.'

Massive wages are given to top youngsters; flash cars and flash women follow. Yet despite the adulation and glamour there is the mundane side of football too: day-long coach trips to away fixtures, endless hotels and being treated like a child by the manager until you are well into your thirties.

Then there is the loneliness. Ex-pro

Tommy Tynan recalls the nights in his club cottage when he first signed for Plymouth: 'Sometimes I sat in my room alone every night of the week. I used to eat on my own and go out on my own. In the end I bought a telly and sat in watching that . . . I resented the fact that no one invited me round to their house or asked me out for a beer.'

Training ends at one o'clock and then the footballer has ten or eleven hours to kill – and usually he doesn't read Proust. Football is a sociable game, and the after-training drinking session or the post-match Wednesday and Saturday night binge is an easy way of filling up the hours.

Tynan, who saw life in the 'soccer factory' at Liverpool, Swansea, Sheffield Wednesday, Lincoln, Newport, Plymouth, Rotherham and Torquay, knows the player's psyche as well as anyone and cites boredom as the biggest reason for some turning to drink and drugs:

'No one wants to go home from half-past one to eleven at night and watch telly. They're all virile males at that age, they like the company of women and going out and they have a lot of money. I have eighteen-year-old lads from Sheffield Wednesday come in my pub and they're on £500 a week. I think the clubs should try and find something else for players to do in the afternoon, like running soccer clinics for kids.'

In an unusually articulate moment, Wimbledon's Vinny Jones spoke eloquently of the need to protect young players:

'The money is hard to handle. Young boys who lived in the slums or were orphans are now getting more money than they could dream of.

'There you are, an honest lad grafting on £100 per week, and all of a sudden at twenty-one years old you are on the front and back pages of newspapers and can't walk down the street. You haven't been taught to handle that. How can you come out from one life to another? We've never been taught to handle spotlights.'

The salaries paid to youngsters are almost unbelievable. When Liverpool signed teenager Mark Kennedy from Millwall in March 1995, it was reported that the eighteen-year-old received a £250,000 signing-on fee spread over three years, a basic wage of £2,500 a week, plus a sponsored car and £850 for every League win.

With the huge wages comes the pressure of expectation, of being a hero to thousands. It's hard for us to believe, but often our £10,000-a-week stars are acutely lacking in confidence and hide behind stimulants of all kinds. Paul Merson, who had so many drink, drug and gambling problems he even contemplated suicide, revealed that after he first snorted cocaine his personality changed: 'Normally I'm quite shy, especially if I'm sober and I wouldn't want to talk to anybody I didn't know. But that night I started rabbiting on to all sorts of people. I felt I could talk to anybody.'

Another self-confessed cocaine user, Mark Dennis, believes that drugs could kill a player. 'The demands of today's game are so great that players need to escape the pressure.'

High wages, boredom, fame, lack of interests outside football, all play a role in causing some to over-indulge in drink and drugs. The sociability of football, the endless fans ready to buy you a beer, has ruined the career of many a star. Any player signing for West Ham might be excused a stiff drink, but Jimmy Greaves was an alcoholic by the time he joined the

ONLY ANOTHER THIRTEEN-AND-A-HALF PINTS TO GO, MERSE...

Hammers in 1970 and ended up requiring psychiatric help.

'I spent about five months in mental hospitals drying out,' recalls Greavesie. 'Then one night I had a couple of pints in the local and that was that. Three or four weeks later I walked out of the loony bin and I've never been back since.' After further visits to Alcoholics Anonymous, Greaves, who admits that his beer and vodka boozing would have killed him if he hadn't stopped, hasn't drunk for nearly twenty years now – despite having to talk about the Endsleigh League like it's important.

Other chapters in this book detail how drink results in countless driving bans, car crashes and night-club fights. Many famous names have been hit hard by booze allegations. In addition to Merson's fourteen pints a night we have had the sad sight of retired Forest manager Brian

A CELEBRATORY BRIAN CLOUGH: 'IT'S A PLEASURE TO MEET YOU, YOUNG MAN . . .'

Clough being found asleep in a ditch and admitting that his family and friends believe he drinks too much: 'My problem is that booze is part and parcel of the business. Drink is always there if you want it, and it is free. You drink to celebrate a victory. I had more to celebrate than most.'

Once away from the game the effects of soccer's alcohol culture often haunt the ex-players. Tony Currie, the former Sheffield United, Leeds and QPR star, drank a bottle of Scotch a day after injury ended his career, before 'crawling out of the gutter' to work as community officer at Sheffield United.

And who now remembers Tommy Caton, the young Manchester City

CLOUGHIE TELLS THE DIRECTORS STRAIGHT: MAKE MINE A DOUBLE.

defender dubbed 'the new Bobby Moore'? After his career at City, Arsenal and Charlton was ended by injury, he drank himself to death at the age of just thirty with two bottles of spirits a day. His wife Gillian told the inquest, 'If he didn't play football he didn't think there was anything else he could do.'

Other players who quit can sometimes turn to drugs. Arsenal's Paul Vaessen had to retire at the age of twenty-one after scoring the winner in the 1979–80 European Cup-Winners' Cup semi-final against Juventus. His future snatched away, he became a homeless heroin addict, blowing £175 a day on smack and almost being killed in a knife attack in London's Old Kent Road after a row over a deal.

After becoming a Christian, Vaessen thankfully ended his drugs nightmare.

In Italy the bans imposed on Argentinians Diego Maradona and Claudio Caniggia for cocaine use hinted at the problem of drugs in football. But it wasn't until 1994 that a number of English players revealed their addictions. It was Mark Dennis who first publicly admitted that he had taken drugs throughout his career, and that football in England was riddled with abuse.

There are those who might argue that playing for Birmingham City would be enough to drive anyone to drugs, and indeed it was at the aptly named Blues that Dennis first took cocaine. The defender – sent off twelve times in his career and booked on seventy-three occasions – joined City's infamous gang of boozers, fighters and drug-takers, whose motto was: 'Win or lose we'll have a toot and a booze.'

A hanger-on around the players would provide cocaine in exchange for match tickets. The players ran their own bar on Saturday nights at the ground, and in the St Andrew's toilets Dennis and pals would snort coke through rolled-up five pound notes. Dennis even took his own razor blade to the players' bar to chop up the designer drug.

It was at Maximilians night-club that Dennis tried cocaine with champagne: 'The combination of the drugs and the bubbles gave me a real buzz.' He also took amyl nitrate while in a lift, sending the elevator upwards to increase the effect.

When he moved to Southampton he stopped taking drugs while sharing a hotel with veterans Frank Worthington and Mick Mills (when Frank Worthington is seen as a steadying influence then we really are talking about a soccer bad boy). But when Dennis moved into a house with his wife he was soon exercising his nasal muscles again. One or two Saints players were doing coke, claims Dennis, although nothing like on the scale at Birmingham.

Dennis suffered flashbacks and anxiety attacks – as, no doubt, did many of his opponents. Southampton's manager, dour ex-Guardsman Lawrie McMenemy, would have been stunned if he had known the true cause of Dennis's erratic behaviour.

McMenemy once sent Dennis to see a psychiatrist after he locked himself into a room prior to an FA Cup tie with Bradford City and said he couldn't play. The paranoid left-back did eventually emerge on to the pitch after being talked out by coach Lew Chatterley, 'but I don't remember a thing about the match'. Team-mate Mark Wright also had to coax Dennis out of a room when he came round to pick him up for training.

During his three years at QPR Dennis says he cleaned up, but after moving to Crystal Palace he began to blow £150 a week on drugs again. He was unhappy about the move, as he wanted to stay at Rangers, and had injury problems.

'Fly Virgin' read the sponsor's logo on Crystal Palace's shirts, and while with the Eagles Dennis certainly was flying high: 'I couldn't remember half the games I played in.' Dennis snorted Charlie at a pub in Sutton and a night-club in Croydon called Cinatras: 'On some days I would feel like a gazelle in training because I'd taken so much cocaine over the weekend.' Until he came down afterwards, that is. 'Sometimes on the field I'd be seeing double,' admitted Dennis, perhaps accounting for a few of his overzealous tackles.

Dennis even tried acid once. 'The fellow sitting opposite me in the pub suddenly grew a gigantic nose – he looked like Phil Thompson' (the ex-Liverpool captain). If that doesn't put kids off taking drugs then nothing will. Your best mate might suddenly turn out to have a conk the size of Matt Le Tissier's. And just imagine encountering Iain Dowie on a bad trip . . .

One of Dennis's fellow players at Birmingham, as well as Southampton, was flamboyant Frank Worthington. When Jim Smith signed Frank for the Blues he might have suspected that a man wearing sunglasses, tight jeans, cowboy boots and a jerkin with a rock and roll band's world tour announced on the back must have been on something – and Worthington has admitted taking cocaine once while at Birmingham City, when he was at a party. 'I used it because of the situation I was in. It was there and I took it,' confessed the ex-England international. After the Merson revelations he also owned up to once taking an upper (a form of amphetamine) to improve his performance before a game in the North American Soccer League in the mid-1980s.

Merson wasn't the only blond striker with cocaine running around his brain. Frank McAvennie also revealed that he had taken coke for four years while at West Ham and Celtic. McAvennie first encountered the drug when he went to a night-club in London's West End to celebrate signing for West Ham in 1985. He saw an international footballer there, who had taken cocaine. 'He was sitting in the corner, crying with his hands on his head.'

That sight shocked McAvennie, and he stayed away from the West End for a year, scoring twenty-eight goals in a season as West Ham finished third in the old Division One, their highest ever position. But he returned to the capital's nightlife, and tried cocaine himself: 'Soon I was a regular on the club scene and what I'd seen that night seemed insignificant.'

It wasn't the best value for money: 'I found myself spending a lot of money getting drunk and then spending money on this drug which sobered me up!' His form slumped at West Ham and he was sold to Celtic, but still regularly flew back to London to go out with his page 3 model girlfriend Jenny Blyth.

When Frank signed for West Ham again in 1989, he was back on the party circuit revelling with pop stars and soap actors, and paying £50 to £75 to dealers for his 'gear'. 'I wasn't addicted to coke. I was addicted to the lifestyle,' Frankie said of his snort-snort score draws, reasoning that 'when you have all this money flung at you, you feel you've got to go to the best places'.

Rather disingenuously, McAvennie claims that he only took the drug when drunk, and never snorted coke less than forty-eight hours before a match, so it didn't affect his form.

In the aftermath of the Merson furore, it also emerged that Billy Kenny had been sacked by Everton after failing a drugs test. Kenny, an immensely promising player and son of the former Everton player Billy Kenny Senior, had been warned several times by the club for going missing and other drug-related bust-ups. After a final rap from manager Mike Walker, Kenny went missing again and was sacked in March 1994. Oldham then signed the midfielder, but only after he had spent four weeks at Altrincham Priory Hospital, a drugs and alcohol centre. The £15,000 medical bill was split between Everton and the Professional Footballers' Association.

In a disastrous period for the image of football there have been almost constant drugs revelations. Another Premier League player was accused of taking speed and Ecstasy while on holiday (although, to be fair, how many young men away from home haven't experimented in similar fashion?), while in November 1994 Fulham's Tony Finnigan was charged with dealing heroin, after he was allegedly found with a kilo of the drug on him. He continued to play for Fulham, however, chairman Jimmy Hill commenting, 'It is a case of innocent until proven guilty.'

Finnigan was found not guilty of the drug-dealing charge in November 1995 – but embarrassingly for Hill and the Cottagers, he was fined £500 for possessing 0.35 grams of heroin found in his personal organizer. Finnigan's lawyer admitted the heroin was for the player's personal use – but surprisingly didn't plead playing for Fulham as mitigating circumstances. O. J. Simpson's lawyer would never have missed that chance of swaying a jury.

Finnigan was arrested in the back of what he later found out was an unmarked police car. Also in the motor was drugs courier Susan Ellis, £100,000 worth of heroin and an undercover policeman posing as a dealer. Ellis was sentenced to four and a half years in jail for trying to sell heroin to the officer.

Merson, Dennis, Worthington, and McAvennie all publicly confessed to their drug-taking in newspapers; just how many other players have addictions but have kept silent?

At least the FA has recognized that a drugs problem now exists. The six-week rehabilitation course that Paul Merson was sent on for his cocaine, alcohol and gambling addictions looks, so far, to have resulted in a reborn talent. The FA has also introduced random drugs testing and – believe it or not – random drinks testing at training grounds and after matches. With the full support of the PFA, the players are being breathalysed. One envisages whole teams being carted off to the alcohol rehab clinic.

Alan Hodson, the FA's assistant director of coaching and medical education, is heading the campaign. 'Players are under extreme pressure for forty-four weeks of the season and there is no break. That's why we want to make sure that they are not turning to drugs or alcohol. There have been many cases of alcohol ruining a player's career.'

The FA's sense of priorities does seem amiss, however. Palace fans wondering why Chris Armstrong's career seemed to have gone to pot were bemused to hear that Armstrong had failed a drugs test in January 1995, testing positive for cannabis. Armstrong was forced to miss a Coca-Cola Cup semi-final while attending a programme of assessment and counselling, in what his manager Alan Smith described as a 'storm in a tea cup'. He argued that the striker had 'apologized and is mentally and physically fit. I can't see what the problem is.'

It is doubtful whether Armstrong's performance was adversely affected by the odd midweek joint, as cannabis is a very low-grade drug and supporters of its decriminalization would argue that it is

British Drugs XI

1. **David Icke** (not on drugs but high on God)
2. **Mark Dennis** (cocaine, acid, amyl nitrate)
3. **Roger Stanislaus** (cocaine)
4. **Billy Kenny** (cocaine)
5. **David Hillier** (cannabis)
6. **Tony Finnigan** (heroin)
7. **Lee Bowyer** (cannabis)
8. **Frank McAvennie** (cocaine and peroxide)
9. **Frank Worthington** (cocaine and an upper)
10. **Chris Armstrong** (cannabis)
11. **Paul Merson** (cocaine and lager top)

Substitutes

12. **Lee Chandler** (cannabis)
13. **Ricky Otto** (cannabis)
14. **Craig Whittington** (cannabis)
15. **Paul Vaessen** (heroin)

medically no more harmful than a glass of whisky. And indeed, the FA Carling Premiership is sponsored by the purveyors of a drug that does much more harm in terms of anti-social behaviour – alcohol.

Significantly, after the Armstrong incident Palace demanded that the names be released of the other nine players who had failed drugs tests – showing the extent of the problem. Two of these were Charlton's eighteen-year-old youngsters Dean Chandler and England youth inter-national Lee Bowyer, who showed traces of cannabis in random tests.

Other cases soon emerged. Arsenal's David Hillier had tested positive for cannabis at Christmas in 1994. He claimed he'd been offered a cigarette at a party, which unknown to him contained dope. But don't joints give off a funny smell, David? Perhaps he had a cold. Hillier was forced to serve a compulsory six-match ban and attend a rehabilitation course. The treatment worked. He was so rehabilitated that he stopped taking drugs and turned to stealing suitcases at Gatwick airport in May 1995.

Birmingham's Ricky Otto was found with cannabis in his car while driving in Hackney, east London, in August 1995. He passed two breath tests but was cautioned by police for the cannabis pos-session. Well, it must have helped to be chilled out for one of Barry Fry's team talks, eh Ricky? The FA wasn't able to take any action as Otto had not been charged with an offence or failed a drugs test. Huddersfield's striker Craig

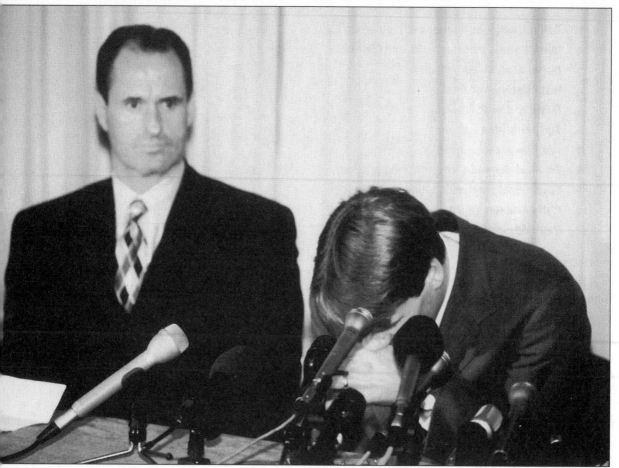

WATCHED BY GEORGE GRAHAM, A TEARFUL PAUL MERSON CONFESSES HIS ADDICTIONS.

Whittington became the first player to fail a drugs test twice. He tested positive for cannabis for the second time in ten months in February 1996. He'd been caught before, in March 1995, and undergone clinical assessment and counselling. After a blow-by-blow account of his offence he was dismissed by Huddersfield.

In February 1996, Leyton Orient's Roger Stanislaus was banned for a year by the FA and sacked by the club after a random test revealed that he had taken a performance-enhancing drug, cocaine, before a match at Barnet. Stanislaus claimed that he had been passed 'some sort of cigarette' at a family funeral on the Thursday before the game. Rather worryingly for O's fans, the club lost to Barnet 3–0. Just imagine the hammering for Orient if they hadn't had a defender on coke. Their fans must have been tempted to reach for 'some sort of cigarette' too.

The FA hearing revealed Stanislaus's funeral story to be a bunch of porkies. Dr David Cowan, head of the King's College drug-testing laboratory in London, testified that to produce the results obtained on the Saturday, Stanislaus would have had to have taken a lethal dose of cocaine on the Thursday of more than one kilogram. This was all the more unlikely when it is considered that even 25 grams of coke can be lethal.

Orient's chairman Barry Hearn promptly sacked the player. 'We felt the good name of Orient as the Littlewoods Community Club of the Year and the very high percentage of young supporters we attract were two of the overriding reasons.' He added that as Stanislaus's story was so heavily contradicted by medical testimony, the club had no alternative but to dismiss him.

There is no doubt that drink and hard drugs can destroy players. Anyone who witnessed Paul Merson break down into tears at a press conference marking his return from six weeks in a clinic had to be moved. Merson had let down his family, the club and the supporters who pay his exorbitant wages – but suddenly the superstar was like a small, lost boy, his tears illuminated in the TV lights, and even fans of rival clubs felt sympathy for a man under intolerable internal pressure.

Merson dabbed at his eyes with a handkerchief and told the nation's media he was an alcoholic. He added: 'I have completely changed. I have started to grow up. This has been the hardest six weeks of my life. I am going to Gamblers Anonymous tonight. That is my night out now.'

Football has to ask itself if it is necessary to pay immature young men thousands of pounds a week without any investment advice, adequate counselling or offers of constructive ways to spend their hours after training. Added to the demand for constant success, the pressure is destroying our brightest young stars.

Think of the words of Mark Dennis. He should have played for England, but now admits: 'If I'm asked if I'd like my career again, I'd say no. Because it got me into drugs. It's so, so bad and I'm embarrassed by it all now. Sometimes I would go to sleep and hope that I wouldn't wake up.'

17

Who's the Idiot on the Bench?

'I have come to the conclusion that nice men do not make the best football managers.'

Graeme Souness

When former Nottingham Forest striker Stan Collymore knocked on Frank Clark's office door one autumn morning in 1994, the £4 million-rated superstar must have known that he was about to receive some words of fatherly advice from a manager renowned for his pipe-and-slippers image. Stan had been spotted in one night-club too many, and Frank, who liked nothing better than relaxing at home of an evening with his Jerry Lee Lewis records, was worried that his much sought-after frontman might end up scoring everything but goals. 'Stan,' said Frank, squeezing his player's shoulder in the buddy-buddy style recommended by big-selling men's magazines, 'I think you need to settle down. Get married. Have kids. Too many late nights in dimly lit bars aren't good for anyone, let alone highly trained athletes like yourself. Come on, Stan,' he beseeched. 'Find yourself a nice girl, eh?'

'Settle down' is the mantra delivered by generations of soccer supremos to players whose fast-lane social life risks speeding them straight to hospital with a busted nose or pickled liver. And in uttering it to Collymore, Frank Clark was merely following in the footsteps of his predecessor at the City Ground. Brian Clough, a man who appended to his autograph the rather ironic phrase, 'be good', was forever urging his more hot-headed charges to snuggle into domestic bliss. Once or twice, Matt Busby might even have suggested to George Best that whichever Miss World he was knocking about with at the time seemed like a home-loving sort of girl. Well, maybe. But who is there to give a manager this same cosy fireside chat over tea and biccies? It's an inescapable fact of football that all bosses are former players – and while age and creaking limbs have a mellowing effect on some, there are others whose yearning for the fancy-free existence as 'one of the lads' never dies away. Graham Taylor insists that the first rule of management is never to fall in love with players. Instead, the game's inglorious history is littered with the names of managers who fell in love with someone, or something, else – with disastrous consequences.

Graeme Souness made public his philosophy of love and romance while playing for Middlesbrough in the early 1970s. Paranoid that his white BMW

2000 might be an IRA target after he received a suspicious phone call, probably from a vengeful team-mate kicked to pieces in that day's five-a-sides, Souness drafted in the cops. With the area sealed off and nosy faces peering from every window, the policeman leading the search shouted that he had found a plastic bag under the seat. Souness called back that there was no need to worry as he knew what was in it. But this didn't satisfy the officer in charge. Four times he demanded to be told the contents of the bag and on each occasion Souness stonewalled. Eventually, his face crimson with embarrassment, he was forced to yell down the street that it was full of Durex. Living in a tittle-tattle North-eastern neighbourhood, the craggy midfielder's womanizing wiles could hardly have been better-advertised if he'd put them on the front page of the *Middlesbrough Evening Gazette*.

A tearaway by his own admission during schooldays in one of the toughest districts of Edinburgh, Souness's motto throughout his playing career with Spurs, 'Boro, Liverpool, Sampdoria and Rangers was 'live hard, play hard'. There were tales of six-up in a one-bedroomed flat in Montreal, and a trans-European drinking tour with Middlesbrough team-mate Eric Carruthers. 'I must confess that, as a fit, healthy nineteen-year-old,' declared one of seventies soccer's lustiest Lotharios, 'I did not need too many hot water bottles, nor did I have to make my own cup of tea in the morning too often.' But the flip side of suave Souness was a reputation as a footballer with razor blades in his boots. This was a view borne out when Frank Worthington called him 'the nastiest, most ruthless man in soccer'. 'He isn't just hard – there is a nasty streak to him,' vouched Worthy.

It was a view amply confirmed when Souness, after becoming player-manager at Glasgow Rangers, was sent off on his debut for committing GBH on George McCluskey and leaving the Hibees' man needing some nine stitches in his knee. 'I suppose I am the kind of player spectators dislike,' he wrote in a failed attempt at self-deprecation. 'My style of play antagonizes them. I think it stems from the unfortunate way I run.' Players who had rubbed up the wrong way against the sandpaper schemer offered other reasons, too. Even his own full-back Jan Bartram joined in, with an article in Copenhagen's biggest-selling daily newspaper. Its less-than-subtle headline read: 'My boss is a hooligan'.

Souness's obsession with aggression dates back to his childhood. At the age of twelve, he went on holiday to Butlin's at Ayr and won first prize in the Body Beautiful contest. Standing on the rostrum in his little white shorts and flip-flops, even then there was that look in his eyes which said: 'Hey, pal, take the ball off me and it's a stud tattoo for you.' This was the boy so desperate to win at all costs that he would cheat at games of Monopoly with his brother Billy, and so convinced that fitness and physical presence were the keys to success on the pitch that he would spend hours preening his pecs and having the aches massaged out of his massive, muscular thighs. 'His body is absolutely beautiful,' confessed the Scottish trainer Jim Steel, clearly unaware of homoerotic connotations. 'He was never off the massage table. I used to spend an hour a day on him.'

But obsession in one area of life leads to neglect in others, and Souness's eight-year marriage to Danielle Wilson broke up in November 1988. Bitter legal wrangles followed – first over custody of their two sons, Fraser and Jordan, and his wife's daughter by her first husband, Chantelle. Then, in March 1995, the pair clashed over the terms of the divorce settlement made six years earlier. Danielle went to the High Court seeking more than the £500,000 she originally received, claiming she had been 'under pressure' when she agreed to the sum. But she failed to provide full details of her finances, as required under a court order, and lawyers acting for her former husband sensationally demanded that she be given a suspended jail sentence.

Home life for the Sounesses was apparently like a match itself: family v. football. But it was clear almost from the start that one team was doomed to defeat. 'I longed for him to set aside time for the family, but he was always much too busy,' confided the heiress to her father Austin's £22 million fortune. 'On the rare occasions he took me out he talked about nothing but football and the good and bad points about players. By the time I left him, I knew more about soccer than most managers.' Perhaps she should have taken over at Anfield.

If the strain of signing Catholic and Celt Maurice Johnston for the hard-line Protestants across Glasgow upped his blood-pressure level a few notches, this was nothing compared to the stress loaded on Souness when he followed Kenny Dalglish into the Liverpool hot-seat in April 1991. He spent £22 million ripping apart an ageing but still talented Liverpool side, without obvious success. And it was almost inevitable that, just one year later, the body worshipped with a near-religious fervour ran up the white flag. 'He's a vain bastard. I thought he was going to tell me he was having another

nose job,' declared assistant manager Phil Boersma when his boss revealed it was a triple heart bypass rather than mere cosmetics that he needed. Boersma may have hoped that the surgeons would slip in a humility implant at the same time.

For a man whose basic intelligence has never been in doubt, the mistake Souness made in hospital can only be attributed to an overzealous anaesthetist. A month before the op, he fell in love. Nothing so foolish about that, since 33-year-old Karen Levy, whom he met in Knutsford's Number 15 wine bar, had classic footballing pedigree. Besides being a stunning blonde divorcee, Levy was an ex-model and a former hostess on *Sale of the Century*. But even Nicholas Parsons would have had trouble smarming away Souness's next deal. He talked about their relationship to the *Sun*, a paper reviled on Merseyside for its coverage of the Hillsborough tragedy. To compound this tactless gaffe, he was then photographed canoodling with Karen on the anniversary of the disaster, oblivious of the anguish the story would cause.

His behaviour was condemned at a club still traumatized by the events at Sheffield three years earlier. In the peculiar circumlocutory style which football officials adopt whenever there's anything serious to be said, chief executive Peter Robinson announced that Souness 'had accepted the board's recommendation that it is inappropriate for the manager of Liverpool to enter into exclusive arrangements with any section of the media'. Sports columnist Michael Parkinson was blunter. He slammed Souness as crass, insensitive and 'plain bloody silly'. The fans put it in even simpler language.

The end was nigh. When Graeme James Souness resigned in January 1994, the opening line of his autobiography, written nine years earlier and fittingly titled *No Half Measures*, had come back to haunt him: 'Being successful has always been more important to me than being popular.' Now he was neither.

But there were still two allies he could count on. In June 1994, Souness whisked Karen Levy to Las Vegas, where they wed in secret at the Treasure Island hotel. He fought back tears and declared it 'one of the greatest days of my life'. She wept with joy and said: 'I am the happiest woman alive.' And, of course, they took a reporter and cameraman from the *Sun* along with them, to record the nuptials of the man dubbed a 'soccer hero' by the ever-loyal tabloid. The families of ninety-five Liverpool fans will have offered a collective toast to the happy couple that night. But you can bet the glass didn't have champagne in it.

GRAEME SOUNESS TIES THE KNOT WITH HIS OWN LITTLE GEM AT THE TASTEFUL TREASURE ISLAND HOTEL IN LAS VEGAS.

'I don't expect to live for ever,' Malcolm Allison once declared, but the legend of Allison will survive long after his trademark fedora, Havana cigar and bottle of Moët have been interred alongside him. The big seven-o is drawing close for Talcy Malcy, but this is no crumbling, fumbling OAP on stage at Croydon's Ashcroft Theatre, just a drop-kick away from the Selhurst Park scene of his most infamous crime. For a man whose playing career at West Ham was ended by tuberculosis and the loss of a lung, Allison is still in rebellious, robust, champagne-quaffing health – ever the charismatic lounge lizard of popular image, and pulling in the punters to hear his and Tommy Docherty's footballing reminiscences. In 1975, when he was forty-seven, he said he wanted to live until he was at least ninety-four. Even now, with the whistle on his management career finally blown in 1992, there are those within soccer's cosy establishment who would happily see this perennial outsider fail in his ambition.

'Big Mal' was a rebel with applause. His mission was to drag English football out of its master-and-servant mentality. He wanted to coach rather than administrate, to learn and apply lessons from overseas, to produce confident, arrogant, stylish teams, reflections of his own self – which people flocked to watch. In 1973, he moved from Maine Road, where he and Joe Mercer had masterminded Manchester City's late-sixties surge to the League Championship, FA Cup and European Cup-Winners' Cup, to take over at First Division rivals Crystal Palace. When he was sacked from Selhurst three years later, the Eagles were grounded in Division Three. But did the fans care? The hell they did. In We All Follow the Palace, long-time supporter Keith Brody insists that under Allison, Palace were truly a football team for the only sustained period in the last twenty-five years: 'Men like Mal don't waste time consolidating because they don't know how. They go for it today.'

Like Souness, Mal the man and Mal the manager are inextricable. An understanding of one is the key to the other. But for Allison, the key does not simply unlock the main entrance. Instead, it provides an opening into countless side-passages of personality. In his classic autobiography, Colours of My Life, he tried to explain this fascinating, multi-faceted psyche. He contrasted his one-dimensional lifestyle as a player – 'My dedication was absolute. I didn't smoke, I didn't drink, and I never had sex within three days of a match. Incredible!' – to his later quest for a more rounded existence through gambling and women. Particularly women. 'I suppose my pleasure in female company, my need for its softness,' he wrote, 'stems to a large extent from the fact that my working life is spent in an entirely male environment. This is very oppressive.'

But there was more than a mere desire to avoid suffocation behind Allison's fascination with Christine Keeler. The woman whose involvement in the Profumo Affair ripped apart a Tory government was something else: a challenge to his ego, especially when he heard in the Star pub in London's Belgravia, one of her haunts, that she had seen him on TV and fancied him: 'I wanted to know and talk with this woman who had caused so much havoc, inspired so many headlines. And perhaps make love to her.' The relationship was brief but revelatory. 'How was it that one young woman could bring such a cloud across so many successful and apparently well-ordered lives?' The answer, even for Allison, was absurdly simple: 'She was a very sexy woman.'

It was not a career-threatening affair. Sleeping with a call-girl, no matter how notorious, was not then classed as a sackable offence on soccer's lengthy chargesheet. But letting a porn queen share the club bath with the players certainly was.

The lads at Selhurst Park knew what Fiona Richmond looked like, but only with a staple through her navel in the pages of *Men Only*. And then in 1976 she turned up at Palace's Langley Park training ground in a Rolls-Royce, alongside Allison resplendent in fur coat and fedora. Big Mal wanted a photo. It was muddy. The players had just finished five-a-sides. And what began as a bit of innocent fun quickly got out of hand – with calamitous consequences for its instigator.

Richmond went in goal alongside keeper Paul Hammond, who found his pneumatic partner rather softer to dive on than the carved-up turf. Jim Cannon, then Palace's captain, recalls Hammond leaping on to her and pulling her top off: 'She had her boobs hanging out, she was so brazen about it. In the end he was rubbing mud all over her and the cameras were taking pictures and then she got in a group with the whole team and that was it . . . or so we thought.'

When the players were in the communal bath back at the ground, Richmond reappeared. 'She walked in with this guy,' Cannon recounted in *We All Follow the Palace*. 'She was only wearing a white robe which she took off and jumped in and I thought . . . well, I ain't getting out. There was a picture of Derek Jeffries, myself, Fiona Richmond and Phil Holder

in the bath and that's all you could see. But I promise you there were four other people underneath the water all holding their breath because they didn't want the cameras to see them.'

The tidal wave caused when the *News of the World* printed the shots was in inverse proportion to the splash when Richmond had actually hopped into the bath. Jim Cannon got a slap round the face from a furious wife, but Allison was swamped. The chairman who had brought him to this footballing backwater in south-east London, Ray Bloye, wanted to ride out the storm but the FA refused to let him. 'The FA told Bloye he had to get rid of me,' Allison recalls, 'for bringing the game into disrepute. When I told them it was a case of mistaken identity, they didn't believe me. I regret it now, of course, but it was just a joke. It was a publicity stunt for her. It got Fiona Richmond on the front page of papers in nineteen countries, and sold about 500,000 copies for Paul Raymond. It got me the sack.'

Malcolm Allison had entered the elite club of £100,000-a-year supremos when he became Manchester City's team manager in 1971. But mere cash could not untangle the knots in a complex personal life. In fact, money made it worse. Allison married Beth in 1953, when he was twenty-six, and in more than twenty years together they had four children. But after a string of liaisons with, among others, Miss UK Jennifer Lowe, Mal was finally kicked into touch when he was spotted in Tramp with bunny girl Serena Williams once too often. Their affair began in 1972, and three years later Allison wrote: 'It has become inevitable that we will marry.' But they didn't and twelve months later the amour was at an end with

Allison blaming his own erratic habits for the break-up. It was a different bunny girl who next wore his wedding ring, although Sally Allison herself bailed out after seven turbulent years in which Malcolm fathered a daughter, Alexis, but also, she claimed, broke her nose and several teeth. Allison took up with school-teacher Lynn Salten, and the couple now live in a modest two-bedroom flat in Yarm, near Middlesbrough, with their daughter Gina.

'I'm hopeless with money because I have never quite been able to assess its worth,' admitted Big Mal back in 1975. Sixteen years later, his life savings were gone – swallowed up in the BCCI bank crash. And the carefree past was starting to catch up with him. In November 1992, he appeared in Epsom County Court to explain why he owed Sally £6,000 in unpaid maintenance, his ex-wife claiming that: 'Since Mal and I split, it has been one long struggle to get him to pay for his child and her upkeep. There have been many court appearances and many promises. But Malcolm seems incapable of keeping them.' He took along a payslip from the club he was then advising, Bristol Rovers, to explain just how straitened were his circumstances. One of the wisest old owls in football was earning the equivalent of a window-cleaner's wage, just £330 a week.

Allison promised to mend his ways. But two months later the maintenance payments stopped again and the Child Support Agency took up the chase. This time there was no income from football to declare: the man who had steered Manchester City to European glory and inspired the players of Crystal Palace, Middlesbrough, Plymouth Argyle and Sporting Lisbon, among countless others, was dispensing words of wisdom to the never-would-bes of the Killingworth Arms pub team.

'Most people in football just sit back and do what they are told to do. Very few are prepared to challenge the way things are done.' Allison's words about Terry Venables could easily be autobiographical. If ever a football manager needed a Frank Clark figure, a personal guru on hand to proffer a calming pat, it's Big Mal. But then he probably wouldn't have listened. Some people are born with their finger on the self-destruct button – and there's nothing else to do but enjoy them before the digit gets too twitchy.

Howard Kendall seemed to have his finger on the self-destruct button, too. In April 1995, the Notts County supremo was sacked after a mere seventy-nine tempestuous days in charge at Meadow Lane, amid allegations of booze binges which left him incapable of managing a team in dire need of an inspirational leader. But only eight months later, Kendall landed the top job at Sheffield United. It probably helped that at the bottom of his CV, the section marked 'Other Useful Information' read: 'Now teetotal. Has lost two stones in weight.'

Howard Kendall was always assured of a place in football's record books. In 1964, he became the youngest player to appear in an FA Cup Final when he turned out for Preston North End at the age of seventeen. He then went on to make 230 appearances for Everton, earning a rightful berth in the club's hall of fame as a skilful and cultured wing-half. And when he went back to Goodison in 1981 after Gordon Lee had been sacked, it was a case of the prodigal son returning: Kendall steered the club to two League championships, and success in both the FA and European Cup-Winners' Cups. But a second spell on Merseyside was less triumphant. According to Tony Cottee, he sometimes made team selections on the flip of a coin: 'Sorry TC, you lost the toss this week, you're number 14. Mo [Johnston], you're number 10.' And when he walked out in December 1993, it was to a bizarre sunshine appointment with the little-known Xanthi in Greece.

However, the lure of English football's mud, sweat and beers was too strong. Kendall cited 'personal reasons' when he quit the Greek club after less than twelve months, and in January 1995 took on the challenge of keeping Notts County in the First Division. Just three days after his appointment, County beat Burnley 3–0, and the dream was up and running.

It didn't last, though. County got to Wembley, and even beat Ascoli 2–1 in the final of the Anglo-Italian Cup, but remained rooted to the foot of the table. And there were rumours of trouble off the pitch. Kendall was billeted in the £71-a-night Nottingham Holiday Inn, where he was reported to be furious that the hotel did not offer room service. Not that it was food he wanted, according to one staff member, who told the *People*: 'Howard would come back in the afternoon and have a couple of glasses of red wine at the bar. Then he would often disappear across the road to Sainsbury's, and you would hear the bottles clinking in his bag as he made his way up to his room.'

Kendall was booted out after he and assistant Russell Slade allegedly turned up drunk for a reserve team game at Leeds. 'Results apart, we were not happy with the way the club was being run,' stated vice-chairman John Mounteney as County drew a veil over the precise details. But assistant secretary Ian Moat broke an official club silence to reveal: 'I regularly had to take Howard Kendall back to his hotel from the ground absolutely legless.'

Some managers have all the luck. When Kendall got an unexpected break at Bramall Lane, and masterminded Sheffield United's shock victory over Arsenal in the 1995–96 FA Cup, there was much innuendo in reports describing the 'sober' suit he was wearing. However, he refused stoically to rise to the bait, and described some of the wilder claims made about his behaviour as 'an absolute disgrace'. 'A lot of things got blown out of proportion,' he deadpanned to Paul Wilson in the *Observer*. And teetotal? No. 'I just haven't had a drink for a while.'

It's a phrase which many managers, seeking liquid solace after yet another crushing defeat, would do well to learn by heart.

1. Stan Flashman – an overweight neurotic who made his name as a ticket tout – became chairman of Barnet, his local club, in May 1985. Football's fattest supremo paid £50,000 for a majority stake in the struggling non-League outfit, which then owed more than £130,000 to the Inland Revenue and was within a week of going into receivership.

2. Flashman was by this time a successful 'ticket broker', as he termed his line of business. That is, he made a very good living by charging extortionate prices for tickets, often obtained from people who weren't meant to sell them. He had a house in *nouveau riche* Totteridge, in the north London suburbs, and a rather less grand office at seedy King's Cross. When trade was good, 'king of the touts' was his preferred self-description.

3. Born in the East End in 1938, 'Stan the Man' began touting in the early 1960s while he was working as a salesman in a Houndsditch warehouse: 'I saw the boys selling tickets outside the ground [White Hart Lane]. I bought a couple, sold them to a punter and made £10. In a couple of hours, I'd made £40. I thought to myself, "When I'm earning £35 a week working from 8.30 a.m. to 5.30 p.m., that's all right."'

4. Flashman married his feisty Scottish wife Helen, a West End night-club hostess, in 1963. They have one son, Mark, a goalkeeper whose modest ability curiously did not prevent him finding his way into the Barnet reserve team.

5. Flashman claims that 'a public servant in a high position' used to supply him with tickets for the Queen's garden parties.

6. When Frank Sinatra performed in Britain in 1977 and demanded that ticket prices be pegged, Flashman bought hundreds and made a killing. His *coup de grâce* was to present an unwitting Sinatra with a bottle of the finest bourbon from the best seats in the house, where he and Helen were sitting.

7. When Manchester United winger Willie Morgan defended his description of Tommy Docherty as 'about the worst manager there has ever been' in the famous libel trial of 1978, Morgan's counsel alleged that Docherty had sold FA Cup Final tickets on the black market. The previous year, defence claimed, Docherty had sold 200 tickets for £7,000, and even invited the buyer into the executive suite at Old Trafford to complete the deal. Guess who?

8. 'Why sleep when you can make money?' is Flashman's life-long motto.

9. Flashman has never denied having a bad temper, or throwing his considerable weight about. He played in goal for Wilton Way school in Hackney, where his teammates remembered that he would bump into anyone who upset him and try to knock them over. He was once so angry at losing to a class-mate in a table tennis tournament that he beat up the umpire.

10. The larger-than-life chairman – variously estimated to weigh between 18 and 25 stones – quickly became a cult figure at Barnet's Underhill ground. Indeed, the team did well under Fat Stan's stewardship. But in March 1989, after he had sold a popular player to Conference rivals Wycombe Wanderers despite Barnet being well-placed to win the title, there was a demonstration by supporters. Flashman chased and grabbed the editor of a fanzine, and threatened a female fan who tried to intervene.

11. After Barnet had reached the Fourth Division play-offs during their first season in the Football League, 1991–92, Flashman sacked then-manager Barry Fry in the latest of a series of spats between the pair. Following a 1–0 win over Blackpool in the first leg of the semi-finals, Fry claimed that 'Flashman came in and said we were crap and that the entire team should be up for transfer. If he wants, he can be manager, chairman and centre-forward next season. I will turn up for the second leg in an unpaid capacity and, if Flashman tries to stop me, we'll have a fight on the centre line and sell tickets for that.'

12. Fat Stan clearly didn't believe in rewarding his players' efforts with FA Cup Final tickets. Despite Barnet receiving forty-seven for the final in 1991, the players got none. In fact, the Football Association revealed that two of the tickets issued to the club had been sold by touts at Wembley. Club captain Duncan Horton declared that none of the tickets had been offered to players or staff, and that Kenny Lowe, who wanted to go to the match, had been forced to buy two tickets from Flashman. What's more, they were from the allocation to Kettering FC.

13. Suspicions of more serious misdeeds at Barnet were first voiced by Fry. He pointed out that the club had raised £1.5 million from transfers over three years, making it a relatively rich little set-up considering its status and average gate, then asked: 'What's happened to it? Your guess is as good as mine. I wouldn't know if we were £100 in credit or £1 million overdrawn.'

14. Flashman became so paranoid about those who criticized his chairmanship of the club that in September 1991 he announced he was placing 'terrace spies' around the ground 'to root out these sarcastic people'. He later claimed that this statement was the work of 'an imposter'.

15. In November 1991, several expletives were bleeped from an interview given by Flashman to BBC Radio 5, in which he blasted: 'The supporters don't matter as far as I'm concerned. They just pay their entrance fee. I don't care whether they come to Barnet or not.' Consistent as ever, he phoned the Beeb back later that day to call Barnet fans 'the best in the country'. This time he didn't say that his earlier comments were the work of an imposter.

16. Two weeks later, Barnet were fined £50,000 by the Football League for failing to keep proper books of accounts and players' contracts. Before the hearing, Flashman grappled with *Daily Mirror* photographer Dale Cherry, tearing his coat, and afterwards pinned *Sun* snapper Paul Welford against a wall. 'He wrapped his hands around my throat as his wife was trying to pull him off,' said a shocked Welford.

17. After the incident with Welford, the *Sun* launched a campaign to 'Ban Fat Stan'. The paper parked a lorry outside Flashman's house carrying the hoarding: 'Ban this fat bully today'.

18. When Barnet managing director Tom Hill resigned in 1992, he revealed that he had often been asked to sign books of blank cheques without knowing who he was signing them for: 'A month before I left the club, Stan asked me to sign two books of 500 cheques.'

19. A Football League probe into the club's finances uncovered a cheque stub for £10,000 made out to 'Neil Warnock'. The then Notts County manager of that name insisted that he had never received any money from Barnet, nor was he expecting any. When Flashman was quizzed on the matter, he refused even to admit that he was the Barnet chairman.

20. Fat Stan finally resigned from Barnet in March 1993, bowed down by the pressure of fans' demonstrations and citing 'health reasons'. He sold his 6,868 shares for a nominal £1 to the incoming chairman Stephen Glynne. Relief all round.

18

Bruce, Bribes and Broken Dreams

'It is like a cloak-and-dagger novel, but sometimes truth is stranger than fiction.'

Chris Vincent, Bruce Grobbelaar's former business partner, on the alleged 'match-fixing' bribery scandal involving Grobbelaar, John Fashanu and Hans Segers, which he exposed in November 1994.

When footballers appear in court, it is usually to answer charges such as drink-driving, assault or, if your name is Peter Storey and you used to play for Arsenal, attempting to import pornographic videos. Their law-breaking indiscretions amuse, titillate and occasionally even genuinely outrage us. Happily, they rarely threaten the integrity of football itself. If players have been breaching the Prevention of Corruption Act 1906 by throwing games for money, however, that is an awful lot more serious business. The very word 'corruption' conjures up sordid images of bent officials, of government ministers on the take and of crooked police officers receiving brown envelopes full of cash. Its dictionary definition – 'corrupt action; bribery; dishonesty; rottenness; impurity' – seems to have no obvious connection with football, especially British football. Here, as any Premiership or Nationwide League player will tell you, the game may not be as sophisticated as in Italy, Brazil or Spain, but at least its participants give 100 per cent honest effort. Indeed, that perspiration is generally thought to embody the same qualities as British football itself: decent, clean, firm (but fair) and, above all, honest.

When Bruce Grobbelaar, John Fashanu and Hans Segers were woken from their beds by squads of detectives at 6.55 a.m. on Tuesday 14 March 1995, that cosy notion was brought into question. The three players' arrest, on suspicion of throwing matches for money, was part of a chain of events which began four months earlier with detailed, explosive allegations in the *Sun* about games which had allegedly been rigged. The trail would end in early 1997 with the trio facing a Crown Court jury charged with corrupting the most popular sport on earth in the very country of its birth. A nation of football fans winced as they watched television pictures of the early-morning swoops, then held their breath and waited for the trial, fearful of what painful truths they might soon learn about the game they adore and some of the men who play it. This wasn't like lovable bad lads such as Tony Adams or Terry Fenwick, Mickey Thomas or Jan Molby being carted off to jail for their sins. For once, nobody laughed. Football scandal suddenly wasn't funny any more.

Normally the highly publicized arrest of three big football stars would shock supporters everywhere. This time, though, few fans were really that surprised. The dawn swoops came towards the end of a season, 1994–95, which will go down in history as the game's equivalent of the Queen's *annus horribilis*. By the time Fash, Grob and Hans Segers were detained, it seemed that any scandal which could hit football had already done so. It was a season of unprecedented sleaze and shame.

Drug-taking by players, well hidden from public gaze until then, suddenly burst on to the front pages. First to confess they had dabbled in illicit substances were Mark Dennis and Frank Worthington, both long out of the game. November, though, brought the news that Arsenal's Paul Merson was addicted to cocaine, alcohol and gambling. 'I'd go out and could have up to fourteen pints of lager top,' revealed Merse. 'I was doing line after line of cocaine throughout the night.' Ex-West Ham star Frank McAvennie's admission soon after that he too had snorted coke during his playing career was less shocking than it might have been, but added to a rapidly emerging, unsavoury picture of a sport riddled with substance-abuse. Early in the new year, on 25 January, Eric Cantona's kung-fu kick on Matthew Simmons, however understandable, again dragged football's name into the mud. Then two incidents the next

month confirmed that hooliganism, such a scourge of the sport in the 1980s, had not gone away and that fans could be far more violent than any sorely provoked Frenchman. On 8 February, Chelsea's supporters invaded the pitch at Stamford Bridge after an FA Cup defeat by First Division Millwall. Exactly a week later, rioting England followers, stirred up by neo-Nazi extremists, forced their team's 'friendly' at Lansdowne Road in Dublin against Jack Charlton's Republic of Ireland to be abandoned after just twenty-seven minutes. Football's public image, already reeling from a series of setbacks almost as damaging as the Heysel, Bradford and Hillsborough disasters, was blackened further when Arsenal sacked George Graham as their manager. He had been given £425,000 by controversial Norwegian agent Rune Hauge soon after persuading his Highbury bosses to buy two of Hauge's clients, Pal Lydersen and John Jensen. Initially, Graham told no one about the money. When these eyebrow-raising payments were later revealed, the Gunners manager insisted the cash was an 'unsolicited gift' and not a bung. Few believed him.

These scandals constitute only a brief selection of the trials and tribulations of English football during 1994–95. That turbulent time also saw Vinny Jones try to bite off a *Daily Mirror* photographer's nose, other players exposed as drug-takers (including cannabis-puffer Chris Armstrong – proof of what Brian Clough used to say, that God intended football to be played on grass) and Paul Ince charged with assaulting a fan just after team-mate Cantona's descent into madness at Selhurst Park. Notts County's decision to sack Howard Kendall, one of the most successful managers of the 1980s, after just seventy-nine days in charge was a reminder of the game's age-old occupational hazard: drink. Kendall's alleged crime: heavy boozing. However, the Premier League's ongoing inquiry into the transfer of around two dozen foreign players to English clubs suggested that money – and the backhander in particular – was the sport's new vice. It was investigating whether any palms had been greased during the deals and thus raised the possibility that some of football's players, managers and agents had been lining their own pockets. In addition, Terry Venables' bitter feud with Spurs supremo Alan Sugar was still in its early stages: that, along with the England coach's Spaghetti Junction-style tangled mess of other legal wrangles, would later cause El Tel to resign his job with the national side. And on 13 March, just twenty-four hours before the three players were arrested, Chelsea captain Dennis Wise was given a three-month stretch at Her Majesty's pleasure for attacking a taxi-driver outside Venables' night-club, Scribes West, and damaging his cab. The once-beautiful game seemed to be reeling from a new disgrace every week.

Despite all this, the arrest of Fash, Grob and Segers on such serious charges constituted a different class of scandal. The secrecy, style and surprise nature of the police swoops, codenamed Operation Navajo, showed just how seriously the boys in blue viewed the affair. Fifty officers were involved, and their chosen tactic – early morning wake-up calls of the most unwelcome kind on their suspects, who were taken away in front of hordes of waiting media personnel – seemed more suited to detaining murderers, armed robbers or escaped psychopaths than professional footballers.

Grobbelaar, the Southampton and Zimbabwe goalie, was still asleep when two unmarked police cars pulled up outside his New Forest cottage at 6.55 a.m. At exactly the same time, other teams of detectives were hammering on Wimbledon 'keeper Hans Segers' front door in nearby Fleet and the £300,000 home owned by John Fashanu, who had made his name with the Crazy Gang but was by then playing for Aston Villa, in the posh north London suburb of St John's Wood. But the *Gladiators* presenter wasn't there. The police's hopes of a co-ordinated series of raids, grabbing all the suspects and seizing boxloads of vital documents at the same time, lay in ruins. Instead his girlfriend Melissa Kassa-Mapsi was the one arrested at the penthouse pad. The controversial hitman – renowned for his aggressive style on the pitch (Fash the Bash) and money-making acumen off it (Fash the Cash) – was only finally nicked fully eight hours later, near Villa's training ground. Not far away from St John's Wood, in Kilburn, a Malaysian businessman called Heng Suan Lim became the fifth person to be arrested. Was he the linkman to the Far East betting syndicates which had allegedly had the matches fixed?

Grobbelaar's trademark smile was noticeably absent when he was taken from his home, looking shocked and bewildered, to a waiting police Cavalier. When he arrived at Southampton central police station at 8.25 a.m. he still appeared distressed. His solicitor, David Rawlinson, said that the colourful keeper strenuously denied all allegations of match-rigging, just as he had done ever since the claims first appeared in the *Sun* four months before. Fashanu, too, maintained he was 'totally innocent'. In fact, a week after the *Sun* first implicated Grobbelaar in the scandal, he had dramatically announced to the world that he was definitely not involved. In an interview, he had insisted that he was not the other unnamed big-name player with whom Grob had purportedly conspired. Fash spoke darkly but vaguely of 'two leading figures' in the game who were trying to discredit him, about his home being bugged, about friends who had been offered bribes to reveal personal details about him and, most damningly, about efforts to tie him to various rackets including money-laundering, drugs-running and the sale of forged British passports. All lies, he said. Press inquiries about his possible links to the match-fixing affair 'were the straw that broke the camel's back', he fumed. 'I have remained silent over the last eighteen months regarding a conspiracy to stitch me up, but I have been logging every event as they happen. There are a number of people, two in particular, who are trying to discredit me. It's only a matter of time before they get me.' That was back in November 1994. A month after the arrests, he spoke out again. This time he lambasted Chris Vincent, the source of the *Sun*'s original story. 'The crux of this whole business is that he and Grobbelaar fell out over a safari park project. It all got very nasty and Vincent wanted revenge,' he insisted. 'I turned up as a middleman trying to help out and the next thing I know I'm being accused of match-fixing. It's nonsense.' Fash maintained that the only reason police had arrested him was 'because they've spent thousands of pounds investigating me and found nothing. So they had to have a big public display to show they're still on the case.'

At the Football Association headquarters in London's Lancaster Gate, chief spokesman David Davies tried not to make a drama out of a crisis. Despite the detention of Fash, Grob and Segers, 'We remain convinced that corruption is not rife in our national sport,' he intoned. The FA's own inquiry would await the outcome of Hampshire Police's investigation. Brendan Batson of the Professional Footballers' Association was equally adamant that the sport was not bent. 'Our biggest concern is that there is a growing perception that the game is riddled with corruption,' he said. 'All of us involved in it know that is simply not the case.' Meanwhile, thousands of miles away in Malaysia, an investigative journalist with long experience of probing the country's shady gambling cartels told a different story. According to Johnson Fernandez's sources, in all six Premier League players had taken bribes. 'The British players who were approached were those with financial problems and those who had bet a lot on horse racing,' he explained. 'They were seen to be vulnerable.' The arrests of 14 March could be 'just the tip of the iceberg', Fernandez continued. 'In Malaysia we have far greater experience of match-fixing and 126 players have been arrested, although forty were later cleared through insufficient evidence. Up to a million pounds is staked on each English match.' Premiership contests 'are incredibly popular here and are shown live on TV every weekend. I heard about a couple of Premier League matches being fixed towards the end of last season.' So who were these six players allegedly involved? 'Easily recognizable, high-profile names,' he said. British libel law meant he could add no more than that.

The arrests represented the biggest disaster of a truly terrible season for English football. It was the first time the spectre of corruption had raised its ugly head in the domestic game for many years. Until the Fash, Grob and Segers affair, most fans had contented themselves with the belief that bribing players was something that only went on in French, Italian, East European and South American football. All those places had recently suffered scandals involving money paid to players or officials to influence the outcome of games. In France, for example, Olympique Marseille were stripped of their European Cup after it emerged that they had given money to certain members of an opposing team not to try too hard against them in an end-of-season league fixture. Britain, though, did have some history of match-fixing. Back in 1965, ten Football League players had been sent to prison for between four months and four years for rigging games. Two England players, Peter Swan and Tony Kay of Sheffield Wednesday, and their team-mate, David Layne, were among them. One of the other known cases of 'buying' or 'selling' games was in the 1970s. Don Revie, the England manager at the time, was claimed to have tried to 'buy' the League Championship while at Leeds United. Revie had allegedly offered three Wolves players up to a thousand pounds to lose against his Yorkshire terriers.

Fashanu, Grobbelaar and Segers were only finally charged several months after their arrest. When they were, the only consolation was that while the *Sun* had originally accused Grobbelaar of throwing or trying to throw six games, the madcap 'keeper was eventually charged over just two specific matches, one while he was playing for Liverpool and the other for the Saints. That, though, did not detract from the gravity of the alleged offences. In all, the three players and the mysterious Malaysian faced six charges. The first said that, contrary to the Criminal Law Act 1977, the four men had jointly 'in London or elsewhere, between the 1st day of February 1991 and the 15th day of March 1995, conspired together and with others known and unknown corruptly to give and corruptly to accept gifts of money as inducements improperly to influence the outcome of football matches or as rewards for having so done.' It was all very heavy stuff.

The first of the two games allegedly 'fixed' was the Newcastle United v. Liverpool game played on 21 November 1993, which Kevin Keegan's resurgent Magpies won 3–0. Fashanu was charged under the Prevention of Corruption Act 1906 with having given Grobbelaar £40,000 four days after the game as payment for throwing the match. The goalie was separately charged with breaching the same law by accepting the cash, allegedly for services rendered in that game. Fashanu, by now retired from football, was further accused of giving Segers £19,000 for 'having improperly influenced the outcome of the Wimbledon versus Liverpool football match played on 22 October 1994', which the Scousers won 3–0. The Dons' Dutch keeper, charged under his full name of Hans Johannes Cornelius Segers, was accused of accepting the cash either just before or soon after the game. The last of the six charges was against Grobbelaar, and alleged: 'At Southampton on 3 November 1994, being an agent of Southampton Football Club, you corruptly accepted from Christopher James Edward Vincent the sum of two thousand pounds as an inducement or reward for doing an act in relation to the affairs or business of your principal, namely for improperly influencing the outcome of a football match or matches.'

In March 1996, after a three-day committal hearing at Eastleigh Magistrates Court, all four were sent for trial at Winchester Crown Court. Chris Vincent, Grobbelaar's ex-close associate, was among those who gave evidence at that stage; he would later become the star witness against his former friend and the others. The legal authorities decided that the men, both individually and together, had a case to answer. For their part the three players insisted they were totally innocent of the charges against them. As they were released on bail to prepare their defence, fans everywhere began the long wait for the trial. It would decide if what was billed as English football's worst-ever scandal was anything like as serious as that. Fellow players who recalled Fashanu's highly committed approach to the game, and Grobbelaar's famous tendency to get shirty with team-mates who made mistakes, found the allegations incredible. Sometimes, however, as Vincent had said, truth is stranger than fiction.